6000095449

 University of
Hertfordshire

College Lane, Hatfield, Herts. AL10 9AB

Learning and Information Services
College Lane Campus Learning Resources Centre, Hatfield

For renewal of Standard and One Week Loans,
please visit the web site **http://www.voyager.herts.ac.uk**

This item must be returned or the loan renewed by the due date.
The University reserves the right to recall items from loan at any time.
A fine will be charged for the late return of items.

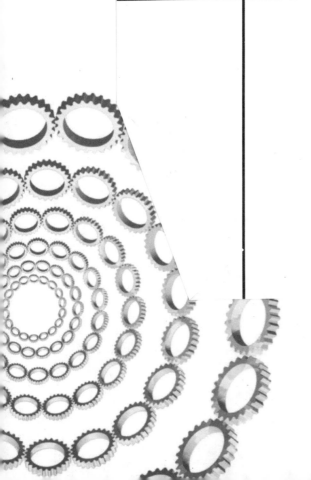

About the Author

Paul Tremblett is a software developer with AudioAudit, Inc. He has written several articles for *Dr. Dobb's Journal*, and is a frequent speaker at technical conferences.

Instant Wireless Java™ with J2ME™

Paul Tremblett

McGraw-Hill/Osborne

New York Chicago San Francisco
Lisbon London Madrid Mexico City Milan
New Delhi San Juan Seoul Singapore Sydney Toronto

McGraw-Hill/Osborne
2600 Tenth Street
Berkeley, California 94710
U.S.A.

To arrange bulk purchase discounts for sales promotions, premiums, or fund-raisers, please contact McGraw-Hill/Osborne at the above address. For information on translations or book distributors outside the U.S.A., please see the International Contact Information page immediately following the index of this book.

Instant Wireless Java™ with J2ME™

1234567890 FGR FGR 0198765432

Book p/n 0-07-219176-7 and CD p/n 0-07-219177-5
parts of
ISBN 0-07-219175-9

Publisher	Brandon A. Nordin
Vice President & Associate Publisher	Scott Rogers
Acquisitions Editors	Rebekah Young & Jim Schachterle
Project Editor	Jennifer Malnick
Acquisitions Coordinators	Paulina Pobocha & Tim Madrid
Technical Editor	Adrian Colyer
Copy Editor	Lunaea Weatherstone
Proofreaders	Paul & Linda Medoff
Indexer	Jack Lewis
Computer Designers	Lauren McCarthy, Tara A. Davis, Jean Butterfield
Illustrators	Michael Mueller, Lyssa Wald
Series Design	Roberta Steele
Cover Design	Eliot Bergman
Series Illustrator	Greg Scott

This book was composed with Corel VENTURA™ Publisher.

This book is dedicated to my wife, Eleanor, who is an integral part of all my accomplishments.

Contents

Acknowledgments

I would like to thank Adrian Colyer for once again providing the feedback and criticisms that are such a vital part of a book such as this. I would also like to thank Mike Bowler of Gargoyle Software. Without his knowledge of how to write a test suite the right way, I might still be trying to get the KMath library to work. A word of gratitude also to Rebekah Young and Paulina Pobocha for all the help they gave me before embarking on other endeavors. I wish them both the best.

Introduction

About This Book

The list of hardware and operating systems to which Java has been ported is as impressive as it is long, so it came as no surprise that when handheld devices started to gain in popularity Java-enabled models of such devices were quick to appear. Porting Java to small devices presented quite a challenge. The Java footprint had grown to the point where any thought of making either the Java 2 Standard Edition (J2SE) or the Java 2 Enterprise Edition (J2EE) available on small devices was entirely out of the question.

So exactly how should Java be ported to small devices? Your first thought might be to trim away all of the functionality not immediately applicable to small devices. While this would reduce the footprint considerably, it wouldn't even come close to solving the problem. The solution to the problem of building a smaller version of Java turned out to be exactly that—build a smaller version of Java. Rather than attacking the problem by reducing the size of an existing platform, the approach was to start from the ground up, borrowing from J2SE where it was appropriate. The new version of Java 2 that resulted from this effort is called Java 2 Micro Edition, or J2ME.

Now, before you run off to look for J2ME so you can download it, you should know that J2ME is not a product but rather a technology that has two kinds of components, configurations, and profiles.

A configuration is a set of low-level APIs and a virtual machine optimized for a family of devices. There are two common configurations in use today, the Connected Device Configuration (CDC) and the Connected Limited Device Configuration (CLDC).

The CDC provides a virtual machine and basic class libraries that support Java applications on such devices as smart communicators, pagers, personal digital assistants (PDAs), and television set-top boxes. These devices typically feature a 32-bit processor and more than 2MB of storage to hold the VM and the libraries. Their need for the functionality of the Java 2 virtual machine feature set is satisfied by the CVM virtual machine. This is a full-featured virtual machine with a small footprint.

The CLDC provides a standard Java platform with a footprint suitable for small, resource-constrained, connected devices. These devices typically feature a 16-bit or 32-bit processor and have 160KB to 512KB total memory to hold the VM and the libraries. They are often powered by batteries and have connectivity to some kind of a network, usually using a wireless, intermittent connection with bandwidth sometimes lower than 9600 bps. The core of the CLDC is the K Virtual Machine (KVM). The "K" designation reflects the fact that the size is measured in kilobytes. The CLDC also features a set of libraries.

A profile is a specification that details a set of APIs built on top of and making use of a configuration. Together they provide a complete runtime environment for a specific kind of device. One example of a profile is the Foundation Profile, which is built on the CDC. It provides a complete J2ME runtime environment for applications targeted at such devices as residential gateways, smartphones, and two-way pagers. Another profile, the Mobile Information Device Profile (MIDP), is built on CLDC and provides a complete J2ME runtime environment for applications that run on such devices as mobile phones and entry-level PDAs. MIDP addresses such issues as user interface, persistent storage, networking, and application life cycle.

This book focuses on MIDP and on MIDlets, which are applications that use the APIs defined by the MIDP and CLDC specifications.

Who Should Read This Book

This book is aimed at those developers who prefer to learn by analyzing and modifying working examples. If you wish, you can simply read the book, but you will probably learn better if you actually run the code. If you really want to master all of the material, you'll want to create you own variation of each of the examples or, better still, write your own examples from scratch using the techniques that are introduced in the chapter you are reading, using the sample code as a guideline.

Before you begin, you should install all of the prerequisite software described in Appendix A.

What This Book Covers

Chapter 1 eases you into the world of MIDlets with a simple example. Because the code is simple, you can concentrate on familiarizing yourself with the tools that you will use to work with the examples in the rest of the book. At the end of the chapter, you should be familiar with both the Java 2 Micro Edition Wireless Toolkit and Forte for Java Community Edition. Most readers will probably prefer to use Forte, but if you wish to use your own favorite IDE, all of the code will compile and run in any environment that supports J2ME.

Chapter2 introduces the MIDP version of several classes that you have already used under Java 2 Standard Edition. At the end of the chapter you will understand that even though you are using the same Java language you've used for years, some classes behave differently under J2ME.

In Chapter 3 you will learn how to associate commands with soft keys and some system keys on handheld devices and how to write code that responds to these commands. You will also see the variety of emulators that are delivered with the Wireless Toolkit.

Chapter 4 will show you that in situations where it is essential that runtime behavior under J2ME is identical to runtime behavior under J2SE, that is exactly the case.

By the time you reach Chapter 5, you'll probably be ready for applications with a richer user interface. In this chapter, you'll learn about `TextBox`, `Form`, `Choice`, and `ChoiceGroup`.

Chapter 6 takes you even further into the user interface. It shows you how to use `DateField` and `Gauge`, which are slightly more complex than the UI components you learned in Chapter 5. The chapter will also teach you how to use the *ItemStateListener* interface.

Chapter 7 covers Portable Network Graphics. You will learn as much as you choose to read about this graphics format. You will see how you can add icons to identify your MIDlets and how you can use icons to make the meaning of certain UI components more apparent to the user.

Chapter 8 teaches you how to add a splash screen to your application. It also presents an example that uses each of the types of `Alert` and associates a distinct image with each type.

Chapter 9 uses several examples to demonstrate the variety of `Tickers` that are available and how you use each of them.

Chapter 10 introduces the concept of persistent data and shows how the RecordStore class is used to provide persistence.

In Chapter 11, you will use what you learned in Chapter 10 to develop a practical application. You will learn how to customize the application for use in different countries.

When you reach Chapter 12, you will know enough to develop a wide variety of applications. By this time, you will realize that the applications you develop will be limited in power if the only resources available are those on the devices you are using. In this chapter, you will learn about the `GenericConnection` Framework and you will see how it can be used to perform network I/O. Once you have networking capabilities available, you can tap into resources on larger computers.

Chapter 13 takes you beyond simple networking. It shows how you can conduct client/server conversions that send queries to applications that use Java Database Connectivity (JDBC) to execute these queries against an enterprise database and return the results to a MIDlet.

Chapter 14 introduces the concept of the "Detached Office," which enables you to use a network connection to download some of your work onto a handheld device, use your portable copy of your work to carry out your daily duties in locations where there is no network connectivity, and to synchronize your work with the corporate database when you return to the office.

In recognition of the web-based world of which many of today's applications are a part, Chapter 15 demonstrates that MIDlets can behave as if they are web-based. You will see that you can send the same HTML form from a handheld device that a browser can send from a desktop computer. You will also see how MIDlets can interact with the Servlets and JavaServer Pages you have already used in J2EE.

Chapter 16 shows you how to add security to a login procedure without using SSL. It also shows how a MIDlet can participate in s server session.

In Chapter 17, you will see how you can develop you own homegrown e-mail application using a server as a message repository.

Our First MIDlet

IN THIS CHAPTER:

Defining a MIDlet

The J2ME Wireless Toolkit

Using KToolbar

Using J2ME with Forte for Java Community Edition

In this chapter, you will develop your first program that uses the MID Profile. You will learn how to write, compile, and deploy a MIDlet in two development environments and will test the MIDlet using two emulators.

Hello MIDP!

Hello.java

It has become a tradition to use the famous *Hello World* program as a starting point for any exploration of a new programming language or API. The program whose source is listed below honors that tradition. As you will see shortly, when it is compiled and deployed, it displays the familiar greeting on MID.

```java
import javax.microedition.midlet.MIDlet;
import javax.microedition.lcdui.Command;
import javax.microedition.lcdui.CommandListener;
import javax.microedition.lcdui.Display;
import javax.microedition.lcdui.Displayable;
import javax.microedition.lcdui.TextBox;

public class Hello extends MIDlet {

    private Display display;

    public Hello() {
        display = Display.getDisplay(this);
    }

    public void startApp() {
        TextBox t = new TextBox("Hello MIDlet", "Hello MIDP!", 256, 0);
        display.setCurrent(t);
    }

    public void pauseApp() {
    }

    public void destroyApp(boolean unconditional) {
    }
}
```

The first thing you notice is that there is more code than would have been required to display "Hello World!" using J2SE.

Whenever you first see a new form of the *Hello World* program, the natural tendency is to look for the statement that displays the message text. In the code just shown, you can quickly spot the following:

```
TextBox t = new TextBox("Hello MIDlet", "Hello MIDP!", 256, 0);
```

You might venture a guess that the presence of a class such as `TextBox` implies that the application runs in a GUI environment. Such a guess would not only be correct but also would come as no surprise. Those of you who have played your favorite game on your cellular phone, pager, or PDA know that applications that run on such devices are graphical in nature. If you examine the `import` statements in the application, you'll see that the `TextBox` class is contained in the package *javax.microedition.lcdui*. The acronyms LCD (liquid crystal display) and UI (user interface) that comprise the third node of the package name leave you with no doubt that you are dealing with a GUI.

Examining the `Hello` class further, you note that it implements `MIDlet`. The MIDP specification contains the following definition of a MIDlet:

> A MIDlet is a Mobile Information Device Profile application. The application must extend this class to allow the application management software to control the MIDlet and to be able to retrieve properties from the application descriptor and notify and request state changes. The methods of this class allow the application management software to create, start, pause, and destroy a MIDlet. A MIDlet is a set of classes designed to be run and controlled by the application management software via this interface. The states allow the application management software to manage the activities of multiple MIDlets within a runtime environment. It can select which MIDlets are active at a given time by starting and pausing them individually. The application management software maintains the state of the MIDlet and invokes methods on the MIDlet to change states. The MIDlet implements these methods to update its internal activities and resource usage as directed by the application management software. The MIDlet can initiate some state changes itself and notifies the application management software of those state changes by invoking the appropriate methods.

Another look at the `import` statements reveals that the `MIDlet` class is contained in the package *javax.microedition.midlet*. If you examine the documentation for this package in Appendix B, you see that it defines the following three abstract methods:

▶   startApp

▶   pauseApp

▶   destroyApp

You would expect to see these methods implemented in any code that extends `MIDlet` and such is indeed the case in the *Hello* application. These methods are not invoked by the application but rather by the application management software. The names of the methods tell exactly when they are invoked.

Deploying the Application Using the J2ME Wireless Toolkit

By now you are probably impatient to run the application, so let's do that. Before you use an emulator to run the application, you must first compile, pre-verify, and deploy it. You can perform these tasks using the J2ME Wireless Toolkit.

NOTE

Before proceeding, you should make sure that you have installed the appropriate software as described in Appendix A. This is especially important if you intend to use Forte for Java in conjunction with the J2ME Wireless Toolkit since the order in which the components are installed makes a difference, as does selection of the Integrated Toolkit option during installation of the Wireless Toolkit.

Starting the Toolkit

There are two ways you can use the J2ME Wireless Toolkit. Let's begin with the easier of the two—the KToolbar, which you run by clicking Start and then selecting

Programs | J2ME Wireless Toolkit | KToolbar. When you do so, the J2ME Wireless
Toolkit begins executing in a window like the one shown next:

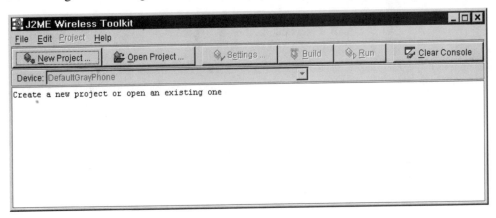

Creating a Project

The Wireless Toolkit uses the concept of a project. A project is associated with a
MIDlet Suite, which is a packaging arrangement that leverages the limited resources
of a Mobile Information Device by allowing multiple MIDP applications to share such
resources. You create a new project by selecting the New Project option from the File
drop-down menu or by simply clicking on the toolbar button labeled New Project.
This results in the appearance of the following dialog box:

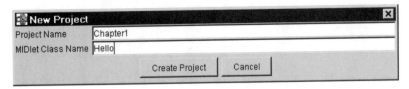

Type **Chapter1** in the Project Name text entry field and **Hello** in the MIDlet
Class Name text entry field.

NOTE

*The project name should not contain any spaces. This restriction might be relaxed in releases of the
J2ME Wireless Toolkit later than the one used to prepare the examples in this book.*

After you have supplied names for the project and the `MIDlet` class, click Create Project, and a dialog box like the one shown next is displayed:

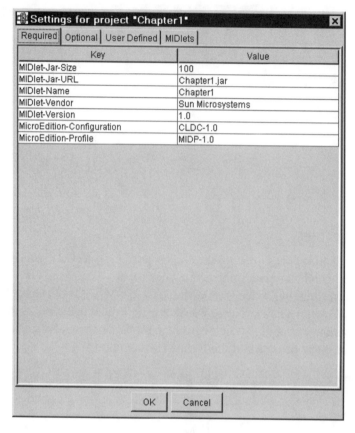

The items in the Key column are MIDlet attributes. The Toolkit saves some of these attributes in a Java Application Descriptor (JAD) file, some in a Manifest file, and some in both files.

The attributes shown are predefined and required. With the exception of *MicroEdition-Configuration* and *MicroEdition-Profile*, they all begin with *MIDlet*. Other attributes are optional. If you click on the Optional tab, you see the following dialog box that you use to specify optional, application-specific attributes. Some attributes are user-defined and must *not* begin with *MIDlet*.

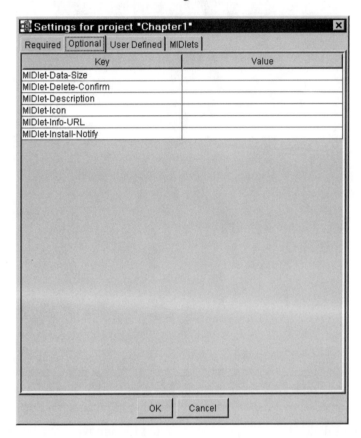

To specify additional attributes, you first click the User Defined tab, then click Add and type the name of a key, as follows:

After you dismiss the Add Property dialog box, you specify a value, as shown here:

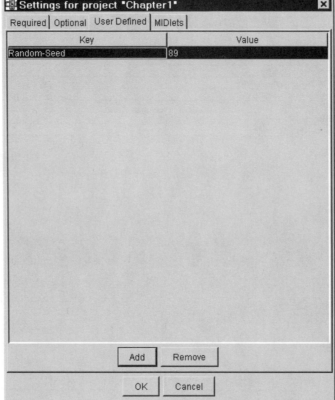

The Settings dialog box also provides a button for removing attributes.

Table 1-1 summarizes the various MIDlet attributes. In addition to describing each attribute, it shows whether the attribute is required or optional and shows the file or files in which it is stored.

 NOTE

The notation J/M in Table 1-1 indicates that the attribute can be found in the JAD file and/or the Manifest.

Attribute Name	Required/Optional	Description	JAD/Manifest
MIDlet-Name	R	The name of the MIDlet Suite that identifies the MIDlets to the user.	J+M
MIDlet-Version	R	The version number of the MIDlet Suite. It takes the form x.y.z where x is the major version, y is the minor version, and z is the micro version.	J+M
MIDlet-Vendor	R	The organization that provides the MIDlet Suite.	J+M
MIDlet-Jar-URL	R	The URL from which the JAR file can be loaded.	J
MIDlet-Jar-Size	R	The size of the JAR file in bytes.	J
MicroEdition-Profile	R	The J2ME profile required. The format is MIDP-x.y.z where x, y, and z are as described for MIDlet-Version.	M
MicroEdition-Configuration	R	The J2ME configuration required. The format is CLDC-x.y.z.	M
MIDlet-Icon	O	The name of a Portable Network Graphics (PNG) file used to represent the MIDlet Suite. The actual file found in the JAR file.	J/M
MIDlet-Description	O	The description of the MIDlet suite.	J/M
MIDlet-Info-URL	O	A URL from which further information describing the MIDlet Suite can be obtained.	J/M
MIDlet-Data-Size	O	The minimum number of bytes of persistent storage required by the MIDlet.	J/M

Table 1-1   *MIDlet Attributes*

Preparing the Source Code

After you dismiss the Settings dialog box, the main window displays instructions like these telling you where you should place your source code. As instructed, copy Hello.java from \Chapter1 on the CD to C:\J2MEWTK\apps\Chapter1\src.

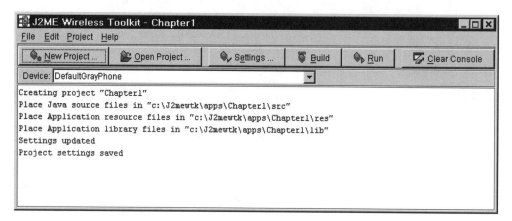

Building the Project

The next step is to build the project. The build operation consists of compiling the source code, pre-verifying the byte code emitted by the compiler, and preparing a JAD file and a Manifest file. You instruct the Toolkit to perform these tasks by selecting the Build option from the Project drop-down menu or by clicking Build on the toolbar. After the Toolkit builds the project, the main window looks like this:

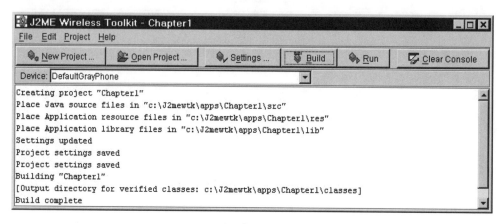

A Short Analysis of the Project

We already stated that the Toolkit generates a JAD file, a Manifest file, and a .class file containing pre-verified byte code. The first two files are stored in the *bin* subdirectory of the directory containing the project. Projects are stored in the *apps* subdirectory of the directory into which you installed the Toolkit. Assuming you installed it in the default directory, you can list the JAD and Manifest files generated by the Toolkit by typing:

```
cd \J2MEWTK\apps\Chapter1\bin
dir
```

The two files you see listed are plain ASCII, so you can use the `type` command to list their contents, as shown next:

```
Command Prompt                                                       _ □ ×

C:\J2MEWTK\apps\Chapter1\bin>type Chapter1.jad
MIDlet-1: Chapter1, Chapter1.png, Hello
MIDlet-Jar-Size: 100
MIDlet-Jar-URL: Chapter1.jar
MIDlet-Name: Chapter1
MIDlet-Vendor: Sun Microsystems
MIDlet-Version: 1.0

C:\J2MEWTK\apps\Chapter1\bin>type MANIFEST.MF
MIDlet-1: Chapter1, Chapter1.png, Hello
MIDlet-Name: Chapter1
MIDlet-Vendor: Sun Microsystems
MIDlet-Version: 1.0
MicroEdition-Configuration: CLDC-1.0
MicroEdition-Profile: MIDP-1.0

C:\J2MEWTK\apps\Chapter1\bin>
```

As you will see later, the .class file is usually packaged in a JAR file that contains other MIDlets belonging to the same MIDlet Suite, as well as the common classes and resources they share as well as a Manifest. This JAR file and the JAD file comprise a MIDlet Suite, as illustrated in Figure 1-1.

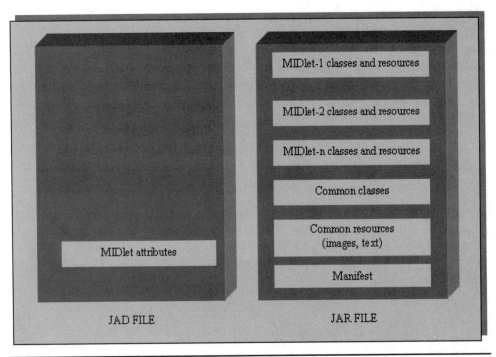

Figure 1-1   *Components of a MIDlet Suite*

Running the Application

All that remains now is to run the application. The Toolkit provides several emulators you can use to test your code. Select one of these from the Device drop-down list beneath the toolbar. After you choose the default device (Default Gray Phone), click Run on the toolbar, and the application is presented in a window containing the emulator, as shown next:

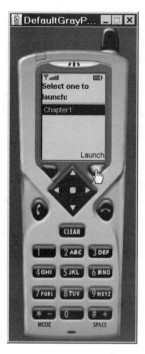

When you press the soft key beneath "Launch" using the hand-shaped cursor, a text box containing the familiar *Hello* greeting is displayed, as shown here:

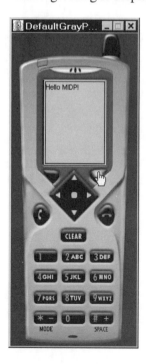

Testing Using Multiple Devices

Although the applications you develop in this book will run on any device that supports the MID specification, the behavior of the application is almost guaranteed to vary from device to device. This is because such characteristics as display size, color support, and keyset vary, as do the number and type of soft buttons and additional keys.

The importance of using a variety of devices to test code cannot be emphasized enough. The Wireless Toolkit supplies a variety of emulators you can use to test your code. There are advantages to using an emulator for testing rather than an actual device. You can develop and test on the same platform with access to debugging tools. It is also easier to recover from errant code that might require resetting a real device.

Table 1-2 describes the characteristics of the emulators supplied with the Wireless Toolkit. We will not show each of the emulators here but will use them to test the examples we develop in subsequent chapters.

Device Type	Display Size	Color Support	Keyset	Soft Buttons	Additional Keys
Default Gray Phone	96×128	256 shades of gray	ITU-T	2	none
Default Color Phone	96×128	256 colors	ITU-T	2	none
Minimum Phone	96×54	Black/white	ITU-T	None	BACK MENU
Motorola i85s	111×100	Black/white	ITU-T	2	MENU
RIMJava Handheld	198×202	Black/white	QWERTY	None	MENU
PalmOS device	Variable, usually 160×160	Variable: Black/white up to 16-bit color	Graffiti and hard buttons	None	MENU HOME

Table 1-2   *Emulator Characteristics*

Using the J2ME Wireless Toolkit with Forte CE

We chose to start with the Ktoolbar because it is easy to use. The price you pay for ease of use in this case is reduced functionality. You discovered, for example, that you had to edit the source code outside of the KToolbar environment. Many developers prefer an Integrated Development Environment (IDE), which allows all aspects of development such as editing source code, compiling, packaging, executing, and debugging to be carried out in a single window or group of related windows. Forte for Java CE (Community Edition) provides such an IDE. It can be freely downloaded from http://java.sun.com. Forte for Java CE integrates with a special module in the Wireless Toolkit so that the full MIDP development cycle can be performed without leaving the IDE.

There are many ways in which you can use Forte for Java to build and run an application. We will now examine one such way.

Starting Forte

You launch Forte by clicking Start and then selecting Programs | Forte for Java CE | Forte for Java CE. The program displays a splash screen followed by a progress report as it loads it components. When loading is complete, you see a screen like this:

Creating a New Project

Like the KToolbar, Forte uses projects; however, in the case of Forte, the amount and type of information associated with a project is far more extensive. For the applications you will develop in this chapter and the remaining chapters, you will create a minimal project, which you start by selecting the Project Manager option from the Project drop-down menu. Forte for Java responds by displaying the following dialog box:

Since you are about to create a project, click on New… and enter **J2MEBook** as the project name, as shown here:

After you enter the project name and click OK, Forte creates and opens the new project, as evidenced by the fact that the Explorer window contains a Project J2MEBook tab, shown next:

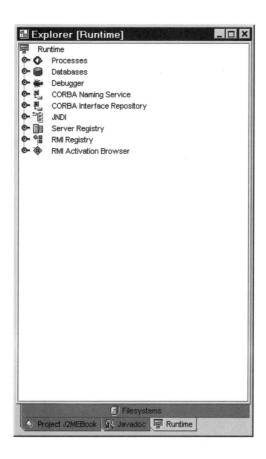

NOTE

Now that you have created a project, you can work through the examples at your own pace. Whenever you close Forte, it saves the state of the active project and restores it during the next startup.

Mounting a Directory

Forte supports the concept of making resources available via a mount point. You are familiar with this concept if you have used UNIX or even if you have shared resources using network drives. For the current project, you will mount the directory c:\OMH.

You start by clicking on the Filesystems tab located immediately above the Project J2MEBook tab in the Explorer window. When you do, a list of the mounted file systems is displayed. Now select Mount Filesystem… from the File drop-down menu in Forte's main window, and this dialog box is displayed:

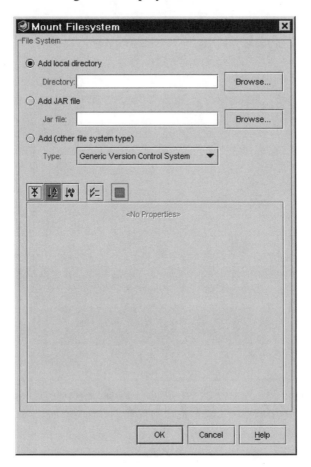

    Click the Browse button located to the right of the Directory: text field beneath the Add local directory radio button and navigate the file system until you reach the directory you wish to mount, in this case c:\OMH. After the appropriate directory has been selected, when you click OK, "c:\OMH" is displayed in the Directory text field. Now click OK at the bottom of the Mount Filesystem dialog box, and the mounted directory is displayed in the Explorer window, as shown next. This mounted directory becomes the relative root for the package you are about to create in the next section.

NOTE

The examples in the book were developed using Preliminary Release 3.0 of Forte for Java CE and Beta 1.0.3 of the Java 2 Micro Edition Wireless Toolkit. One of the "features" of this combination is that the file midpapi.zip, which contains the MIDP classes, is not in the CLASSPATH. To make this file available, it was necessary to mount this file. You should first try deploying your applications without mounting it. If compilation fails with messages that the classes specified by your `import` *statements cannot be found, then mount midpapi.zip by selecting the Add JAR file radio button in the Mount Filesystems dialog box.*

Creating a Package

Good Java programming practice suggests that programmers should use packages. The de facto standard for naming a packages states that the first two nodes of the package name should be the two top-level nodes of an Internet domain in reverse order. This guarantees uniqueness among companies. The third and subsequent nodes in the package name should be chosen so as to guarantee that the package name is unique within the domain. I have registered paulsjavabooks.com and so you can create the package com.paulsjavabooks.instantj2me.Chapter1.

You create the package by right-clicking on the directory you mounted and selecting New Package, as shown next:

After you click New Package, a dialog box containing a request for the package name is displayed. Type **com.paulsjavabooks.instantj2me.Chapter1** into the Name text field, as shown here:

After you type the package name and click OK, the contents of the Explorer window are updated to reflect the addition of the package. The Explorer window now looks like this:

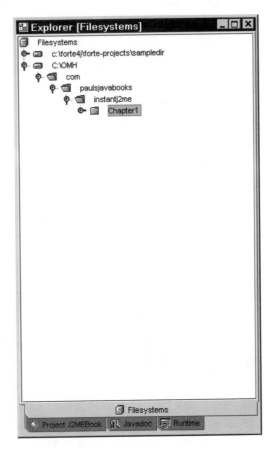

Creating a MIDlet Suite

MIDlet applications are part of a MIDlet Suite, so the next task is to create a MIDlet Suite. To do so, you first select the subdirectory corresponding to the last node of the package name (Chapter1) and right-click. Then select New | MIDP | MIDlet Suite, as shown here:

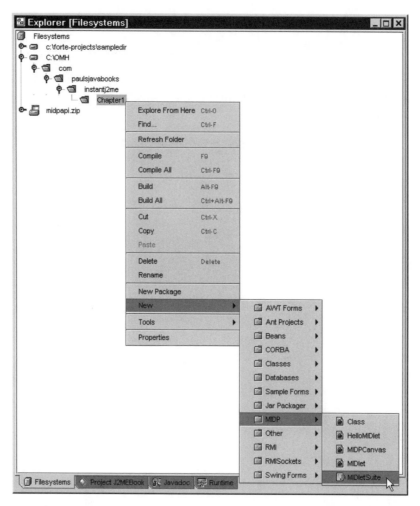

NOTE

It's important that you select the correct subdirectory. Accidentally creating a MIDlet Suite in the wrong subdirectory is the most common mistake and is a source of endless frustration.

When you carry out the steps just outlined, a Wizard like the one shown next appears. It contains a text field into which you type a name for the MIDlet Suite—in this case, **Hello.**

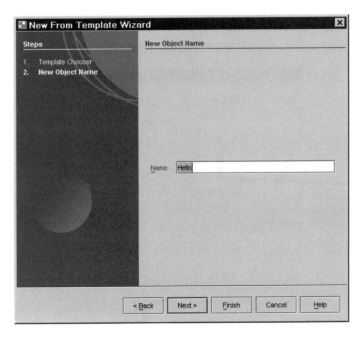

Now, click Next> and the Wizard's second window appears. From the Template drop-down list, select MIDlet. The default values supplied for the other fields are the name of the MIDlet and the name of its main class. The window should now look like this:

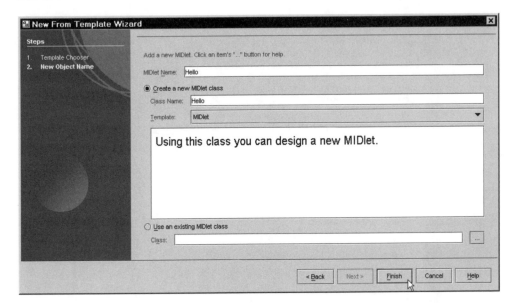

When you click Finish, Forte creates a MIDlet Suite and skeletal source code, and the corresponding icons are displayed in the Explorer window, as shown here:

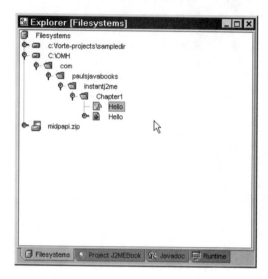

If you double-click on the second of the two new icons, a Source Editor window like the one shown here opens:

```
1  /*
2   * Hello.java
3   *
4   * Created on August 26, 2001, 10:30 PM
5   */
6
7  package com.paulsjavabooks.instantj2me.Chapter1;
8
9  import javax.microedition.midlet.*;
10 import javax.microedition.lcdui.*;
11
12 /**
13  *
14  * @author  paul
15  * @version
16  */
17 public class Hello extends javax.microedition.midlet.MIDlet {
18     public void startApp() {
19     }
20
21     public void pauseApp() {
22     }
23
24     public void destroyApp(boolean unconditional) {
25     }
26 }
27
```

Observe that the code contains comments and tags in a format suitable for use by the *javadoc* utility. It also contains an appropriate `package` statement and empty implementations of the three methods declared as abstract in the `MIDlet` class.

Any changes you need to make to the source can be made in the Source Editor window. As you modify the code, you can compile it without ever leaving the Source Editor by right-clicking anywhere in the window and selecting Compile. You should modify the source so that it looks like this:

```
/*
 * Hello.java
 *
 * Created on August 26, 2001, 10:30 PM
 */

package com.paulsjavabooks.instantj2me.Chapter1;

import javax.microedition.midlet.*;
import javax.microedition.lcdui.*;

/**
 *
 * @author   paul_tremblett
 * @version 1.0
 */
public class Hello extends MIDlet {

    private Display display;

    public Hello() {
        display = Display.getDisplay(this);
    }

    public void startApp() {
        TextBox t = new TextBox("Hello MIDlet", "Hello MIDP!", 256, 0);
        display.setCurrent(t);
    }

    public void pauseApp() {
    }

    public void destroyApp(boolean unconditional) {
    }
}
```

Running the Application

You are finally ready to run the application. You do so from the Explorer window by right-clicking on the MIDlet Suite icon and selecting Execute, as shown next:

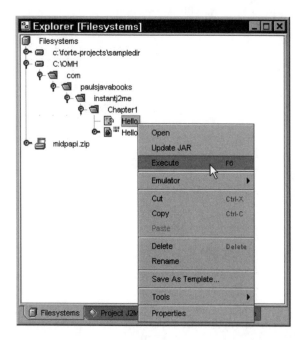

Forte now compiles and pre-verifies the source code, updates the MIDlet Suite, and launches the emulator, which looks like the one shown next:

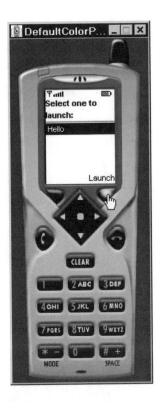

From here, you use the application in exactly the same manner as you did when you launched it from the KToolbar.

Dynamic Content

IN THIS CHAPTER:

The Date Class
The Calendar Class
Time Zones

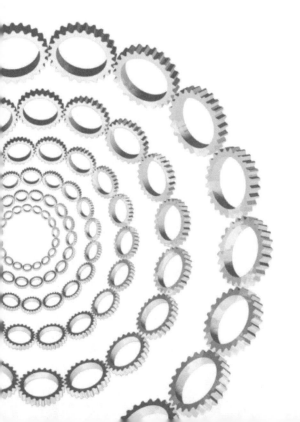

I n the last chapter, the message your program displayed was static. In this chapter, you will deal with a form of dynamic data, the current time. When you first learned Java, you used the `Date` class, which represents a specific instant in time with millisecond precision. We will compare the subset of the `Date` class used in MIDP to the implementation you have previously used in J2SE. We will also explore the related classes `Calendar` and `TimeZone`.

Comparing Implementations of the Date Class

Table 2-1 shows that whether you use J2SE or MIDP, you use identical constructors to create instances of the `Date` class.

Table 2-2, which compares the methods that you can invoke against a `Date` object in the J2SE and MIDP environments, clearly reinforces the fact that MIDP classes offer less functionality than the equivalent classes from J2SE.

NOTE

Strictly speaking, the `Date`, `Calendar`, *and* `TimeZone` *classes are CLDC classes that are available to MIDP by virtue of the fact that MIDP is built on CLDC. Since we are limiting our examples in the book to MIDlets, we will describe all classes and interfaces as belonging to MIDP.*

\OMH\DateTime.java

We will now examine the behavior of an instance of the `Date` class in the J2SE and MIDP environments. Here is a stand-alone J2SE application that creates an instance of `Date` and displays it:

```
import java.util.Date;

public class DateTime {

  public static void main(String[] args) {
    System.out.println(new Date());
  }
}
```

J2SE	MIDP
Date()	Date()
Date(long date)	Date(long date)

Table 2-1   *Constructors of the Date Class*

J2SE	MIDP
after(Date when)	
before(Date when)	
clone()	
compareTo(Date anotherDate)	
compareTo(Object o)	
equals(Object o)	equals(Object o)
getTime()	getTime()
hashCode()	hashCode()
setTime(long time)	setTime(long time)
toString()	

Table 2-2   *Methods of the Date Class*

When you execute this code, you see output like this:

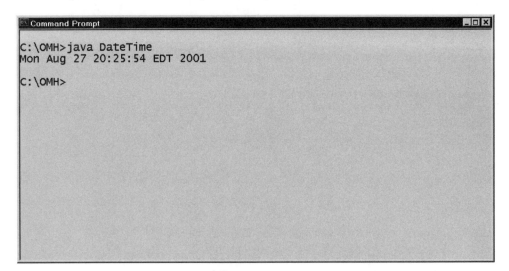

```
C:\OMH>java DateTime
Mon Aug 27 20:25:54 EDT 2001

C:\OMH>
```

\OMH\com\paulsjavabooks\instantj2me\Chapter2\DateMIDlet1.java

Now examine the following equivalent code written as a MIDlet:

```
/*
 * DateMIDlet1.java
 *
```

```
 * Created on August 27, 2001, 8:12 PM
 */

package com.paulsjavabooks.instantj2me.Chapter2;

import java.util.Date;

import javax.microedition.midlet.*;
import javax.microedition.lcdui.*;

/**
 *
 * @author  paul_tremblett
 * @version 1.0
 */
public class DateMIDlet1 extends javax.microedition.midlet.MIDlet {

  private Display display;

    public void startApp() {
        display = Display.getDisplay(this);
        TextBox t = new TextBox("Date MIDlet",
          new Date().toString(), 256, 0);
        display.setCurrent(t);
    }

    public void pauseApp() {
    }

    public void destroyApp(boolean unconditional) {
    }
}
```

Using the procedure presented in Chapter 1, create the package Chapter2 under com\paulsjavabooks\instantj2me; and in the Chapter2 directory create a MIDlet Suite named DateMIDlet1 containing the class DateMIDlet1. When you execute the MIDlet, you see the following output:

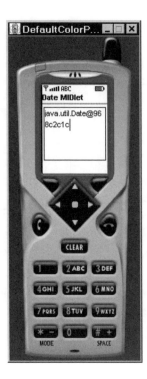

This output is not exactly what was expected, so let's examine the MIDlet. The text you see in the display area is generated by the following code:

```
TextBox t = new TextBox("Date MIDlet", new Date().toString(), 256, 0);
```

Based on experience you have gained from using dates in J2SE, you would expect `new Date().toString()` to return a String in the format:

> *dow mon dd hh:mm:ss zzz yyyy*

where:

- ▶ *dow* is the day of the week (Sun, Mon, Tue, Wed, Thu, Fri, Sat)
- ▶ *mon* is the month (Jan, Feb, Mar, Apr, May, Jun, Jul, Aug, Sep, Oct, Nov, Dec)
- ▶ *dd* is the day of the month (01 through 31), as two decimal digits

- ▶ *hh* is the hour of the day (00 through 23), as two decimal digits
- ▶ *mm* is the minute within the hour (00 through 59), as two decimal digits
- ▶ *ss* is the second within the minute (00 through 59), as two decimal digits
- ▶ *zzz* is the time zone
- ▶ *yyyy* is the year, as four decimal digits

What you see displayed instead is familiar to you as the representation of an object returned by the `toString` method inherited from class `Object` by a class that does not provide its own implementation of `toString`. A quick check of Table 2-2 reveals that this is exactly the case. The important lesson here is that you should not blindly write Java code for MIDP assuming that it will behave exactly like code you write for J2SE. If you do, you should expect an occasional surprise.

The Calendar Class

The problem you encountered in the last example leads you to look for an alternate solution. Such a solution involves using the `Calendar` class. Table 2-3 compares the constructors you can use to create instances of `Calendar` using J2SE and MIDP. Once again, you'll notice the reduced functionality offered by MIDP classes as evidenced by the fact that the `Calendar` class provides a single constructor. You deal with time zones by using the static method `getInstance`, which takes a `TimeZone` object as an argument.

Table 2-4 compares methods of the `Calendar` class available for use under J2SE and MIDP. Once again, you'll notice that MIDP offers less than one-third of the number of methods provided by J2SE. The apparent lack of functionality of the `Date` and `Calendar` classes might lead you to conclude that MIDP can only be used to write trivial programs. Over time, you will see that MIDP does provide you with a sufficient number of methods to implement solutions for most common problems.

J2SE	MIDP
Calendar()	Calendar()
Calendar(TimeZone zone, Locale aLocale)	

Table 2-3   *Constructors of the Calendar Class*

J2SE	MIDP
add(int field, int amount)	
after(Object when)	after(Object when)
before(Object when)	before(Object when)
clear( )	
clear(int field)	
clone( )	
complete( )	
computeFields( )	
computeTime( )	
equals(Object obj)	equals(Object obj)
get(int field)	get(int field)
getActualMaximum(int field)	
getActualMinimum(int field)	
getAvailableLocales( )	
getFirstDayOfWeek( )	
getGreatestMinimum(int field)	
getInstance( )	getInstance( )
getInstance(Locale aLocale)	
getInstance(TimeZone zone)	getInstance(TimeZone zone)
getInstance(TimeZone zone, Locale aLocale)	
getLeastMaximum(int field)	
getMaximum(int field)	
getMinimalDaysInFirstWeek( )	
getMinimum(int field)	
getTime( )	getTime( )
getTimeInMillis( )	getTimeInMillis( )
getTimeZone( )	getTimeZone( )
hashCode( )	
internalGet(int field)	
isLenient( )	
isSet(int field)	
roll(int field, boolean up)	
roll(int field, int amount)	

Table 2-4   *Methods of the Calendar Class*

J2SE	MIDP
set(int field, int value)	set(int field, int value)
set(int year, int month, int date)	
set(int year, int month, int date, int hour, int minute)	
set(int year, int month, int date, int hour, int minute, int second)	
setFirstDayOfWeek(int value)	
setLenient(boolean lenient)	
setMinimalDaysInFirstWeek(int value)	
setTime(Date date)	setTime(Date date)
setTimeInMillis(long millis)	setTimeInMillis(long millis)
setTimeZone(TimeZone value)	setTimeZone(TimeZone value)
toString( )	toString( )

Table 2-4   *Methods of the Calendar Class* (continued)

OMH\com\paulsjavabooks\instantj2me\Chapter2\DateMIDlet2.java

Now, let's return to the issue of correcting the strange, undesirable behavior exhibited by our first example. Take a look at the following code:

```
/*
 * DateMIDlet2.java
 *
 * Created on August 27, 2001, 9:32 PM
 */

package com.paulsjavabooks.instantj2me.Chapter2;

import java.util.Calendar;

import javax.microedition.midlet.*;
import javax.microedition.lcdui.*;

/**
 *
 * @author  paul_tremblett
 * @version 1.0
 */
public class DateMIDlet2 extends javax.microedition.midlet.MIDlet {

    private Display display;
```

```
public void startApp() {
    display = Display.getDisplay(this);
    TextBox t = new TextBox("Date MIDlet",
      Calendar.getInstance().toString(), 256, 0);
    display.setCurrent(t);
}

public void pauseApp() {
}

public void destroyApp(boolean unconditional) {
}
}
```

Instead of creating an instance of Date and invoking its toString method, which proved to be the cause of the unanticipated output from the execution of the first program, this version of the MIDlet invokes the toString method against an instance of Calendar.

When you run it, it generates the following output, which looks much more like what we intended when we wrote the first application:

We started the chapter by showing the behavior of code written for J2SE and then developing what we hoped would be a MIDP equivalent. Since you now have a working MIDlet, let's reverse the process by writing a proposed J2SE equivalent version that uses the `Calendar` class and see what happens. Since we are more interested in comparing the behavior of the `Calendar` class under J2SE to its behavior under MIDP, we simplify things by creating a single instance of `Calendar` and displaying the String returned by its `toString` method. Here is the code:

\OMH\CalTest.java

```
import java.util.Calendar;

public class CalTest {

  public static void main(String[] args) {

  System.out.println(Calendar.getInstance().toString());
  }
}
```

This is the output produced by the program:

```
Command Prompt                                          _ □ ☒

C:\OMH>java CalTest
java.util.GregorianCalendar[time=998964497612,areFieldsSet=true,areAllF
ieldsSet=true,lenient=true,zone=java.util.SimpleTimeZone[id=America/New
_York,offset=-18000000,dstSavings=3600000,useDaylight=true,startYear=0,
startMode=3,startMonth=3,startDay=1,startDayOfWeek=1,startTime=7200000,
startTimeMode=0,endMode=2,endMonth=9,endDay=-1,endDayOfWeek=1,endTime=7
200000,endTimeMode=0],firstDayOfWeek=1,minimalDaysInFirstWeek=1,ERA=1,Y
EAR=2001,MONTH=7,WEEK_OF_YEAR=35,WEEK_OF_MONTH=5,DAY_OF_MONTH=27,DAY_OF
_YEAR=239,DAY_OF_WEEK=2,DAY_OF_WEEK_IN_MONTH=4,AM_PM=1,HOUR=10,HOUR_OF_
DAY=22,MINUTE=8,SECOND=17,MILLISECOND=612,ZONE_OFFSET=-18000000,DST_OFF
SET=3600000]

C:\OMH>_
```

Once again, the output is not what you expected. It is obvious that MIDP and J2SE have very different implementations of the `toString` method of the `Calendar` class. This not only reinforces what you learned earlier about being careful when porting code, but it also demonstrates that you should be as careful when you port from MIDP to J2SE as when you port from J2SE to MIDP.

The TimeZone Class

One of the forms of the `getInstance` method of the MIDP class `Calendar` takes a `TimeZone` object as a parameter. This would imply that MIDP supports the concept of time zones. You will now see the extent to which this is true. Table 2-5 shows that the MIDP implementation of the `TimeZone` class has a single constructor like its J2SE counterpart.

As you might expect, Table 2-6 shows that the MIDP implementation of `TimeZone` offers less functionality. What the table does not point out is that the MIDP specification states that only a single time zone, GMT, must be supported.

Time Zones Under MIDP

\OMH\com\paulsjavabooks\instantj2me\Chapter2\TimeZoneMIDlet.java

Here is a MIDlet that lists all available time zones:

```
/*
 * TimeZoneMIDlet.java
 *
 * Created on August 28, 2001, 6:19 PM
 */

package com.paulsjavabooks.instantj2me.Chapter2;

import javax.microedition.midlet.*;
import javax.microedition.lcdui.*;

import java.util.TimeZone;
```

```
/**
 *
 * @author  paul_tremblett
 * @version 1.0
 */
public class TimeZoneMIDlet extends javax.microedition.midlet.MIDlet {

  private Display display;

    public void startApp() {
        display = Display.getDisplay(this);
        String[] timeZoneList = TimeZone.getAvailableIDs();
        StringBuffer sb = new StringBuffer();
        for (int i = 0; i < timeZoneList.length; ++i) {
          sb.append(timeZoneList[i]);
          sb.append('\n');
        }
        TextBox t = new TextBox("Time Zone List",
          sb.toString(), 256, 0);
        display.setCurrent(t);
    }

    public void pauseApp() {
    }

    public void destroyApp(boolean unconditional) {
    }
}
```

J2SE	MIDP
TimeZone()	TimeZone()

Table 2-5   *Constructors of the TimeZone Class*

J2SE	MIDP
clone()	
getAvailableIDs()	getAvailableIDs()
getAvailableIDs(int rawOffset)	
getDefault()	getDefault()
getDisplayName()	
getDisplayName(boolean daylight, int style)	
getDisplayName(boolean daylight, int style, Locale locale)	
getDisplayName(Locale locale)	
getID()	getID()
getOffset(int era, int year, int month, int day, int dayOfWeek, int milliseconds)	getOffset(int era, int year, int month, int day, int dayOfWeek, int milliseconds)
getRawOffset()	getRawOffset()
getTimeZone(String id)	getTimeZone(String id)
hasSameRules(TimeZone other)	
inDaylightTime(Date date)	
setDefault(TimeZone zone)	
setID(String ID)	
setRawOffset(int offsetMillis)	
useDaylightTime()	useDaylightTime()

Table 2-6 *Methods of the TimeZone Class*

The application simply iterates through the array of Strings returned by the `getAvailableIDs` method, appends each ID in the list to a StringBuffer, and appends a newline character. When the iteration has been completed, it converts the StringBuffer to a String and displays it.

When you run the application, it produces the following rather sparse output:

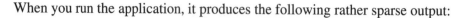

J2SE
\OMH\TimeZonesJ2SE.java

Here is the J2SE equivalent of the application that lists all available time zones:

```java
import java.util.TimeZone;

public class TimeZonesJ2SE {

  public static void main(String[] args) {
    String[] zoneList = TimeZone.getAvailableIDs();
    for (int i = 0; i < zoneList.length; ++i) {
      System.out.println(zoneList[i]);
    }
    System.out.println("There are " + zoneList.length +
      " time zones available");
  }
}
```

When you compile and run this program, it produces so much output that it scrolls off the window. The last lines it displays are here.

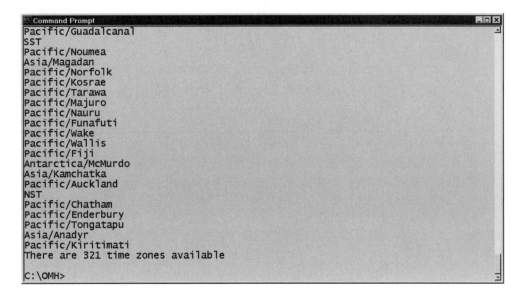

Command and CommandListener

IN THIS CHAPTER:

A second version of Hello World

Emulators and more emulators

The Command class

The CommandListener interface

An inner class as a listener

I n order to keep the examples presented in the first two chapters simple, we omitted an important element of any meaningful program, user interaction. In this chapter, we demonstrate how the `Command` class and the `CommandListener` interface are used to provide such interaction.

A Second Version of Hello World

\OMH\com\paulsjavabooks\instantj2me\Chapter3\Hello2.java

Here is the code for a second version of the *Hello* application:

```
/*
 * Hello2.java
 *
 * Created on September 11, 2001, 9:53 PM
 */

package com.paulsjavabooks.instantj2me.Chapter3;

import javax.microedition.midlet.*;
import javax.microedition.lcdui.*;

/**
 *
 * @author  paul_tremblett
 * @version 1.0
 */
public class Hello2 extends javax.microedition.midlet.MIDlet
        implements CommandListener {

  private Command cmdExit;
  private Display display;
```

```
public Hello2() {
  display = Display.getDisplay(this);
  cmdExit = new Command("Exit", Command.SCREEN, 2);
}

public void startApp() {
  TextBox t = new TextBox("Hello MIDlet", "Hello MIDP!", 256, 0);

  t.addCommand(cmdExit);
  t.setCommandListener(this);

  display.setCurrent(t);
}

public void pauseApp() {
}

public void destroyApp(boolean unconditional) {
}

public void commandAction(Command cmd, Displayable disp) {
  if (cmd == cmdExit) {
    destroyApp(false);
    notifyDestroyed();
  }
}
}
```

In addition to extending MIDlet, Hello2 implements CommandListener. The documentation states that this interface is used by applications that need to receive high-level events. You can see from Appendix B that CommandListener defines a single method commandAction, which takes two arguments. The first argument is a command object and the second is a displayable.

We will take a closer look at the CommandListener interface and the Command class shortly. For now, let's run the application. Observing its runtime behavior will prove helpful when we discuss the Command class.

Running the Second Version of Hello World

You use either the KToolbar or Forte for Java to prepare the application for execution as you learned earlier. Regardless of which method you choose, when you run the application using the Default Color Phone, you see a window like the one shown here:

At first glance, things look the same. The difference between this version and the previous version manifests itself when you click the button pointed to by the hand-shaped cursor. When you do so, the emulator displays "Hello MIDP!" as it did before, but this time the text "Exit" is displayed above the leftmost soft button, as shown next. When you press the button, the application terminates and you are once again looking at the original display.

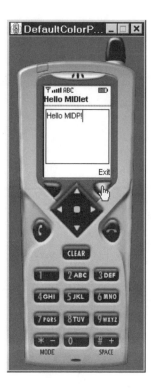

Running Using Different Emulators

We have already mentioned the importance of using multiple devices to test your applications. In Table 1-2 we showed the characteristics of the emulators that come with the J2ME Wireless Toolkit. We will now observe `Hello2` running in several of these emulators.

The way you specify the emulator you wish to use depends on whether you are using the KToolbar or Forte. We start with the KToolbar because it is easier. When you load a project using the toolbar's Open Project button, the Device drop-down list becomes active. You then simply select the desired device from the list.

If you are using Forte for Java, you begin the process of specifying an emulator by right-clicking on the Hello2 MIDlet Suite icon, as shown here:

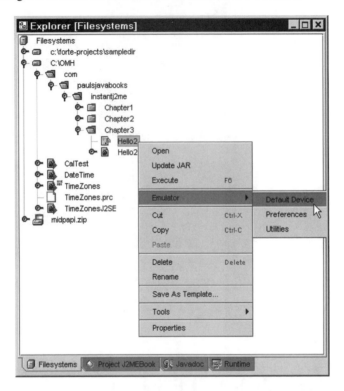

When the Default Device dialog box is displayed, select "Minimum Phone" from the drop-down list, as shown here:

After you have selected an emulator, click OK to dismiss the dialog. You then execute your application again. This time you'll observe that the window that appears is labeled Minimum Phone and the emulator it contains does indeed look different from the Default Color Phone.

You start the application by pressing the roller button located beneath the hand-shaped cursor. When you do so, the message "Hello MIDP!" is displayed, as shown next:

The text "Exit" that served as a label in the Default Color Phone emulator is noticeably absent. The rightmost button beneath the display, which is pointed to by the hand-shaped cursor, bears the permanent label "Menu" etched into the body of the phone. When you press this button, a menu containing the single item Exit is displayed, as shown next:

If the menu contained more than one item, you would use the roller button to traverse the list. The item selected by moving the roller button is displayed in inverted colors. In this case, the Exit item is selected. When you press the roller button, the application terminates and the window once again looks like the original display.

Using the procedure just illustrated, you next select the *Pager* emulator.
This time, when you execute the application, the initial display looks like this:

When you use the *Pager* emulator, you start the application by pressing Select,
which is located beneath the hand-shaped cursor. Once again, you see "Hello
MIDP!" displayed, as shown next:

Like the Minimal Phone, the Pager emulator features a Menu button that is permanently labeled. When you press this button, a menu like the one shown next is displayed:

If the menu contained more than one item, you could use the up and down arrow buttons at the bottom of the emulator to traverse the list. When an item is selected, it is displayed in inverted colors. In this case, the Exit menu item is selected. When you press Select, the application terminates.

Establishing the Mind-set Required to Work with LCDUI

In Chapter 1, we stated that applications behave differently when run on different devices. In this chapter, we demonstrated the truth of that statement. The emulators listed in Table 1-2 and used in the previous section to run the *Hello2* application represent but a tiny subset of an ever-growing universe of devices. The Mobile Information Device Profile Expert Group (MIDPEG) states in the specification that "MIDs span a potentially wide set of capabilities. Rather than try to address all such capabilities, the MIDPEG agreed to limit the set of APIs specified, addressing only those APIs that were considered absolute requirements to achieve broad portability."

In addition to being limited, the APIs tend to lean toward the abstract. This is especially true of user interface APIs. The task of transforming these abstractions to a real-world interface is left to the implementation that runs on a given device.

Programmers who use this interface quickly discover they have far less control over the behavior of their application than they did when they wrote the same applications for Windows or X Windows. The best you can hope to do in many cases is to make suggestions and leave the rest to the implementation. The hardest part of using the LCDUI in most cases is not letting this loss of control discourage you.

One other characteristic that can contribute to a painful transition from traditional GUI programming to writing MID applications is screen real estate. There really is no other way to say it—the screen on even the largest MID is small.

You can take heart in knowing that even though MIDs are relatively new, numerous MID applications have already been developed. Knowing this serves the twofold purpose of reminding you that MID development, although frustrating at first, is indeed possible, and giving you examples you can follow as you develop your own applications.

With that sermonette out of the way, we now look a little deeper into MID programming.

The Command Class

The "Exit" text that was displayed in each of the emulators as either a label associated with a soft button or an item in a menu is a visual representation of a Command object. The spec defines the Command class as follows:

> The Command class is a construct that encapsulates the semantic information of an action. The behavior that the command activates is not encapsulated in this object. This means that command contains only information about 'command' not the actual action that happens when command is activated. The action is defined in a CommandListener associated with the screen. Command objects are *presented* in the user interface and the way they are presented may depend on the semantic information contained within the command.

> Commands may be implemented in any user interface construct that has semantics for activating a single action. This, for example, can be a soft button, item in a menu, or some other direct user interface construct. For example, a speech interface may present these commands as voice tags.

> The mapping to concrete user interface constructs may also depend on the total number of the commands. For example, if an application asks for more abstract commands than can be mapped onto the available physical buttons on a device, the device may use an alternate human interface such as a menu. For example, the abstract commands that cannot be mapped onto physical buttons are placed in a menu and the label 'Menu' is mapped onto one of the programmable buttons.

In the *Hello2* application, the Command object is created by the following line of code:

```
cmdExit = new Command("Exit", Command.SCREEN, 2);
```

Now let's discuss each of the three arguments passed to the constructor.

Command Label

The first argument an application passes to the constructor when creating an instance of the Command class is a String that the application *requests* to be shown to the user to represent the command. In your *Hello2* application, the label is "Exit." The implementation may override the request and display a system-specific label that is more appropriate for this command on this device. The exception is when the command is of type *SCREEN*. We discuss command types in the next section.

Command Type

The second argument an application passes to the constructor when creating an instance of Command is an int that specifies a command type. The application uses the command type to notify the implementation of the *intent* of the command. If the device has a standard placement for the specified type of command, the implementation can follow the style of the device using the command type as a guideline. Keep in mind that the best the application can do is to signal intent. The ultimate decision regarding placement is made by the implementation.

The defined command types are listed in Table 3-1.

Command Priority

The final argument an application passes to the constructor is an int that specifies the priority or relative importance the application wishes to assign to this command relative to other commands on the screen. Low numbers indicate a high relative priority. As a general rule, the implementation places the greatest weight on the type of command when deciding placement and uses priority to resolve placement of commands of a similar type. The implementation might, for example, place the command with the highest priority next to a soft button if one is available for use and place commands of a lower priority (higher number) in a menu. As was the case with command type, you must keep in mind that the best the application can do is *suggest*. The ultimate decision is made by the implementation.

Type	Assigned Number	Description
BACK	2	A navigation command that returns the user to the logically previous screen.
CANCEL	3	A command that is the standard negative answer to a dialog box implementation by the current screen.
EXIT	7	A command used for exiting from the application.
HELP	5	A command that specifies a request for online help.
ITEM	8	A command the application uses to hint to the implementation that the command is specific to an item on the screen.
OK	4	A command that is the standard positive answer to a dialog box implementation by the current screen.
SCREEN	1	Specifies an application-defined command that applies to the current screen.
STOP	6	A command that will stop some currently running process, operation, etc.

Table 3-1   *Defined Command Types*

It is entirely possible for a screen to contain multiple commands of the same type and priority. In such a case, the implementation chooses the order in which they are presented.

CommandListener

We have already stated that a command contains information but not behavior. The behavior of a Command object is contained in an action that is defined in a CommandListener associated with the screen.

CommandListener is an interface that is implemented by your *Hello2* class. The interface defines the single method commandAction. The implementation of this method in Hello2 looks like this:

```
public void commandAction(Command cmd, Displayable disp) {
    if (cmd == cmdExit) {
      destroyApp(false);
      notifyDestroyed();
    }
}
```

To understand how CommandListener works, start by examining the TextBox class. You can see from the documentation that TextBox extends Screen, which in turn extends Displayable. When you examine the list of methods defined in Displayable, we see that addCommand is used to add a command to the displayable. The implementation determines where and how the command is displayed. In your *Hello2* application, the command is added by the following line of code:

```
t.addCommand(cmdExit);
```

You set a listener for commands by invoking the setCommandListener method as follows:

```
t.setCommandListener(this);
```

Now, when the user selects Exit by either pressing a soft button that bears the corresponding label or selecting a menu item, the command is passed as an argument to the actionCommand method. The implementation of actionCommand in *Hello2* invokes the MIDlet's destroyApp method, which signals the MIDlet to terminate and enter the *destroyed* state. A MIDlet that enters the destroyed state must release all resources and save any persistent data. (We will discuss persistent data in Chapter 10.) Your actionCommand method then invokes notifyDestroyed, which notifies the application management software that the MIDlet has entered the destroyed state. The application management software will then know not to attempt a subsequent invocation of the MIDlet's destoyApp method and will consider it safe to reclaim any resources that were held by the MIDlet.

Using an Inner Class to Implement a CommandListener

Since the concept of listeners is not new to most of you, you probably know that inner classes are often used to implement a listener. Let's now examine a trivial application that uses inner classes to implement two listeners. The application displays the current date and provides the user with a means of specifying whether

the date should be displayed in the normal format DD/MM/YYYY or in the format
MM/DD/YYYY that is used in the United States. Here is the code:

\OMH\com\paulsjavabooks\instantj2me\Chapter3\DateExample.java

```
package com.paulsjavabooks.instantj2me.Chapter3;

import javax.microedition.midlet.*;
import javax.microedition.lcdui.*;

import java.util.Calendar;

public class DateExample extends javax.microedition.midlet.MIDlet {

  private Command cmdSetDateType;
  private Command cmdDisplayDate;
  private Command cmdExit;

  private Command cmdSetDateTypeUSA;
  private Command cmdSetDateTypeNormal;

  private TextBox textBox1;
  private TextBox textBox2;

  private CommandListener listener1;
  private CommandListener listener2;

  private Display display;

  private static final String TEXT1 =
    "TextBox 1\nUse Menu";
  private static final String TEXT2 =
    "TextBox 2\nUseMenu";
  private static final String SLASH = "/";

  private static final int DATE_FORMAT_USA = 1;
  private static final int DATE_FORMAT_NORMAL = 2;
```

```java
    private int dateFormat = DATE_FORMAT_NORMAL;

    public DateExample() {
      display = Display.getDisplay(this);
      cmdSetDateType =
        new Command("Set Date Type",Command.SCREEN,2);
      cmdExit =
        new Command("Exit", Command.EXIT, 1);
      cmdSetDateTypeUSA =
        new Command("USA", Command.SCREEN, 2);
      cmdSetDateTypeNormal =
        new Command("Normal", Command.SCREEN, 2);
      cmdDisplayDate =
        new Command("Display Date", Command.SCREEN, 2);
      dateFormat = DATE_FORMAT_USA;
    }

    public void startApp() {
      textBox1 = new TextBox("Date MIDlet", null, 256, 0);
      textBox1.addCommand(cmdSetDateType);
      textBox1.addCommand(cmdDisplayDate);
      textBox1.addCommand(cmdExit);

      listener1 = (CommandListener)new TextBoxListener1();
      textBox1.setCommandListener(listener1);

      textBox2 = new TextBox("Date ", null, 256, 0);
      textBox2.addCommand(cmdSetDateTypeUSA);
      textBox2.addCommand(cmdSetDateTypeNormal);

      listener2 = (CommandListener)new TextBoxListener2();
      textBox2.setCommandListener(listener2);

      textBox1.setString(TEXT1);
      display.setCurrent(textBox1);
    }

    public void pauseApp() {
    }

    public void destroyApp(boolean unconditional) {
    }
```

```
private void setActiveTextBox(TextBox tb) {
  display.setCurrent(tb);
}

class TextBoxListener1 implements CommandListener {

  public void commandAction(Command cmd, Displayable disp) {
    System.out.println("in TextBoxListener1");
    if (cmd == cmdExit) {
      destroyApp(false);
      notifyDestroyed();
    }
    else if (cmd == cmdSetDateType) {
      textBox2.setString(TEXT2);
      setActiveTextBox(textBox2);
    }
    else {
      Calendar cal = Calendar.getInstance();
      StringBuffer sb = new StringBuffer();
      if (dateFormat == DATE_FORMAT_USA) {
        sb.append(Integer.toString(cal.get(Calendar.MONTH)))
          .append(SLASH)
          .append(Integer.toString(cal.get(Calendar.DAY_OF_MONTH)));
      }
      else {
        sb.append(Integer.toString(cal.get(Calendar.DAY_OF_MONTH)))
          .append(SLASH)
          .append(Integer.toString(cal.get(Calendar.MONTH)));
      }
      sb.append(SLASH)
        .append(Integer.toString(cal.get(Calendar.YEAR)));
      textBox1.setString(sb.toString() + "\n" + TEXT1);
    }
  }
}

class TextBoxListener2 implements CommandListener {

  public void commandAction(Command cmd, Displayable disp) {
    System.out.println("in TextBoxListener2");
```

```
     if (cmd == cmdExit) {
       destroyApp(false);
       notifyDestroyed();
     }
     else {
       if (cmd == cmdSetDateTypeUSA) {
        dateFormat = DATE_FORMAT_USA;
       }
       else {
         dateFormat = DATE_FORMAT_NORMAL;
       }
       textBox1.setString(TEXT1);
       setActiveTextBox(textBox1);
     }
   }
  }
}
```

The first thing you'll notice about `DateTimeExample` is that it does not implement `CommandListener` like the *Hello2* example. Instead, it contains two inner classes that implement `CommandListener` and therefore also contain implementations of the `commandAction` method. The only reason we chose to use two listeners is simply to show that, if appropriate, an application can have multiple listeners. As you navigate through the application, notice that the `TextBoxListener1` object can use the `setActiveTextBox` method to make the `TextBoxListener2` object the active `TextBox` and vice versa. The constructor of `DateTimeExample` adds `textBoxListener1` to `textBox1` and `textBoxListener2` to `textBox2`. Therefore, when `textBox1` is active, the `commandAction` method of `textBoxListener1` is invoked, and when `textBox2` is active, the `commandAction` method of `textBoxListener2` is invoked.

NOTE

The sole purpose of this example is to illustrate how inner classes can be used to implement a `CommandListener`. As you run the application, it becomes obvious that it leaves much to be desired from a navigational point of view. When you learn about displayables other than `TextBox` in later chapters, you will be able to rewrite the application using a more suitable displayable such the `List` class, which is a screen containing a list of choices.

Running the DateExample Application

You can run the application using the Pager and Default Gray Phone emulators and observe how the implementation presents the options for date format as a menu and as soft button labels, respectively.

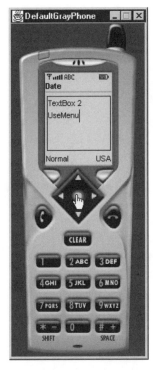

Using Random Numbers

IN THIS CHAPTER:

A comparison to J2SE

Demonstrating the behavior of random number sequences

An application that uses random numbers

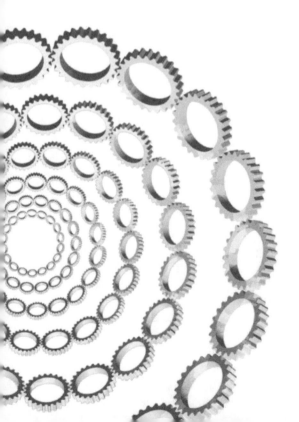

I n Chapter 2, we explored Calendar, Date, and TimeZone. These classes are all contained in the *java.util* package. We pointed out that the MIDP implementation of these classes is different from the J2SE implementation. In this chapter, we will continue our exploration of the *java.util* package by taking a look at the Random class.

Interchangeability Between J2SE and MIDP

Tables 4-1 and 4-2 show comparisons between the constructors and methods of the Random class under J2SE and MIDP. By now, a comment about reduced functionality under MIDP is unnecessary.

Java code should behave identically under J2ME and J2SE. The documentation of Random states that if two instances of Random are created with the same seed, and the same sequence of method calls is made for each, they will generate and return identical sequences of numbers. You prove this by running identical code under J2ME and J2SE.

A Random Sequence Under J2SE

\OMH\RanGen1.java

Start by generating a sequence of ten random numbers under J2SE. Here is the code:

```
import java.util.Random;

public class RanGen1 {

  public static void main(String[] args) {
    Random rand = new Random(171);
    for (int i = 0; i < 10; ++i) {
      System.out.println(rand.nextInt());
    }
  }
}
```

J2SE	MIDP
Random()	Random()
Random(long seed)	Random(long seed)

Table 4-1   *Constructors of the Random Class*

J2SE	MIDP
next(int bits)	next(int bits)
nextBoolean()	
nextBytes(byte[] bytes)	
nextDouble()	
nextFloat()	
nextGaussian()	
nextInt()	nextInt()
nextInt(int n)	
nextLong()	nextLong()
setSeed(long seed)	setSeed(long seed)

Table 4-2   *Methods of the Random Class*

When you run this code, you'll observe output like that shown here:

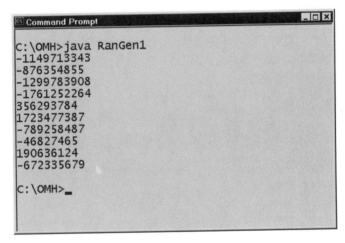

```
C:\OMH>java RanGen1
-1149713343
-876354855
-1299783908
-1761252264
356293784
1723477387
-789258487
-46827465
190636124
-672335679

C:\OMH>_
```

A Random Sequence Under MIDP

\OMH\com\paulsjavabooks\instantj2me\Chapter4\RanGen2.java

Here is the MIDP equivalent of the J2SE code you just ran:

```
/*
 * RanGen2.java
 *
```

```
 * Created on September 12, 2001, 9:00 PM
 */

package com.paulsjavabooks.instantj2me.Chapter4;

import javax.microedition.midlet.*;
import javax.microedition.lcdui.*;

import java.util.Random;

/**
 *
 * @author  paul_tremblett
 * @version 1.0
 */
public class RanGen2 extends javax.microedition.midlet.MIDlet
    implements CommandListener {

  private Display display;
  private Form f;
  private Command cmdExit;
  private StringItem nums;

  public void startApp() {
    display = Display.getDisplay(this);
    f = new Form("Random Numbers");
    String s = generateRandoms();
    nums = new StringItem(null,s);
    f.append(nums);
    cmdExit = new Command("Exit",Command.EXIT,1);
    f.addCommand(cmdExit);
    f.setCommandListener(this);
    display.setCurrent(f);
  }

  public void pauseApp() {
  }

  public void destroyApp(boolean unconditional) {
  }

  public void commandAction(Command cmd, Displayable disp) {
    if (cmd == cmdExit) {
      destroyApp(false);
```

```
      notifyDestroyed();
   }
}

public String generateRandoms() {
  StringBuffer sb = new StringBuffer();
  Random rand = new Random(171);
  for (int i = 0; i < 10; ++i) {
    int ri = rand.nextInt();
    sb.append(Integer.toString(ri));
    sb.append('\n');
  }
  return sb.toString();
  }
}
```

You will observe that you create an instance of Random and invoke its nextInt method in exactly the same manner as you did in your J2SE code. When you compile, pre-verify, and run the code using the RIM emulator, it generates the following output:

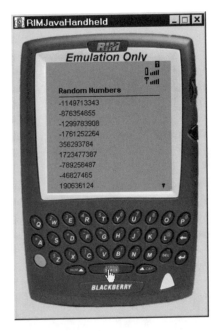

When you compare the random numbers generated by both versions of the code, you see that they are identical. This means that Java applications that rely on generation of a predictable, reproducible sequence of random numbers can be ported with confidence from J2SE to MIDP.

Generating Lottery Numbers

OMH\com\Paulsjavabooks\instantj2me\Chapter4\Lottery.java

We all know that having a computer "pick" lottery numbers for us has absolutely no effect on our odds of winning. However, for those who enjoy the fun of using a PDA to select lottery numbers, we present an application that does so. Here is the code:

```java
/*
 * Lottery.java
 *
 * Created on September 13, 2001, 7:33 PM
 */

package com.paulsjavabooks.instantj2me.Chapter4;

import javax.microedition.midlet.*;
import javax.microedition.lcdui.*;

import java.util.Hashtable;
import java.util.Random;

/**
 *
 * @author  paul tremblett
 * @version 1.0
 */
public class Lottery extends javax.microedition.midlet.MIDlet
    implements CommandListener {

  private Command cmdMore;
  private Command cmdExit;
  private Form f;
  private Display display;
  private StringItem nums;

  private int maxValue;
  private int numNumbers;

  private Random rand;

  public void startApp() {
```

```
    numNumbers = Integer.parseInt(getAppProperty("NUM_NUMBERS"));
    maxValue = Integer.parseInt(getAppProperty("MAX_VALUE"));
    rand = new Random(System.currentTimeMillis());
    display = Display.getDisplay(this);
    f = new Form("Lottery Numbers");
    nums = new StringItem(null,null);
    f.append(nums);
    cmdMore = new Command("More",Command.SCREEN,1);
    cmdExit = new Command("Exit",Command.EXIT,1);
    f.addCommand(cmdMore);
    f.addCommand(cmdExit);
    f.setCommandListener(this);
    nums.setText(generateNumbers());
    display.setCurrent(f);
}

public void pauseApp() {
}

public void destroyApp(boolean unconditional) {
}

public void commandAction(Command cmd, Displayable d) {
  if (cmd == cmdExit) {
    destroyApp(false);
    notifyDestroyed();
  }
  else if (cmd == cmdMore) {
    nums.setText(generateNumbers());
  }
}

private String generateNumbers() {
  StringBuffer sb = new StringBuffer();
  boolean[] duplicate = new boolean[maxValue + 1];

  for (int i = 0; i < duplicate.length; ++i) {
    duplicate[i] = false;
  }

  int x = 0;
  int ct = 0;
```

```
      Hashtable ht = new Hashtable();
      while (ct < numNumbers) {
        int ri = 1 + Math.abs(rand.nextInt() % maxValue);
        if (!duplicate[ri]) {
          duplicate[ri] = true;
          sb.append(Integer.toString(ri));
          sb.append(' ');
          ++ct;
        }
      }
  return sb.toString();
    }
}
```

This code does the following:

▶ Retrieves the values of the properties named MAX_VALUE and NUM_NUMBERS, which specify the value of the largest random number to be selected and how many random numbers constitute a set

▶ Creates a random number generator seeded with a number based on the current time

▶ Generates a random integer between 1 and the specified maximum value

▶ Checks if the number that was generated has been previously generated

▶ If the number has not been previously generated, appends it to a `StringBuffer`

▶ Updates the array that keeps track of duplicates

▶ Repeats the previous four steps until a complete set of unique values has been generated

▶ Displays the contents of the `StringBuffer`

Running the Lottery Application

After you have compiled the MIDlet, double-click on the MIDlet Suite icon. When the resulting dialog box appears, enter **NUM_NUMBERS** into the entry field to the right of the New Tag button. Repeat the process to enter **MAX_VALUE**. After the new tags have been added, specify values for them, as shown here:

User Interaction Using the MIDP API

IN THIS CHAPTER:

More about TextBox
The Form class
The Choice interface
The ChoiceGroup class

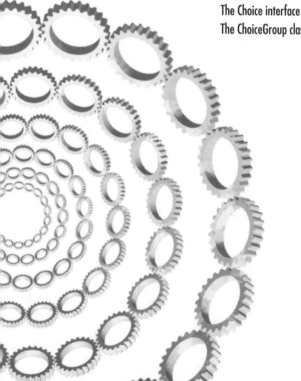

One of the most important qualities of an application is its ability to interact with the user. The MIDP specification describes a user interface that is simple, yet sufficiently powerful to provide the user of a MID with a way to interact with a MIDlet. In this chapter, we will discuss some of the UI elements and present sample programs that demonstrate how to use them.

A Closer Look at TextBox

In Chapter 1, you used an instance of TextBox to display a simple "Hello" greeting. In Chapter 3, based on your observation that TextBox inherited from Displayable, you used the addCommand method to add several commands with which the user could interact. In both these chapters, you used the instance of TextBox to display text; however, there is much more to the TextBox class, and we will now examine it in greater detail.

The documentation defines TextBox as a screen that allows the user to enter and edit text. If you run the *Hello World* example from Chapter 1, you discover that you can modify or even delete the original greeting, as shown here:

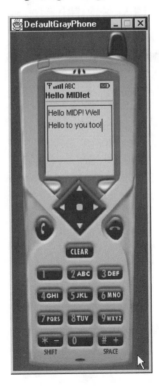

NOTE

The mechanism used to enter text depends on the type of MID being used. In the previous example, we used the Default Gray Phone, which features an ITU-T keyset. On this keyset, you type a character using a "tap code." Each button on the keypad is marked with a number and/or one or more letters or symbols. The display typically contains a mode indicator that shows whether the key that is tapped next will produce an uppercase letter, a lowercase letter, a number, or a symbol. One key on the keypad is used to switch modes. In the case of Default Gray Phone, it is the SHIFT key. When the mode indicator indicates numeric, the next key tapped generates the number marked on that key. When the mode indicator indicates uppercase alpha or lowercase alpha, the next key tapped will generate one of the letters marked on that key. The letter it generates depends on the number of times the key is tapped. In the case of the key labeled "2 ABC," if you tap once, the letter A is generated. Tapping twice generates B, and tapping three times generates C. If you tap four times, depending on the device, either the number 2 or the letter A is generated. Pausing longer than a timeout interval defined by the device advances the cursor on the display to the next position.

The best way to get an idea of how the tap code works if you have not already used it is to experiment. At first, it all seems awkward, but you will find that with a little practice you can actually become rather proficient at composing lengthy e-mails using the pad on a cellular phone. The Pager emulator features a QWERTY keyset. Entering data using such a keyset requires no explanation.

If you examine the documentation for the constructor of class `TextBox`, you see that it takes four parameters. The first is a String that specifies the label that is displayed by the implementation to identify this instance of `TextBox`. The second parameter is a string that specifies the initial contents of the text editing area. If this parameter is `null`, the text editing area is empty. The third parameter is an int that must have a value greater than zero. This value specifies the maximum capacity in characters. As an applications programmer, you can only *suggest* a value for maximum capacity. The implementation in the device can override the value you suggest. Good programming practice dictates that whenever you create an instance of `TextBox`, you should invoke the `getMaxSize` method to determine the actual size and use that size in your code. The fourth parameter is an int that the application uses to request the implementation restrict the user's input. Table 5-1 shows the types of restrictions that can be requested.

Field Name	Restriction
ANY	The user is allowed to enter any text.
EMAILADDR	The user is to enter an e-mail address.
NUMERIC	The user is allowed to enter only an integer value. The first character may be a minus sign.
PASSWORD	The data the user enters is to be considered confidential and is not to be displayed as it is typed. Each character typed is to be replaced by an implementation-defined "mask" character. The actual text is delivered to the application.
PHONENUMBER	The user is allowed to enter a phone number. What constitutes a phone number is specific to the device and to the device's network. It may be as little as a single digit (speed dialing is an example) and may contain nonnumeric characters.
URL	The user is allowed to enter a Uniform Resource Locator (URL).

Table 5-1   *TextBox Constraints*

Experimenting More with TextBox

\OMH\com\paulsjavabooks\Chapter5\TextBoxExample2.java

Take a look at the following MIDlet:

```
/*
 * TextBoxExample2.java
 *
 * Created on May 20, 2001, 8:44 PM
 */


package com.paulsjavabooks.instantj2me.Chapter5;

import javax.microedition.midlet.*;
import javax.microedition.lcdui.*;

/**
 * A simple application to demonstrate TextBox
 *
 * @author  paul_tremblett
```

```
 * @version 1.0
 */
public class TextBoxExample2 extends MIDlet
    implements CommandListener {

  private TextBox t;

  private Command cmdCompare;
  private Command cmdExit;
  private Display display;

  private String msg =
    "Mr. Hughes hid in Dylan's shoes wearin' his disguise.";

  public TextBoxExample2() {
    display = Display.getDisplay(this);
    cmdCompare = new Command("Compare", Command.SCREEN, 2);
    cmdExit = new Command("Exit", Command.SCREEN, 2);
  }

  public void startApp() {
    t = new TextBox("TextBoxExample2", msg, 256, 0);

    t.addCommand(cmdCompare);
    t.addCommand(cmdExit);
    t.setCommandListener(this);

    display.setCurrent(t);
  }

  public void pauseApp() {
  }

  public void destroyApp(boolean unconditional) {
  }

  public void commandAction(Command cmd, Displayable disp) {
    if (cmd == cmdExit) {
      destroyApp(false);
      notifyDestroyed();
    }
```

```
    else if (cmd == cmdCompare) {
      (t.setString((msg.compareTo(t.getString()) == 0) ?
        "SAME" : "CHANGED");
      t.removeCommand(cmdCompare);
    }
  }
}
```

The constructor obtains the `Display` instance that is unique to the MIDlet and stores it in the instance variable `display`. It then creates two instances of `Command`, `cmdCompare`, and `cmdExit`.

When the MIDlet enters the *Active* state, the `startApp` method creates an instance of `TextBox` with a title of "TextBox Example 2," which it assigns to the instance variable `t`. The initial contents are obtained from the instance variable `msg`, which is a String whose value is "Mr. Hughes hid in Dylan's shoes wearin' his disguise." The `startApp` method then sets the current instance of the MIDlet as a listener to `t`. It then requests that `t` be made visible on the display by passing it as an argument to the `setCurrent` method of `display`.

If the user selects the Compare option, the implementation on the device invokes the `commandAction` method indicating that a command event has occurred on `t`. When the method determines that the command it is processing is `cmdCompare`, it invokes the `getString` method to obtain the current contents of `t`, which it compares to the original contents. It then invokes the `setString` method to replace the contents of `t` with "SAME" or "CHANGED," depending on the result of the comparison. Since `cmdCompare` now serves no useful purpose, the `commandAction` method removes it using `t.removeCommand(cmdCompare)`.

If the `commandAction` method is invoked in response to the user selecting the Exit option, it signals the MIDlet to terminate and enter the *Destroyed* state by invoking `destroyApp`. It then invokes `notifyDestroyed` to notify the application management software that it has entered the *Destroyed* state.

Running

You can use either KToolbar or Forte to build the MIDlet. In either case, when you start it in the emulator, it looks like this:

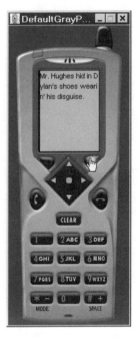

You can use the left-arrow key on the diamond-shaped arrangement of keys beneath the display to backspace the cursor and then use the keypad to alter the text so that it now looks like this:

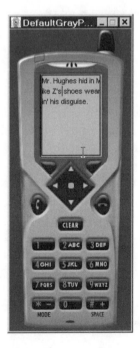

When you select the Compare option, the MIDlet detects the changes you made to the `TextBox` and displays this message:

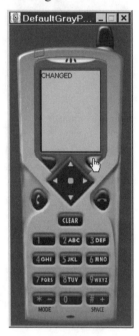

The Form Class

In the last example, we displayed a single `Displayable`, a `TextBox`, on the `Display` object that is unique to the MIDlet. This is a rather sparse user interface and would be woefully inadequate for all but the most trivial applications. The user interface in a real-world MIDlet usually consists of one or more Forms. A Form is a screen that contains an arbitrary mixture of items such as images, read-only text fields, editable text fields, editable date fields, gauges, and choice groups. We will now see how to use a Form.

A Form can contain any component that is a subclass of the `Item` class. The `Form` class provides two constructors. The first takes a single argument, a String that is used as the Form's title. When this constructor is used, an empty `Form` is created and items are added later using methods we will discuss shortly. The second constructor takes an additional argument, an array of `Item`s. If this array is `null`, an empty `Form` is created; otherwise, a Form containing the items in the array is created. Items in a non-empty `Form` are referred to by their indexes, which are consecutive integers. If a Form contains *n* items, the index of the first item is zero, and the index of the last item is *n*-1.

Adding Components to a Form

Before we discuss how to add items to a `Form`, you should be aware that items in a `Form` are subject to the following restrictions:

▶ An item may be placed within at most one Form. If an application attempts to add an item to a Form and that item is already owned by another Form, including the one to which the attempted addition is targeted, an `IllegalStateException` is thrown.

▶ For focusable items like `TextField`, `DateField`, `Gauge`, and `ChoiceGroup` that involve user input, the layout policy is vertical. This means that a new line is started for each such item.

▶ For Strings and images, which do not involve user interaction, the layout policy is horizontal. Successive instances of such items are filled in horizontal lines. This can be changed by insertion of a newline. Text is wrapped and images are clipped to fit the width of the display. There is no horizontal scrolling.

▶ After a Form has been created, its contents can be modified by using the `append`, `insert` and `delete` methods to add and delete `Items` or using the `set` method to modify an `Item`. You should usually invoke these methods when the `Form` is not visible to the user. To do otherwise would prove confusing to the user.

▶ A user can scroll and traverse from `Item` to `Item` indefinitely. If the user modifies the state of an interactive `Item` within the Form, the system notifies the application by invoking the `itemStateChanged` method of a listener that was declared with the `setItemStateListener` method.

▶ If a Form is visible on the display when the application makes a change to its contents, the changes take place immediately. The application programmer does not have to request that the display be refreshed.

TextField

The first `Item` we will add to a Form is a `TextField`, which is an editable text component. When you create a `TextField`, you specify a maximum number of characters that can be stored in the `TextField`. You should not confuse this maximum capacity with the number of characters visible on the display. The implementation might display only a portion of the contents and provide an automatic scrolling mechanism. The maximum capacity is enforced both upon the user and the application

programmer. If the user attempts to enter data that would cause the maximum
capacity to be exceeded, the data is not accepted. If the application programmer
invokes any of the methods that set or modify the contents of an instance of
TextField and execution of that method would result in the maximum capacity
being exceeded, the method throws an IllegalArgumentException.

As was the case with TextBox, the maximum size suggested by the application
programmer can be overridden by the implementation. You should use the defensive
programming technique of invoking the getMaxSize method to determine the
actual maximum size.

A TextField shares the same concept of constraints as we already described
when we discussed TextBox. Table 5-1 lists these constraints.

TextField Example

OMH\com\paulsjavabooks\instantj2me\Chapter5\TempConvMid.java

Here is the source code for a MIDlet that uses a TextField:

```
/*
 * TempConvMid.java
 *
 * Created on May 22, 2001, 10:04 PM
 */

package com.paulsjavabooks.instantj2me.Chapter5;

import javax.microedition.midlet.*;
import javax.microedition.lcdui.*;

import com.paulsjavabooks.instantj2me.Math.*;

/**
 *
 * @author  paul_tremblett
 * @version 1.0
 */
public class TempConvMid extends MIDlet implements CommandListener {

    private Display display;
    private Command cmdExit;
    private Command cmdConvert;
    private Command cmdOK;
```

```
private Form form1;
private Form form2;
private TextField tempField;
private StringItem convertedTemp;

  public void startApp() {
    display = Display.getDisplay(this);

    cmdConvert = new Command("Convert",Command.SCREEN,1);
    cmdExit = new Command("Exit",Command.SCREEN,1);
    cmdOK = new Command("OK",Command.SCREEN,1);

    form1 = new Form("TmpCnv");
    tempField = new TextField("Temp:",null,10,TextField.ANY);
    form1.addCommand(cmdConvert);
    form1.addCommand(cmdExit);
    form1.setCommandListener(this);
    form1.append(tempField);

    form2 = new Form("Result");
    convertedTemp = new StringItem(null, null);
    form2.append(convertedTemp);
    form2.addCommand(cmdOK);
    form2.setCommandListener(this);

    display.setCurrent(form1);
  }

  public void pauseApp() {
  }

  public void destroyApp(boolean unconditional) {
  }

  public void commandAction(Command cmd, Displayable d) {

    String displayString = null;

    if (cmd == cmdExit) {
      destroyApp(false);
      notifyDestroyed();
    }
    else if (cmd == cmdConvert) {
```

```
        String s = tempField.getString();
        displayString = convertTemp(s);
        convertedTemp.setText(displayString);
        display.setCurrent(form2);
      }
      else if (cmd == cmdOK) {
        tempField.setString(null);
        display.setCurrent(form1);
      }
    }

    private String convertTemp(String s) {
      char c = s.charAt(s.length() - 1);
      String ts = null;
      try {
        switch (c) {
          case 'C':
          case 'c':
            ts = cToF(s.substring(0,s.length() - 1));
            break;
          case 'F':
          case 'f':
            ts = fToC(s.substring(0,s.length() - 1));
            break;
          default:
            ts = "**ERROR**";
        }
      }
      catch(KMathException e) {
        ts = "**ERROR**";
      }
      finally {
        return ts;
      }
    }

    private String cToF(String c) throws KMathException {
      String cx9 = KMath.multiply(c,"9");
      String temp = KMath.divide(cx9,"5");
      String f = KMath.add(temp,"32");
      return f;
```

```
    }

    private String fToC(String f) throws KMathException {
        String fm32 = KMath.subtract(f,"32");
        String temp = KMath.multiply(fm32,"5");
        String c = KMath.divide(temp,"9");
        return c;
    }
}
```

The MIDlet's `startApp` method creates three commands, `cmdConvert`, `cmdExit`, and `cmdOK`. It then creates an instance of `Form` with the title "TmpCnv." It then creates an instance of `TextField` with the label "Temp:", no initial contents, and a maximum capacity of 10 that can accept any input the user enters. It then adds the `cmdConvert` and `cmdExit` commands to the Form, sets the current MIDlet as a command listener, and invokes the `append` method to add the instance of `TextField`.

Next, the `startApp` method creates a second `Form` with the title "Result." It adds to this Form a `StringItem`. As its name implies, a `StringItem` is an `Item` that can contain a String. A `StringItem` is display-only and this particular instance is used to display the result of temperature conversion. Since the `StringItem` is display-only, the user cannot modify the displayed value as was the case when `TextBox` was used. After the `startApp` method appends the `StringItem` to the Form, it adds the `cmdOK` command and sets the current MIDlet as a command listener.

The `commandAction` method determines the command that caused the method to be invoked. If it was `cmdExit`, the application terminates and enters the *Destroyed* state. If the command was `cmdConvert`, the contents of the `TextField` are obtained and passed to the `convertTemp` method. The String that is returned is used to set the contents of the `StringItem` and the Form containing the `StringItem` is made visible. If the command is `cmdOK`, the `StringItem` is reset and the Form containing the `TextField` is displayed so that the user can enter another temperature to convert.

The `convertTemp` method examines the last character of the temperature that the user entered. If the last character is *C*, it invokes the `cToF` method to convert Celsius to Fahrenheit. If the last character is *F*, it invokes the `fToC` method to convert Fahrenheit to Celsius.

Providing Floating Point Math

J2ME does not provide support for floating point. Some commercial floating point math libraries are available. To make development easier, the CD contains a trivial floating point math library called KMath. It does not pretend to be efficient and it is anything but a model of good programming. Its most attractive feature is that it is free. The listing is shown at the end of this chapter.

After you have created the MIDlet Suite, you should double-click on the MIDlet Suite icon, select the Content tab and add the directory containing the math library as shown here:

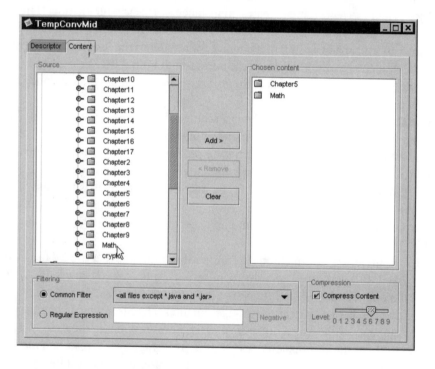

Running TextFieldExample

As is the case with all MIDlets, the runtime behavior depends on the device that is used. We will use the Motorola i85s phone. When you first launch the MIDlet, it looks like the following:

Press MENU and enter a temperature using *C* or *F* as the terminating character to indicate Celsius or Farenheit. Let's use 98.6F, human body temperature. The display looks like this:

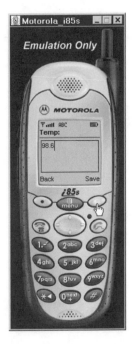

When you press Save, the soft key corresponding to the Convert command appears and the display looks like this:

When you press Convert, the command is processed, the temperature is converted, and it is displayed as follows:

The Choice Interface

Making a selection is another aspect of a user interface. Choice allows this. In the previous example, you indicated the temperature scale by using a terminating *C* or *F*. This does not come naturally to users, and most desktop applications would provide two radio buttons that the user would click to indicate the temperature scale. You will now see how to do the same in a MIDlet.

The Choice interface defines an API that allows the user to make one or more selections from a predefined number of choices. The two LCDUI components that implement this interface are ChoiceGroup and List.

Each element in the Choice is composed of a text String and an optional image. We will discuss images in the next chapter. The implementation is not required to display the image and may ignore it if it exceeds the capacity of the device to display it. If it is displayed, it will be displayed adjacent to the text portion of the Choice element. The image and the text are treated as a unit. If an element is wider than the width of the display, the implementation provides the user with a means to see the whole element. This is often achieved by wrapping the element to multiple lines. When the implementation uses such wrapping, it must clearly indicate to the user that the second and subsequent lines are part of the wrapped element and not a new element.

As was the case with a Form, elements in a Choice object are referred to by their indexes, which are consecutive integers. If a Choice object contains *n* elements, the index of the first element is zero, and the index of the last element is *n*-1. After a Choice object has been created, elements may be appended, inserted, and deleted.

There are three types of Choices. The first two are exclusive choice and multiple choice, which are implemented by both ChoiceGroup and List. The third, implicit choice, is valid only for List.

The exclusive choice presents a series of elements with which the user can interact. As this interaction takes place, a visual representation of the selected state of each element is the list is maintained. At any time, only one item can be selected. If the list is created empty and one or more items is subsequently added, the implementation chooses one element to designate as selected. The only way the user can unselect an element is to select another element. You will recognize this behavior as that of the radio buttons you use in desktop applications and indeed the implementations on most MIDs represent exclusive-choice as radio buttons.

The multiple choice presents a series of elements from which the user can select one or more. Unlike exclusive choice, an element in a multiple choice can be unselected. You will recognize this behavior as that of check boxes, which is how the implementations on most MIDs represent multiple choice.

The selected state of an element is a property of that element and remains with the element until the element is deleted. If an element is shifted as the result of additions or deletions, its selected state does not change. Likewise, if the contents of an element are changed, the selected state remains the same.

We will discuss implicit choice in Chapter 8.

ChoiceGroup

A ChoiceGroup is a group of selectable elements that can be placed within a Form. It may allow single or multiple choices. The exact appearance of the ChoiceGroup depends on the implementation in the MID. The only requirement is that single choice and multiple choice use different visual representations. As we mentioned earlier, in most cases, the implementation uses what we recognize as radio buttons for single choice and check boxes for multiple choice.

An Example of ChoiceGroup
\OMH\com\paulsjavabooks\instantj2me\Chapter5\TempConv2Mid.java

Here is the source code for a MIDlet that uses a ChoiceGroup:

```
/*
 * TempConv2Mid.java
 *
 * Created on June 21, 2001, 10:48 PM
 */


package com.paulsjavabooks.instantj2me.Chapter5;

import javax.microedition.midlet.*;
import javax.microedition.lcdui.*;

import com.paulsjavabooks.instantj2me.Math.*;

/**
 *
 * @author  paul_tremblett
 * @version 1.0
 */
public class TempConv2Mid extends MIDlet implements CommandListener {

  private Display display;
  private Command cmdExit;
```

```java
private Command cmdConvert;
private Command cmdOK;
private Form form1;
private Form form2;
private TextField tempField;
private ChoiceGroup tempChoice;
private StringItem convertedTemp;

  public void startApp() {
    display = Display.getDisplay(this);

    cmdConvert = new Command("Convert",Command.SCREEN,1);
    cmdExit = new Command("Exit",Command.SCREEN,1);
    cmdOK = new Command("OK",Command.SCREEN,1);

    form1 = new Form("TmpCnv");
    tempField = new TextField("Temp:",null,10,TextField.ANY);
    form1.addCommand(cmdConvert);
    form1.addCommand(cmdExit);
    form1.setCommandListener(this);
    form1.append(tempField);
    String[] tempType = {"Celsius","Farenheit"};
    tempChoice =
      new ChoiceGroup("Temp Type",Choice.EXCLUSIVE,tempType,null);
    form1.append(tempChoice);

    form2 = new Form("Result");
    convertedTemp = new StringItem(null, null);
    form2.append(convertedTemp);
    form2.addCommand(cmdOK);
    form2.setCommandListener(this);

    display.setCurrent(form1);
  }

  public void pauseApp() {
  }

  public void destroyApp(boolean unconditional) {
  }

  public void commandAction(Command cmd, Displayable d) {
```

```
    String displayString = null;

    if (cmd == cmdExit) {
      destroyApp(false);
      notifyDestroyed();
    }
    else if (cmd == cmdConvert) {
      String s = tempField.getString();
      displayString = convertTemp(s);
      convertedTemp.setText(displayString);
      display.setCurrent(form2);
    }
    else if (cmd == cmdOK) {
      tempField.setString(null);
      display.setCurrent(form1);
    }
  }

  private String convertTemp(String s) {
    char c = s.charAt(s.length() - 1);
    StringBuffer tsb = new StringBuffer();
    try {
      switch (tempChoice.getSelectedIndex()) {
        case 0:
          tsb.append(cToF(s));
          tsb.append('F');
          break;
        case 1:
          tsb.append(fToC(s));
          tsb.append('C');
          break;
        default:
          tsb.append("**ERROR**");
      }
    }
    catch(KMathException e) {
      tsb.append("**ERROR**");
    }
    finally {
      return tsb.toString();
    }
  }
```

```
private String cToF(String c) throws KMathException {
    String cx9 = KMath.multiply(c,"9");
    String temp = KMath.divide(cx9,"5");
    String f = KMath.add(temp,"32");
    return f;
}

private String fToC(String f) throws KMathException {
    String fm32 = KMath.subtract(f,"32");
    String temp = KMath.multiply(fm32,"5");
    String c = KMath.divide(temp,"9");
    return c;
}
}
```

Running

Before you attempt to run the application, make sure you have included the
KMath library.

As you know by now, runtime behavior depends on the device being used.
Let's use the RIM-Blackberry-957. The initial display looks like this:

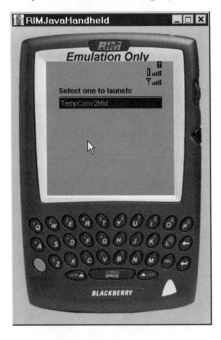

Beneath the hand icon is a thumbwheel with three visible notches. You use the upper and lower notches to scroll and the middle notch to make a selection. If you press the middle position, the display changes to look like this:

Now press the SPACE BAR on the keyboard and the MIDlet launches. It displays a screen that looks like this:

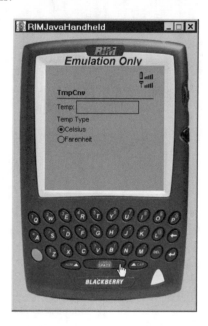

Notice that the two elements you added to the `Form` are presented in a vertical layout. The `TextField` is identified by its label Temp:. The `ChoiceGroup` is identified by its title Temp Type and is visually represented as radio buttons.

Press the NUM key and use the mouse to click the keys on the keypad to enter a temperature as shown. Notice that you do not enter the trailing character *C* or *F* as in the earlier example.

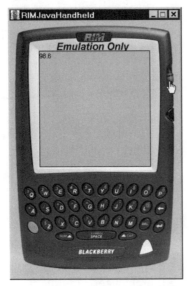

When you have entered the number, press the middle button on the thumbwheel, and you will see the following menu:

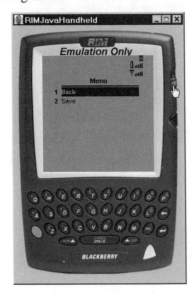

Save the number by first clicking on the lower notch of the thumbwheel to select Save and then pressing the SPACE BAR on the keyboard. The display now looks like this:

You can now use the thumbwheel to highlight which of the two radio buttons you wish to select. You select a highlighted radio button by pressing the SPACE BAR. Select Farenheit and press the thumbwheel's middle position. The following menu is presented:

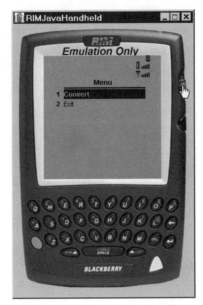

Press the SPACE BAR to send the command to the application. The application performs the conversion and the result is displayed as follows:

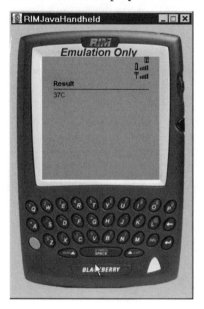

Access the menu again by pressing the middle notch of the thumbwheel. The menu contains the single item, OK, as shown here:

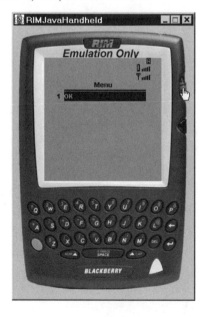

When you press the middle notch of the thumbwheel, the display first form becomes visible again and you can enter other temperatures. When you have converted as many temperatures as you wish, press the button below the thumbwheel and select Exit from the menu.

KMath Source

The KMath library consists of three packages. The source code is presented here:

KMath.java

\OMH\com\paulsjavabooks\instantj2me\Math\KMath.java

```java
/*
 * KMath.java
 *
 * Created on June 19, 2001, 1:47 PM
 */

package com.paulsjavabooks.instantj2me.Math;

/**
 *
 * @author  paul_tre
 * @version
 */
public final class KMath {

  protected static int MAX_FIELD_WIDTH = 10;

  private KMath() {
  }

  public static void setMaxFieldWidth(int width) {
    MAX_FIELD_WIDTH = width;
  }

  public static String add(String s1, String s2)
      throws KMathException {
    QuasiScientificNotation qsn1 =
      new QuasiScientificNotation(s1);
    QuasiScientificNotation qsn2 =
```

```java
        new QuasiScientificNotation(s2);
    qsn1.add(qsn2);
    return qsn1.toString();
  }

  public static String subtract(String s1, String s2)
      throws KMathException {
    QuasiScientificNotation qsn1 =
      new QuasiScientificNotation(s1);
    QuasiScientificNotation qsn2 =
      new QuasiScientificNotation(s2);
    qsn1.subtract(qsn2);
    return qsn1.toString();
  }

  public static String multiply(String s1, String s2)
      throws KMathException {
    QuasiScientificNotation qsn1 =
      new QuasiScientificNotation(s1);
    QuasiScientificNotation qsn2 =
      new QuasiScientificNotation(s2);
    qsn1.multiply(qsn2);
    return qsn1.toString();
  }

  public static String divide(String s1, String s2)
      throws KMathException {
    QuasiScientificNotation qsn1 =
      new QuasiScientificNotation(s1);
    QuasiScientificNotation qsn2 =
      new QuasiScientificNotation(s2);
    qsn1.divide(qsn2);
    return qsn1.toString();
  }
}
```

QuasiScientificNotation.java

\OMH\com\paulsjavabooks\instantj2me\Math\QuasiScientificNotation.java

```java
/*
 * QuasiScientificNotation.java
 *
 * Created on June 19, 2001, 1:45 PM
```

```
 */

package com.paulsjavabooks.instantj2me.Math;

/**
 *
 * @author  paul_tre
 * @version
 */
public class QuasiScientificNotation {

  private int sign = 1;
  private String mantissaLeftOfDecimal = "0";
  private String mantissaRightOfDecimal = "0";
  private int exponent = 0;

  private static final int LESS_THAN = -1;
  private static final int EQUAL = 0;
  private static final int GREATER_THAN = 1;

  protected QuasiScientificNotation(String s)
      throws KMathException {
    if (s.toUpperCase().indexOf('E') >= 0) {
      parseScientificNotation(s);
    }
    else {
      parseFloatingPointString(s);
    }
  }

  private void parseScientificNotation(String s)
      throws KMathException {
    String ws = s;
    char possibleSign = ws.charAt(0);
    switch (possibleSign) {
      case '+':
        ws = ws.substring(1);
        break;
      case '-':
        sign = -1;
        ws = ws.substring(1);
        break;
      default:
```

```
        break;
    }
    int dx = ws.indexOf('.');
    int ex = ws.toUpperCase().indexOf('E');
    switch (compare(dx,0)) {
      case LESS_THAN:
        mantissaLeftOfDecimal = ws.substring(0,ex);
        mantissaRightOfDecimal = "0";
        break;
      case EQUAL:
        mantissaLeftOfDecimal = "0";
        mantissaRightOfDecimal = ws.substring(0,ex);
        break;
      case GREATER_THAN:
        mantissaLeftOfDecimal = ws.substring(0,dx);
        mantissaRightOfDecimal = ws.substring(dx+1,ex);
        break;
    }
    try {
      exponent = Integer.parseInt(ws.substring(ex+1));
    }
    catch (NumberFormatException e) {
      throw new KMathException("KMath Exception: " + e.getMessage());
    }
    normalize();
}

private int compare(int val1, int val2) {
  if (val1 > val2)
    return GREATER_THAN;
  else if (val1 < val2)
    return LESS_THAN;
  else return EQUAL;
}

private void parseFloatingPointString(String s) {

  StringBuffer mlsb = new StringBuffer();
  StringBuffer mrsb = new StringBuffer();
  int ix = 0;
  boolean gotd = false;
  String ws = s;
  if (ws.startsWith("+")) {
```

```
      ix = 1;
    }
    else if (ws.startsWith("-")) {
      sign = -1;
      ix = 1;
    }
    while (ws.charAt(ix) == '0') {
      ++ix;
    }
    for (;ix < ws.length(); ++ix) {
      if (ws.charAt(ix) == '.') {
        gotd = true;
      }
      else {
        if (mlsb.length() == 0) {
          if (ws.charAt(ix) != '0') {
            mlsb.append(ws.substring(ix,ix + 1));
          }
          if (gotd) {
            —exponent;
          };
        }
        else {
          if (!gotd) {
          ++exponent;
          }
          mrsb.append(ws.charAt(ix));
        }
      }
    }
    if (mrsb.length() == 0) {
      mrsb.append('0');
    }
    if (mlsb.length() == 0) {
      mlsb.append('0');
    }
    mantissaLeftOfDecimal = mlsb.toString();
    mantissaRightOfDecimal = mrsb.toString();
  }

  public void add (QuasiScientificNotation addend)
      throws KMathException {
    this.normalize();
```

```
  addend.normalize();
  if (this.exponent != addend.exponent) {
    this.useExponent(addend.exponent);
  }
  if ((this.sign * addend.sign) < 0) {
    subtractLesserFromGreater(addend);
    return;
  }
  String rs = stringAddJustifiedLeft(this.mantissaRightOfDecimal,
    addend.mantissaRightOfDecimal);
  long carryOver = 0l;
  if ((rs.length() > this.mantissaRightOfDecimal.length()) &&
      (rs.length() > addend.mantissaRightOfDecimal.length())) {
    carryOver = 1l;
    mantissaRightOfDecimal = rs.substring(1);
  }
  else {
    mantissaRightOfDecimal = rs;
  }
  long lsum = stringAdd(this.mantissaLeftOfDecimal,
    addend.mantissaLeftOfDecimal);
  lsum += carryOver;
  mantissaLeftOfDecimal = Long.toString(lsum);
  normalize();
}

private void subtractLesserFromGreater(QuasiScientificNotation val)
    throws KMathException {
  try {
    if (Long.parseLong(this.mantissaLeftOfDecimal) >
        Long.parseLong(val.mantissaLeftOfDecimal)) {
      QuasiScientificNotation diff =subtract(this,val);
      this.mantissaLeftOfDecimal = diff.mantissaLeftOfDecimal;
      this.mantissaRightOfDecimal = diff.mantissaRightOfDecimal;
      this.exponent = diff.exponent;
    }
    else if (Long.parseLong(val.mantissaLeftOfDecimal) >
            Long.parseLong(this.mantissaLeftOfDecimal)) {
      QuasiScientificNotation diff =subtract(val,this);
      this.mantissaLeftOfDecimal = diff.mantissaLeftOfDecimal;
      this.mantissaRightOfDecimal = diff.mantissaRightOfDecimal;
      this.exponent = diff.exponent;
      sign *= -1;
```

```
        }
      else {
        StringBuffer sb1 = new StringBuffer(this.mantissaRightOfDecimal);
        StringBuffer sb2 = new StringBuffer(val.mantissaRightOfDecimal);
        int len1 = sb1.length();
        int len2 = sb2.length();
        if (len1 > len2) {
          for (int i = len2; i < len1; ++i) {
            sb2.append('0');
          }
        }
        else if (len2 > len1) {
          for (int i = len1; i < len2; ++i) {
            sb1.append('0');
          }
        }
        for (int i = 0; i < sb1.length(); ++i) {
          if (sb1.charAt(i) > sb2.charAt(i)) {
            QuasiScientificNotation diff =subtract(this,val);
            this.mantissaLeftOfDecimal = diff.mantissaLeftOfDecimal;
            this.mantissaRightOfDecimal = diff.mantissaRightOfDecimal;
            this.exponent = diff.exponent;
            return;
          }
          else if (sb2.charAt(i) > sb1.charAt(i)) {
            QuasiScientificNotation diff =subtract(val,this);
            this.mantissaLeftOfDecimal = diff.mantissaLeftOfDecimal;
            this.mantissaRightOfDecimal = diff.mantissaRightOfDecimal;
            this.exponent = diff.exponent;
            sign *= -1;
            return;
          }
        }
        this.mantissaLeftOfDecimal = "0";
        this.mantissaRightOfDecimal = "0";
        this.exponent = 1;
      }
    }
  catch (NumberFormatException e) {
    throw new KMathException("KMath exception: " + e.getMessage());
  }
}
```

```
private QuasiScientificNotation subtract(QuasiScientificNotation v1,
    QuasiScientificNotation v2) throws KMathException {
  if (v1.exponent != v2.exponent) {
    v1.useExponent(v2.exponent);
  }
  try {
    long sl = Long.parseLong(v1.mantissaLeftOfDecimal) -
      Long.parseLong(v2.mantissaLeftOfDecimal);
    String sr = stringSubtractJustifiedLeft(v1.mantissaRightOfDecimal,
      v2.mantissaRightOfDecimal);
    long borrow = 0l;
    if (sr.startsWith("-")) {
      borrow = 1l;
      sr = sr.substring(1);
    }
    QuasiScientificNotation qsn =
      new QuasiScientificNotation(Long.toString(sl - borrow) + "." +
      sr + "E" + Integer.toString(v1.exponent));
    qsn.normalize();
    return qsn;
  }
  catch (NumberFormatException e) {
    throw new KMathException("KMath exception: " + e.getMessage());
  }
}

private boolean isAllZeroes(String s) {
  boolean tf = true;
  for (int i = 0; i < s.length(); ++i) {
    if (s.charAt(i) != '0') {
      tf = false;
      break;
    }
  }
  return tf;
}

private void normalize() {
  if ((isAllZeroes(mantissaLeftOfDecimal)) &&
      (isAllZeroes(mantissaRightOfDecimal))) {
    this.sign = 1;
    this.mantissaLeftOfDecimal = "0";
```

```
      this.mantissaRightOfDecimal = "0";
      this.exponent = 0;
      return;
    }
    int nzx = -1;
    for (int i = 0; i < mantissaLeftOfDecimal.length();++i) {
      if (mantissaLeftOfDecimal.charAt(i) != '0') {
        nzx = i;
        break;
      }
    }
    StringBuffer sbl = new StringBuffer();
    StringBuffer sbr = new StringBuffer();
    if (nzx < 0) {
      for (nzx = 0; nzx < mantissaRightOfDecimal.length(); ++nzx) {
        —exponent;
        if (mantissaRightOfDecimal .charAt(nzx) != '0') {
          mantissaLeftOfDecimal =
            mantissaRightOfDecimal.substring(nzx,nzx+1);
          if (nzx == (mantissaRightOfDecimal.length() -1)) {
            mantissaRightOfDecimal = "";
          }
          else {
            mantissaRightOfDecimal =
              mantissaRightOfDecimal.substring(nzx+1);
          }
          break;
        }
      }
    }
    else {
      if (nzx != (mantissaLeftOfDecimal.length() -1)) {
        mantissaRightOfDecimal =
          mantissaLeftOfDecimal.substring(nzx+1) +
          mantissaRightOfDecimal;
        exponent += mantissaLeftOfDecimal.length() - (nzx +1);
      }
      mantissaLeftOfDecimal = mantissaLeftOfDecimal.substring(nzx,nzx+1);
    }
    StringBuffer rsb = new StringBuffer(mantissaRightOfDecimal);
    int rlen = rsb.length();
    for (int i = rlen - 1; i > 0; —i) {
      if (rsb.charAt(i) == '0') {
```

```
        —rlen;
      }
      else {
        break;
      }
    }
    if (rlen < mantissaRightOfDecimal.length()) {
      rsb.setLength(rlen);
      mantissaRightOfDecimal = rsb.toString();
    }
  }
}


private String stringAddJustifiedLeft(String s1, String s2)
      throws KMathException {
    int len1 = s1.length();
    int len2 = s2.length();
    int lenMax = Math.max(len1,len2);
    try {
      long sum1 = Long.parseLong(s1);
      long sum2 = Long.parseLong(s2);
      if (len1 > len2) {
        for (int i = len2; i < len1; ++i) {
          sum2 *= 10l;
        }
      }
      else if (len2 > len1) {
        for (int i = len1; i < len2; ++i) {
          sum1 *= 10l;
        }
      }
      String sum12 = Long.toString(sum1 + sum2);
      StringBuffer sblp = new StringBuffer();
      for (int i = sum12.length(); i < lenMax; ++i) {
        sblp.append('0');
      }
      return sblp.append(Long.toString(sum1+sum2)).toString();
    }
    catch(NumberFormatException e) {
      throw new KMathException("KMath exception: " + e.getMessage());
    }
}

private String stringSubtractJustifiedLeft(String s1, String s2)
```

```java
        throws KMathException {
    int len1 = s1.length();
    int len2 = s2.length();
    int lenMax = Math.max(len1,len2);
    try {
      long val1 = Long.parseLong(s1);
      long val2 = Long.parseLong(s2);
      if (len1 > len2) {
        for (int i = len2; i < len1; ++i) {
          val2 *= 101;
        }
      }
      else if (len2 > len1) {
        for (int i = len1; i < len2; ++i) {
          val1 *= 101;
        }
      }
      StringBuffer sblp = new StringBuffer();
      if (val2 > val1) {
        long m = 11;
        for (int i = 0; i < lenMax; ++i) {
          m *= 101;
        }
        val1 += m;
        sblp.append('-');
      }
      String diff12 = Long.toString(val1 - val2);
      for (int i = diff12.length(); i < lenMax; ++i) {
        sblp.append('0');
      }
      sblp.append(diff12);
      return sblp.toString();
    }
    catch (NumberFormatException e) {
      throw new KMathException("KMath exception: " + e.getMessage());
    }
  }

  private long stringAdd(String s1, String s2)
      throws KMathException {
    try {
      long sum1 = Long.parseLong(s1);
      long sum2 = Long.parseLong(s2);
```

```
      return sum1 + sum2;
    }
  catch (NumberFormatException e) {
    throw new KMathException("KMath exception: " + e.getMessage());
  }
}

public void subtract (QuasiScientificNotation subtrahend)
    throws KMathException {
  if ((this.sign * subtrahend.sign) < 0) {
    subtrahend.sign *= -1;
    add(subtrahend);
    sign = -1;
  }
  else {
    this.normalize();
    subtrahend.normalize();
    if (this.exponent != subtrahend.exponent) {
      this.useExponent(subtrahend.exponent);
    }
    subtractLesserFromGreater(subtrahend);
  }
  normalize();
}

public void multiply (QuasiScientificNotation multiplier)
    throws KMathException {
  try {
    this.normalize();
    multiplier.normalize();
    this.shiftDecimal(-1);
    multiplier.shiftDecimal(-1);
    long m1 = Long.parseLong(this.mantissaRightOfDecimal);
    long m2 = Long.parseLong(multiplier.mantissaRightOfDecimal);
    int nd = this.mantissaRightOfDecimal.length() +
      multiplier.mantissaRightOfDecimal.length();
    String m1m2 = Long.toString(m1 * m2);
    exponent = this.exponent + multiplier.exponent;
    sign = this.sign * multiplier.sign;
    if (m1m2.length() > nd) {
      mantissaLeftOfDecimal = m1m2.substring(0,1);
      mantissaRightOfDecimal = m1m2.substring(1);
      exponent += 1;
```

```
      }
      else if (m1m2.length() < nd) {
        mantissaLeftOfDecimal = "0";
        mantissaRightOfDecimal = "0" + m1m2;
      }
      else {
        mantissaLeftOfDecimal = "0";
        mantissaRightOfDecimal = m1m2;
      }
      normalize();
    }
    catch (NumberFormatException e) {
      throw new KMathException("KMath exception: " + e.getMessage());
    }
  }


  public void divide (QuasiScientificNotation dividend)
      throws KMathException {
    try {
      this.normalize();
      dividend.normalize();
      if (("0".equals(dividend.mantissaLeftOfDecimal)) &&
          (isAllZeroes(dividend.mantissaRightOfDecimal))) {
        throw new KMathException("division by zero");
      }
      int lv1 = Math.abs(Integer.parseInt(this.mantissaLeftOfDecimal));
      int lv2 = Math.abs(Integer.parseInt(dividend.mantissaLeftOfDecimal));
      if (lv1 <= lv2) {
        shiftRight(1);
      }
      long val1 = Long.parseLong(this.mantissaLeftOfDecimal +
          this.mantissaRightOfDecimal + "0000");
      long val2 = Long.parseLong(dividend.mantissaLeftOfDecimal +
          dividend.mantissaRightOfDecimal);
      long adj = 1l;
      while (val1 <= val2) {
        val1 *= 10l;
        --exponent;
      }
      String result = Long.toString(val1/val2);
      this.mantissaLeftOfDecimal = result.substring(0,1);
      this.mantissaRightOfDecimal = result.substring(1);
```

```
      this.exponent -= dividend.exponent;
      sign = this.sign / dividend.sign;
      this.normalize();
    }
    catch (NumberFormatException e) {
      throw new KMathException("KMath exception: " + e.getMessage());
    }
  }

  public void useExponent(int newExponent) {
    if (newExponent == exponent) {
      return;
    }
    int adj = exponent - newExponent;
    shiftDecimal(adj);
  }

  public void shiftDecimal(int ct) {
    if (ct < 0) {
      shiftLeft(-ct);
    }
    else {
      shiftRight(ct);
    }
  }

  private void shiftLeft(int ct) {
    int lenLeft = mantissaLeftOfDecimal.length();
    int newLenLeft = lenLeft - ct;
    if (newLenLeft <= 0) {
      StringBuffer padding = new StringBuffer();
      for (int i = lenLeft; i < (ct + 1); ++i) {
        padding.append('0');
      }
      mantissaLeftOfDecimal =
        padding.append(mantissaLeftOfDecimal).toString();
      lenLeft = mantissaLeftOfDecimal.length();
    }
    String strippedFromLeft =
      mantissaLeftOfDecimal.substring(lenLeft - ct);
    mantissaRightOfDecimal =
      strippedFromLeft + mantissaRightOfDecimal;
    mantissaLeftOfDecimal =
```

```
        mantissaLeftOfDecimal.substring(0,lenLeft -ct);
    exponent += ct;
  }

  private void shiftRight(int ct) {
    int lenRight = mantissaRightOfDecimal.length();
    int newLenRight = ct + 1;
    if (newLenRight > lenRight) {
      StringBuffer padding = new StringBuffer();
      for (int i = 0; i < (newLenRight - ct); ++i) {
        padding.append('0');
      }
      mantissaRightOfDecimal =
        mantissaRightOfDecimal + padding.toString();
      lenRight = mantissaRightOfDecimal.length();
    }
    String strippedFromRight = mantissaRightOfDecimal.substring(0,ct);
    mantissaLeftOfDecimal = mantissaLeftOfDecimal + strippedFromRight;
    mantissaRightOfDecimal = mantissaRightOfDecimal.substring(ct);
    exponent -= ct;
  }

  public String toString() {
    this.normalize();
    boolean isWholeNumber = false;
    int len = 0;
    if (sign < 0) {
      ++len;
    }
    switch (compare(exponent,0)) {
      case LESS_THAN:
        int absexp = Math.abs(exponent);
          len += absexp;
        len++;
        if (!isAllZeroes(mantissaRightOfDecimal)) {
          len += mantissaRightOfDecimal.length();
        }
        break;
      case EQUAL:
      case GREATER_THAN:
        len += mantissaLeftOfDecimal.length();
        len += exponent;
        if (!isAllZeroes(mantissaRightOfDecimal)) {
          ++len;
```

```
      }
      len += mantissaRightOfDecimal.length();
      break;
  }
  if (len > KMath.MAX_FIELD_WIDTH) {
    return this.asScientificNotation();
  }
  else if (isWholeNumber) {
    return this.asWholeNumber();
  }
  else {
    return this.asFloatingPoint();
  }
}

private String asScientificNotation() {
  return ((sign < 0) ? "-" : "") +mantissaLeftOfDecimal +
    "." + mantissaRightOfDecimal +
    "E" + Integer.toString(exponent);
}

private String asFloatingPoint() {
  StringBuffer sb = new StringBuffer();
  if (sign < 0) {
    sb.append('-');
  }
  switch (compare(exponent,0)) {
    case LESS_THAN:
      sb.append(".");
      int exp = -exponent;
      for (int i = mantissaLeftOfDecimal.length(); i < exp; ++i) {
        sb.append('0');
      }
      sb.append(mantissaLeftOfDecimal);
      sb.append(mantissaRightOfDecimal);
      break;
    case EQUAL:
      sb.append(mantissaLeftOfDecimal);
      sb.append(".");
      sb.append(mantissaRightOfDecimal);
      break;
    case GREATER_THAN:
      sb.append(mantissaLeftOfDecimal);
      int lr = mantissaRightOfDecimal.length();
```

```java
      switch(compare(exponent,lr)) {
        case LESS_THAN:
          sb.append(mantissaRightOfDecimal.substring(0,lr-1));
          sb.append('.');
          sb.append(mantissaRightOfDecimal.substring(lr));
          break;
        case EQUAL:
          sb.append(mantissaRightOfDecimal);
          break;
        case GREATER_THAN:
          sb.append(mantissaRightOfDecimal);
          for (int i = lr; i < exponent; ++i) {
            sb.append('0');
          }
          break;
      }
    }
    if (sb.charAt(sb.length()-1) == '.') {
      sb.deleteCharAt(sb.length() -1);
    }
    return sb.toString();
  }

  private String asWholeNumber() {
    StringBuffer sb = new StringBuffer();
    if (sign < 0) {
      sb.append('-');
    }
    sb.append(mantissaLeftOfDecimal);
    if ((mantissaRightOfDecimal.equals("0")) &&
        (exponent == 0)) {
      return sb.toString();
    }
    sb.append(mantissaRightOfDecimal);
    if (mantissaRightOfDecimal.length() < exponent) {
      for (int i = mantissaRightOfDecimal.length(); i < exponent; ++i) {
        sb.append('0');
      }
    }
    return sb.toString();
  }
}
```

KMathException.java

\OMH\com\paulsjavabooks\instantj2me\Math\KMathException.java

```java
/*
 * KMathException.java
 *
 * Created on June 19, 2001, 1:46 PM
 */

package com.paulsjavabooks.instantj2me.Math;

/**
 *
 * @author  paul_tre
 * @version
 */

public class KMathException extends Exception {

  public KMathException() {
    super();
  }

  public KMathException(String msg) {
    super(msg);
  }
}
```

Advanced UI Components

IN THIS CHAPTER:

I n Chapter 5, we used UI components that enabled us to input data and to make selections. In this chapter, we will continue our exploration of the UI by examining two slightly more complex components, `DateField` and `Gauge`. We will also discuss the `ItemStateListener` interface that applications use when they need to receive events that indicate changes in the internal state of interactive items within a form.

The DateField Item

We have already built examples that use the `Date` and `Calendar` classes, so you know that even though these classes are not as rich in functionality as their J2SE counterparts, handling dates and times in MIDP applications is not difficult. If you were restricted to using only `TextField` to accept input, what you would find difficult is accepting a date/time from a user, verifying that the input truly represents a valid date/time, and saving it in a usable form. Fortunately, MIDP solves this problem by providing the `DateField` class.

A `DateField` is a subclass of `Item` that provides an editable component for presenting date and time information that may be placed in a form. The value of the component can be specified when the component is created or left unset. When the implementation displays the component, it provides a clear visual indication of whether the component is initialized or uninitialized. An instance of `DateField` can accept date or time information or both by specifying one of the static fields DATE, TIME, or DATE_TIME.

An Example of DateField

\OMH\com\paulsjavabooks\instantj2me\Chapter6\DateFieldExample.java

Take a look at the following code:

```
/*
 * DateFieldExample.java
 *
 * Created on June 25, 2001, 10:09 PM
 */

package com.paulsjavabooks.instantj2me.Chapter6;
```

```java
import java.util.Calendar;
import javax.microedition.midlet.*;
import javax.microedition.lcdui.*;


/**
 *
 * @author  paul_tremblett
 * @version 1.0
 */
public class DateFieldExample extends MIDlet implements CommandListener {


  private Display display;
  private Command cmdExit;
  private Command cmdOK;
  private Form form1;
  private Form form2;
  private DateField df1;
  private DateField df2;
  private StringItem statusMessage;
  private int state = REQUESTING_DATE_1;
  private Calendar cal1;
  private Calendar cal2;

  private static final int REQUESTING_DATE_1 = 0;
  private static final int CONFIRMING_DATE_1 = 1;
  private static final int REQUESTING_DATE_2 = 2;
  private static final int REPORTING_COMPARISON = 3;

  private static final String title1 = "Date 1";
  private static final String title2 = "Date 2";
  private static final String rtitle = "Result";

  public void startApp() {
    display = Display.getDisplay(this);

    cmdExit = new Command("Exit",Command.SCREEN,1);
    cmdOK = new Command("OK",Command.SCREEN,1);

    df1 = new DateField("Set 1",DateField.DATE_TIME);
    statusMessage = new StringItem(null,null);
```

```
  form1 = new Form(title1);
  form1.addCommand(cmdOK);
  form1.addCommand(cmdExit);
  form1.setCommandListener(this);
  form1.append(df1);

  form2 = new Form(rtitle);
  form2.addCommand(cmdOK);
  form2.setCommandListener(this);
  statusMessage.setText("Date 1 accepted\nEnter Date 2");
  form2.append(statusMessage);

  display.setCurrent(form1);
}

public void pauseApp() {
}

public void destroyApp(boolean unconditional) {
}
  public void commandAction(Command cmd, Displayable d) {

    if (cmd == cmdExit) {
      destroyApp(false);
      notifyDestroyed();
    }
    else if (cmd == cmdOK) {
      switch (state) {
        case REQUESTING_DATE_1:
          if (df1.getDate() == null) {
            break;
          }
          cal1 = Calendar.getInstance();
          cal1.setTime(df1.getDate());
          state = CONFIRMING_DATE_1;
          display.setCurrent(form2);
          break;
        case CONFIRMING_DATE_1:
          form1.setTitle(title2);
          form1.delete(0);
          df2 = new DateField("Set D2",DateField.DATE_TIME);
          form1.append(df2);
          state = REQUESTING_DATE_2;
```

```
            display.setCurrent(form1);
            break;
        case REQUESTING_DATE_2:
            if (df2.getDate() == null) {
                break;
            }
            cal2 = Calendar.getInstance();
            cal2.setTime(df2.getDate());
            String s = new String();
            if (cal1.before(cal2)) {
                s= "DT1 BEFORE DT2";
            }
            else if (cal1.after(cal2)) {
                s= "DT1 AFTER DT2";
            }
            else {
                s= "DT1 SAME AS DT2";
            }
            statusMessage.setText(s);
            state = REPORTING_COMPARISON;
            display.setCurrent(form2);
            break;
        case REPORTING_COMPARISON:
            form1.setTitle(title1);
            form1.delete(0);
            df1 = new DateField("Set Date",DateField.DATE_TIME);
            form1.append(df1);
            state = REQUESTING_DATE_1;
            display.setCurrent(form1);
            break;
        }
    }
}
}
```

The application contains two forms. One is used to accept two sets of date/time input from the user, and the other is used to provide the user with instructions and to display the application's output. This output is a simple report of whether the first date/time entered by the user is before, after, or coincident with the second date/time.

The startApp method creates an uninitialized instance of DateField and adds it to the first form. It also creates and adds the appropriate commands and sets a listener. It then creates the second form to which it adds a `StringItem` that will be used to provide instructions and report results. For each set of date/time pairs the user enters, the application transitions through the following states:

- ▶ REQUESTING_DATE_1
- ▶ CONFIRMING_DATE_1
- ▶ REQUESTING_DATE_2
- ▶ REPORTING_COMPARISON

The `startApp` method sets the initial state to REQUESTING_DATE_1.

When the `commandAction` method detects that it has been invoked in response to an OK command, it examines the `state` instance variable and carries out the operations shown in Table 6-1.

Running the DateField Example

As is the case with all MIDlets, the exact runtime behavior depends on the device on which the application is running. Let's use the Motorola i85s.

When you launch the application, the initial display looks like this:

State	Operation
REQUESTING_DATE_1	Creates an instance of `Calendar`. Invokes the `Calendar`'s `setTime` method using the information obtained from the `DateField` as an argument. Updates the `state` instance variable to CONFIRMING_DATE_1. Sets the second form as current to inform user that first date has been accepted and to request second date.
CONFIRMING_DATE_1	Updates title of form 1. Deletes `DateField` from form 1. Creates uninitialized `DateField`. Adds `DateField` to form. Updates `state` instance variable to REQUESTING_DATE_2. Sets first form as current form to accept second date/time from user.
REQUESTING_DATE_2	Creates a second instance of `Calendar`. Invokes the `Calendar`'s `setTime` method using the information obtained from the second `DateField` as an argument. Determines whether first date/time is before, after, or equal to the second date/time. Updates the text of `statusMessage` to reflect result of comparison. Updates the `state` instance variable to REPORTING_COMPARISON. Sets the second form as current form to report result.
REPORTING_COMPARISON	Updates title of form 1. Deletes `DateField` from form 1. Creates uninitialized `DateField`. Adds `DateField` to form. Updates `state` instance variable to REQUESTING_DATE_1. Sets first form as current form to repeat user input procedure.

Table 6-1   *State Transitions for DateField Example*

Notice that the implementation gives a clear visual indication that the `DateField` component is uninitialized by presenting the date as <date> and the time as <time>. When you press the scroll-down button, the date becomes highlighted, as shown here:

When you press Menu, the editable `DateField` component is displayed. You can use the scroll-up and scroll-down buttons to select the year field, the date field, or the days of the month. When the year or month fields are selected, you can use the scroll-left and scroll-right buttons to modify their values. When the days of the month are selected, you can use the scroll-left and scroll-right buttons to select the previous or next day, or you can use the scroll-up and scroll-down buttons to change the day to one week earlier or one week later. Here is what the display looks like when 8 June 2001 is selected:

After you press Save, the `DateField` is no longed uninitialized and the emulator looks like this:

If you use the scroll-down button to select the time field and then press Menu, a graphical representation of the time component of the `DateField` is displayed. You can use the scroll buttons to modify the time. If you set the time to 10:15 A.M. and press Save, the emulator looks like this:

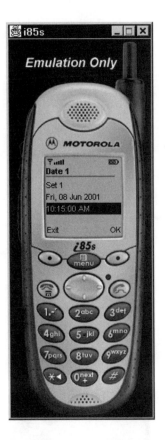

The `DateField` component now shows the values you selected for the date and time portions. When you are satisfied that these are the values you want, press OK and the application presents the second form, which notifies you that the first date has been accepted and requests that you enter the second date. When you press OK, the application presents another screen that contains an uninitialized `DateField`. If you set the date/time to 3:45 P.M. on 1 July 2002, press Save, and then press OK, the application compares the two date/time pairs you entered and reports the result of the comparison, as shown here:

When you press OK this time, the application starts the entire process over and displays the first screen you saw.

Of particular interest to application programmers is the fact that not only can a powerful user interface be presented with a minimal amount of code, but also the date/time validation code you might have expected to deal with is nowhere to be seen.

The Gauge Item

Providing a graphical rather than a simple textual presentation of certain kinds of data has a much greater impact. If an application is performing a lengthy operation, a progress bar gives the user a much better idea of how much time is remaining in the operation than simply reporting the percent of completion as a number.

Similarly, less mental effort is required to realize how much room is left in a record store when the value is represented as a series of nine black bars and one clear bar than if the same value is presented as "10%." The LCDUI provides a displayable item that can be used to present data graphically.

The Gauge class implements a bar graph display of a value intended for use in a form. A gauge can display values ranging from zero to a maximum that was specified when the gauge was created. This range should be kept small and the application should normalize its data to fit within the range. Since screen size varies from device to device, the number of visual states (typically, clear or black bars) that represent a range of values will not always be the same. In many cases, a single visual state represents more than one value within the range.

There are two types of gauge, non-interactive and interactive. As the names imply, the user is permitted to modify the value of an interactive Gauge but not of a non-interactive Gauge. An application is allowed to modify the value of both types of gauge.

An Example of a Non-Interactive Gauge

\OMH\com\paulsjavabooks\instantj2me\Chapter6\NonInteractiveGaugeExample.java

The best way to understand how a gauge works is to use one in a program. Let's pretend that you have written an application that must contact a remote host to obtain data. If contacting the host takes ten seconds and the user is left guessing as to what is happening, the ten seconds are perceived by the user as being much longer. To address this issue, you provide a progress bar that the application updates once per second. Now the user perceives the ten seconds as ten seconds.

Examine the following code that simulates contacting a host:

```
/*
 * NonInteractiveGaugeExample.java
 *
 * Created on June 26, 2001, 10:32 PM
 */

package com.paulsjavabooks.instantj2me.Chapter6;

import javax.microedition.midlet.*;
import javax.microedition.lcdui.*;


/**
```

```
 *
 * @author  paul_tremblett
 * @version 1.0
 */
public class NonInteractiveGaugeExample extends MIDlet
    implements CommandListener {

  private Display display;
  private Form f1;
  private Form f2;
  private Command cmdOK;
  private Command cmdStop;
  private StringItem contactingHost;
  private StringItem statusMessage;

  Thread t;

  int elapsedTime = 0;

  class RunnableGauge extends Gauge implements Runnable {

    int max;

    NonInteractiveGaugeExample owner;

    public RunnableGauge(NonInteractiveGaugeExample owner,
        int max, int initial) {
      super("Progress",false,max,initial);
      this.owner = owner;
      this.max = max;
    }

    public void run() {
      for (int i = 0; i < max; ++i) {
        try {
          Thread.sleep(1000l);
        }
        catch (InterruptedException e) {
        }
        synchronized (owner) {
          if (elapsedTime < 0) {
            break;
          }
          else {
```

```
        ++elapsedTime;
        setValue(elapsedTime);
       }
      }
    }
    if (elapsedTime < 0) {
      owner.statusMessage.setText("ABORTED");
    }
    else {
      owner.statusMessage.setText("HOST CONTACTED");
      owner.display.setCurrent(owner.f2);
    }
  }
}

public void startApp() {
  display = Display.getDisplay(this);
  f1 = new Form("Gauge Demo");
  cmdStop = new Command("STOP",Command.STOP,1);
  f1.addCommand(cmdStop);
  RunnableGauge bgt = new RunnableGauge(this,10,0);
  f1.append(bgt);
  contactingHost = new StringItem(null,"Contacting Host...");
  f1.append(contactingHost);
  f1.setCommandListener(this);

  f2 = new Form("Main Menu");
  statusMessage = new StringItem(null,null);
  f2.append(statusMessage);
  cmdOK = new Command("OK",Command.SCREEN,1);
  f2.addCommand(cmdOK);
  f2.setCommandListener(this);

  t = new Thread(bgt);
  t.start();

  display.setCurrent(f1);
}

public void pauseApp() {
}

public void destroyApp(boolean unconditional) {
}
```

```
public void commandAction(Command cmd, Displayable d) {
  if (cmd == cmdStop) {
    synchronized(this) {
      elapsedTime = -1;
    }
    try {
      t.join();
      display.setCurrent(f2);
    }
    catch (InterruptedException e) {
    }
  }
  else if (cmd == cmdOK) {
    destroyApp(false);
    notifyDestroyed();
  }
}
}
```

Notice that the application contains an inner class RunnableGauge that subclasses gauge and implements Runnable. The startApp method creates an instance of this inner class and adds it to a form. To provide the user with a means of aborting the application before the host has been contacted, startApp adds a STOP command to the form. It is highly recommended that all applications use such a STOP command whenever the Gauge control is used as a progress indicator. You should realize that such a command does not automatically stop anything. That work is carried out by the commandAction method that handles the command. The STOP command simply hints to the application that this command might be used to prematurely terminate some operation.

Since the RunnableGauge class implements Runnable, an instance of it can be used to create a thread, and the startApp method does exactly that. It creates and starts the thread with the following code:

```
t = new Thread(bgt);
t.start();
```

The RunnableGauge executes ten iterations of a for loop. In each iteration, it sleeps for a second, and when it awakens, it checks whether the value of elapsedTime is less than zero. If it is, this indicates that the user has pressed the STOP button and the thread breaks out of the for loop. If elapsedTime is not less than zero, the thread increments elapsedTime and passes the updated value as an argument to the `setValue` method, which sets the value of the gauge. We have already pointed out that any change made to an `Item` in a form is reflected as the change is made. The application program does not have to request that the display be refreshed.

When the loop terminates, the thread checks the value of `elapsedTime`. If it is less than zero, indicating that the user has pressed the STOP button, the code passes a String with a value of ABORTED to the `setText` method of `statusMessage`. If `elapsedTime` is not less than zero, the code passes a String with a value of HOST CONTACTED to the `setText` method and makes the form containing `statusMessage` the current form.

The `commandAction` method determines whether the STOP button has been pressed and sets the value of `elapsedTime` to –1. It then invokes the `join` method to wait for the thread to terminate, and when the `join` method returns, it then makes the form containing `statusMessage` the current form.

Running the Non-Interactive Gauge Example

When you launch the *NonInteractiveGauge* MIDlet, the initial display contains a Form with two elements, the gauge and a `StringItem` whose value is CONTACTING HOST. It looks like this:

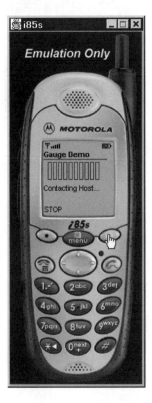

As the thread in the application executes its `for` loop, the gauge is updated and looks like this:

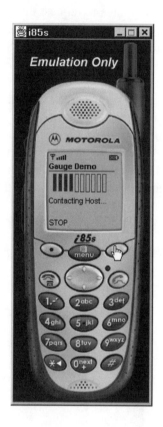

If you do not interrupt the application, it runs for approximately ten seconds and displays a second form containing a `StringItem` whose value is HOST CONTACTED, as shown here:

If you press STOP, the `for` loop terminates prematurely and the application displays a form containing a `StringItem` whose text informs the user that the operation has been aborted. It looks like this:

The ItemStateListener Interface

In the examples we have discussed up to this point, the applications were not aware of changes the user made to items in a form at the time those changes were made. Most applications are not interested in every change the user makes to an item. Rather, they invoke a "getter" method to obtain a value from the item after the user finishes interacting with the item and sends a command to the application by pressing a button. There are, however, situations in which the application needs to be aware of changes to an item as those changes are made. When this is the case, the application can use the `ItemStateListener` interface by invoking the `addItemStateListener` method on the form containing the item(s) the application wishes to monitor.

The single method in the `ItemStateListener` interface is `itemState-Changed`. It is called when the user changes the internal state of an item. A change can occur when a user

▶ Changes the selected value(s) in a `ChoiceGroup`

▶ Adjusts the value of an interactive `Gauge`

▶ Enters or modifies the value in a `TextField`

▶ Enters a new date or time in a `DateField`

The implementation decides what constitutes a change to an item. For example, one implementation of text editing in a `TextField` might consider every keystroke a change, while another implementation might consider the value changed only when all text has been entered and Save has been pressed. The application can rely on the following:

▶ The listener will be called to notify the application of a change to an `Item` before a change is made to another item.

▶ The listener will be called before any command is delivered to the Form's `CommandListener` if it has one.

▶ If the application itself makes a change to an item, the listener will not be called.

An Example of an Interactive Gauge

\OMH\com\paulsjavabooks\instantj2me\Chapter6\InteractiveGaugeExample.java

Here is the source code for a simple MIDlet that allows the user to change the value of a variable using an interactive `Gauge`:

```
/*
 * InteractiveGaugeExample.java
 *
 * Created on June 26, 2001, 10:32 PM
 */

package com.paulsjavabooks.instantj2me.Chapter6;

import javax.microedition.midlet.*;
import javax.microedition.lcdui.*;
```

```java
/**
 *
 * @author  paul_tremblett
 * @version 1.0
 */
public class InteractiveGaugeExample extends MIDlet
    implements CommandListener, ItemStateListener {

  private Display display;
  private Form f;
  private Command cmdOK;
  private Gauge g;
  private StringItem currentValue;

  public void startApp() {
    display = Display.getDisplay(this);
    f = new Form("Demo");
    g = new Gauge("Interactive Gauge",true,10,5);
    f.setItemStateListener(this);
    f.append(g);
    currentValue =
      new StringItem("Current:",Integer.toString(g.getValue()));
    f.append(currentValue);
    cmdOK = new Command("OK",Command.SCREEN,1);
    f.addCommand(cmdOK);
    f.setCommandListener(this);
    display.setCurrent(f);
  }

  public void pauseApp() {
  }

  public void destroyApp(boolean unconditional) {
  }

  public void commandAction(Command cmd, Displayable d) {
    if (cmd == cmdOK) {
      destroyApp(false);
      notifyDestroyed();
    }
  }
```

```
public void itemStateChanged(Item item) {
  if (item == g) {
    System.out.println(g.getValue());
    currentValue.setText(Integer.toString(g.getValue()));
  }
 }
}
```

The `startApp` method creates a form to which it adds a gauge. The second parameter passed to the gauge's constructor is `true`. This indicates that the gauge is interactive. The `startApp` method uses `f.setItemStateListener(this)` to indicate that the MIDlet itself is the listener. This means that the MIDlet contains an implementation of the `itemStateChanged` method. If you examine this method, you see that it invokes the gauge's `getValue` method to obtain the int representing the value and converts this `int` to a String, which it uses to update the value of `currentValue`, a `StringItem` with the label "Current Value:".

Running the Interactive Gauge Example

When you launch the MIDlet, the initial display looks like this:

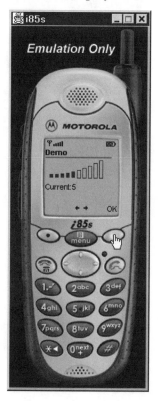

Each time you press the scroll-up button, the gauge is updated by the implementation and the `StringItem` is updated by the listener. After you press the scroll-up button three times, the display looks like this:

Press the scroll-down button six times and the gauge will be updated in the opposite direction until it looks like this:

You will discover that it is impossible to set the gauge to a value that is outside the range that was specified when it was created. This applies also to the application.

Using Graphics in MIDlets

IN THIS CHAPTER:

Portable Network Graphics

Associating an icon with a MIDlet

Adding images to ChoiceGroup items

Our exploration of the LCDUI has taken us from the simple `TextField` and `ChoiceGroup` in Chapter 5 to the more complex `DateField` and `Gauge` in Chapter 6. We will now examine another important aspect of any user interface, the visual appeal offered by icons and images.

Portable Network Graphics

The MID Profile states that implementations are required to support images stored in the PNG (Portable Network Graphics) format, version 1.0. The PNG Specification presents PNG as an extensible file format for the lossless, portable, well-compressed storage of raster images. It further states the following:

▶ PNG is simple and so is easily implemented.

▶ PNG is legally unencumbered.

▶ PNG is flexible and allows for future expansion and private add-ons.

▶ PNG is robust, providing both full file integrity checking and simple detection of common transmission errors.

NOTE

The remainder of this section is included to satisfy the curiosity of those readers who might be wondering about some of the internals of PNG. You can safely skip this material if you are more interested in how to incorporate PNG into your applications than in what it looks like or how it works.

The initial motivation that drove the PNG effort was to provide a replacement for GIF. It retained many of the features offered by GIF, but added the following:

▶ Truecolor images of up to 48 bits per pixel

▶ Grayscale images of up to 16 bits per pixel

▶ Full alpha channel (general transparency masks)

▶ Image gamma information, which supports automatic display of images with correct brightness/contrast, regardless of the machines used to originate and display the image

▶ Reliable, straightforward detection of file corruption

▶ Faster initial presentation in progressive display mode

A PNG Image

If you think of a PNG image conceptually rather than physically, it is a rectangular array of pixels with pixels appearing left to right in each scanline, with scanlines appearing top to bottom. The size of each pixel is determined by the number of bits per sample in the image data and is referred to as the *bit depth*.

PNG provides for three types of pixels. The first type is the *indexed-color* pixel. To use this type of pixel, you supply a palette of colors. The number of entries in the palette is the image bit depth. Each pixel is represented by a single sample that is a direct index into the palette. The second type of pixel is a *grayscale* pixel, which is represented by a single sample that is a grayscale level ranging from black to white where 0 represents black and the largest value for the bit depth represents white. The third type of pixel is the *truecolor* pixel, which is represented by three samples: red, green, and blue. Each sample ranges from black, which is represented by 0, to a maximum, which is red, green, or blue. The bit depth is the size of the sample and not the total size of the pixel. The second two types of pixels can also include an additional sample called the *alpha* sample, which represents transparency information. The value contained in this sample can range from 0 to $(2^{bitdepth})-1$, where a value of 0 indicates that the pixel is completely transparent and the maximum value indicates that the pixel is completely opaque.

A PNG File

The previous section described a PNG image stored in memory. Most often, you will be dealing with PNG images stored in files. A PNG file consists of a PNG *signature* followed by a series of three or more *chunks*.

PNG Signature

A signature is nothing more than a unique series of values that identifies a file's type. The signature of a PNG file consists of eight bytes. The first byte is a hex 89. The second three bytes are the ASCII characters P, N, and G. The next two bytes are the CR-LF sequence \r\n. This is followed by a CONTROL-Z, and the signature is terminated with a line-feed. The complete sequence in hexadecimal is 89 50 4e 47 0d 0a 1a 0a. A PNG signature does not contain a version number. Format extensions are handled by the chunks, which are described in the next section.

PNG Chunks

Chunks contain the actual data that comprises the image. Every chunk consists of four fields. The first field is the length, which is a 4-byte unsigned integer that specifies the number of bytes in the chunk's data field. This value, like all integers used by PNG, is in network byte order. The most significant byte (MSB) appears first and the remaining bytes appear in order of decreasing significance up to the least significant byte (LSB). Within each byte, the highest bit, representing a value of 128, is numbered as bit 7 and the lowest bit, representing 0, is numbered as bit 0. The second field of a chunk is a 4-byte chunk type code. The value of each byte in the type code is restricted to ASCII uppercase and lowercase, letters but the type code field is viewed as four binary values rather than a String. The third field consists of the chunk's data bytes and can be from 0 to $(2^{31})-1$ in length. The final field is a Cyclic Redundancy Check (CRC), which is calculated using the bytes from the chunk type code and the data, but not from the length field.

Chunk Properties

The four ASCII letters that make up the type code field are also called the chunk name. The case of the letters in a chunk name conveys certain information about properties of the chunk. Bit 5 of an ASCII letter determines whether the letter is uppercase (0) or lowercase (1) so the case of each of the four letters in a chunk name represents the following properties of the chunk, as shown in Table 7-1.

A critical chunk is necessary for successful display of the file's contents and must be understood and properly rendered by all implementations. An ancillary chunk is optional. A public chunk is one that appears in the PNG specification or is registered in the list of PNG special-purpose public chunk types. A private or unregistered chunk is one that an application defines for its own purpose.

The "safe to copy" property is of interest to PNG editors and is used to guarantee proper handling of chunks as a file is being modified.

Byte Within Type Code	Value of Bit 5	Property
First	0	Critical
First	1	Ancillary
Second	0	Public
Second	1	Private
Third	0	Reserved (always 0 in Version 1)
Third	1	Possibly used in future
Fourth	0	Unsafe to copy
Fourth	1	Safe to copy

Table 7-1   *Meaning of Property Bits*

Critical Chunks

Table 7-2 lists information about the critical chunks. Notice that each letter of the name is uppercase. This indicates that the chunk is critical, public, and safe to copy.

Ancillary Chunks

Table 7-3 lists some ancillary chunks, as indicated by the first letter of each name being lowercase. The second letter of each name is uppercase, so all of the named chunks are public.

NOTE

The PNG (Portable Network Graphics) Specification, Version 1.0 W3C Recommendation, October 1, 1996, is available at http://www.w3.org/TR/REC-png.html. It is also available as RFC 2083 at http://www.ietf.org/rfc/rfc2083.txt.

Chunk Name	Description	Notes
IHDR	Image Header Contains width, height, bit depth, color type, compression method, filter method, and interlace method.	Must appear first.
PLTE	Palette Contains 1 to 256 palette entries. Each entry is a three-byte sequence of this form: Red (0=black,255=red) Green (0=black,255=green) Blue(0=black,255=blue)	Must appear for color type 3 (indexed color). May appear for color types 2 and 6 (truecolor and truecolor with alpha). Must not appear for color type 4 (grayscale with alpha channel). Chunk length must be divisible by 3.
IDAT	Image Data Contains the actual image data.	At least one such chunk must appear. Multiple IDAT chunks can appear. Multiple IDAT chunks must be consecutive with no intervening chunks.
IEND	Image Trailer	Must appear last.

Table 7-2   *Critical Chunks*

Chunk Name	Description
bKGD	Background color
cHRM	Primary chromaticities and white point
gAMA	Image gamma
hIST	Image histogram
pHYs	Physical pixel dimensions
sBIT	Significant bits
tEXt	Textual data
tIMe	Image last-modification time
tRNS	Transparency
zTXt	Compressed textual data

Table 7-3   *Ancillary Chunks*

MIDP Support for PNG

All MIDP implementations *must* support the critical chunks specified by PNG. A MIDP implementation *may* support any or all of the ancillary chunks, but *should* silently ignore any ancillary chunks it does not support.

The `Image` class is used to hold graphical data. An application can contain many `Image` objects. These objects exist in off-screen memory and are independent of the display device. One or more of an application's `Image` objects can be painted on the display, or they can all be invisible to the user. An `Image` object is painted only when the application issues an explicit command.

There are two categories of images, *mutable* and *immutable*. The type most often used is the immutable image, which is usually created by loading data from resource bundles, from files, or from the network. Once created, an immutable image cannot be modified. Mutable images, on the other hand, can be modified by the application after they are created and are usually used for drawing.

Associating Images with MIDlets

Look back for a minute at the *Hello World* MIDlet in Chapter 1. When you executed it, it looked like this:

Now start the Example application that was delivered with the J2ME Wireless Toolkit. To do so from the KToolbar, open the "example" project, click Build, select Default Color Phone as the device, and click Run. When the application starts, the emulator looks like this:

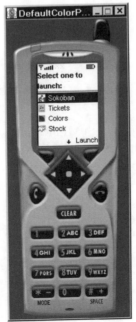

The presence of the icons makes this application more visually appealing than the *Hello World* application. You will now learn how to add icons to your applications.

Let's start by creating a package named Chapter7 and adding the two MIDlet classes, `Hello` and `Goodbye`. The code is contained on the CD, but we will not show it here, since it is simply two copies of our original *Hello* MIDlet with the package names, the class names, and the greetings appropriately modified. Add each class by right-clicking the Chapter7 icon and selecting New | MIDP. Instead of then selecting MIDlet Suite as you have done in earlier examples, select MIDlet. When the Wizard is displayed, enter the name of the class, and press Finish. Then copy the source code into the skeletons generated by the IDE. After you have added the two new MIDlets, the Explorer window looks like this:

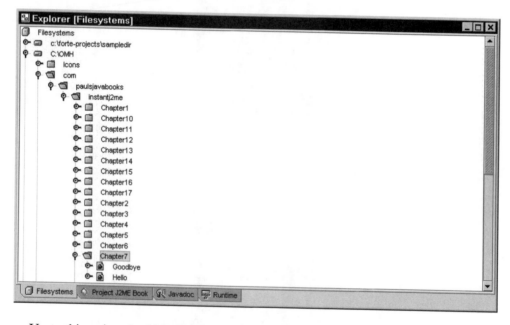

Up to this point, the JAR file in each MIDlet Suite we prepared contained exactly one class file. The *example* suite you just accessed from KToolbar contains multiple applications. Since we are aiming to achieve the look and feel of *example*, let's include multiple applications as well. Start by right-clicking on Chapter7 in the Explorer window and selecting New MIDP | MIDlet Suite. When the Wizard is displayed, type **HelloGoodbye**, as shown here:

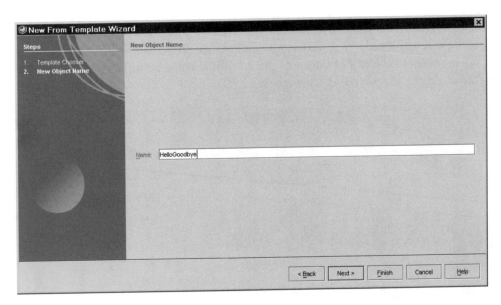

Now press Next>. When the Wizard displays the next screen, you'll be doing something a little different from what you did in prior examples. Instead of simply leaving the Create a new MIDlet class radio button checked, press the radio button labeled "Use an existing MIDlet class." Then press the button labeled "…" in the lower right of the dialog box and navigate through the window that appears until you reach c:\OMH\com\paulsjavabooks\instantj2me\Chapter7. When you do, select Hello and press OK. When the main window is displayed, change the MIDlet Name to Hello. The Wizard should now look like this:

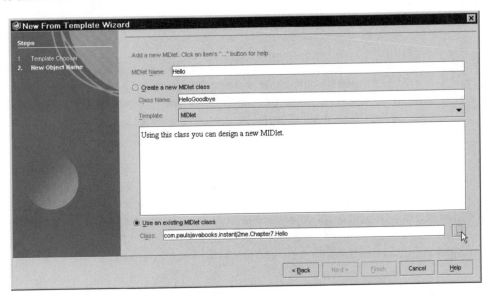

Press <Back and then Finish. Double-click the MIDlet Suite icon and, when the descriptor is displayed, enter **MIDlet-2** into the text entry field at the bottom of the window. Press the New Tag button to the left of the entry field. The new tag is added to those already displayed, as shown here:

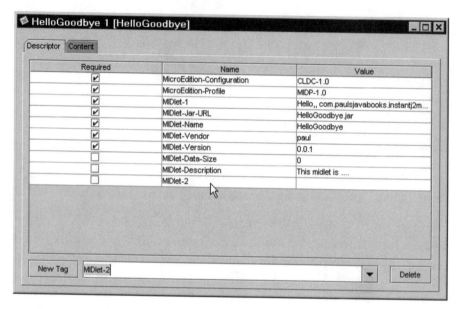

The new tag, MIDlet-2, represents the second MIDlet in the suite. You can add others using sequential numbers. After you add a new tag, you must assign it a value. Assign the following value to MIDlet-2:

```
So Long,/Icons/Goodbye.png,com.paulsjavabooks.instantj2me.Chapter7.Goodbye
```

NOTE

You modify the value of a name by double-clicking the Value column in the appropriate row. This gives that cell the focus so you can enter and/or modify text. It is important that you press ENTER after you finish typing. If you do not, the changes you make will not be accepted.

The value you just entered is actually three comma-delimited fields. The first is the MIDlet name that is displayed when the MIDlet Suite is loaded. The second is the name of the icon displayed next to the MIDlet name. The third is the name of the MIDlet class. If you compare what you just typed to the value of MIDlet-1, you'll notice that no icon is specified for the latter. As a matter of fact, if you examine the descriptor for each of the examples you've developed up until now, you'll see that the same is true of them as well, and that is why no icons were displayed.

You should next modify the value of MIDlet-1 to include /Icons/Hello.png as its icon. If you have unzipped MIDlets.zip from the CD, the Icons directory has already been created. If not, you must create it by right-clicking the filesystem named c:\OMH, selecting New Package, and entering **Icons** in the dialog that appears. You must then copy Hello.png and Goodbye.png into this directory.

NOTE

When you develop your own applications, you will use an image editor that supports PNG to create icons. There are many such editors available. The icons used for the two applications here were prepared by typing the character sequences colon, hyphen, right-parenthesis, and colon, hyphen, left-parenthesis into Microsoft Word, using HyperSnap-DX to capture the regions containing the faces into which Word converted these sequences, and saving the captured regions as PNG files. They are shown here:

NOTE

The icon associated with a MIDlet can be placed anywhere, but you will find it is easier to keep track of things if you place them all in a common directory.

Now return to the dialog in which you entered values for MIDlet-1 and MIDlet-2 and press the Content tab. Use the Add button to add the Icons directory to the group box labeled Chosen Content. When you have finished, the dialog should look like this:

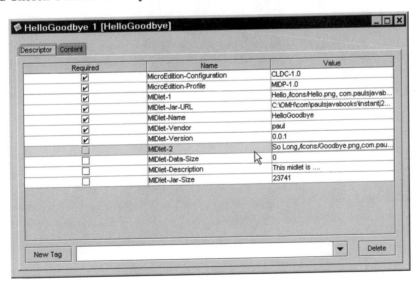

Running Hello/Goodbye

The suite is now ready to run. Right-click the MIDlet Suite icon labeled HelloGoodbye and select Execute. When you do so, an emulator window like this appears:

Isn't that more visually appealing than the simple text you saw in Chapter 1? Now launch the *Hello* application by pressing the Launch button. When you do, this now familiar greeting is displayed:

Press Exit, and you are once again looking at the list of applications that can be launched. Use the scroll-down button to select So Long!, as shown here:

This time, when you press Launch, the following message is displayed:

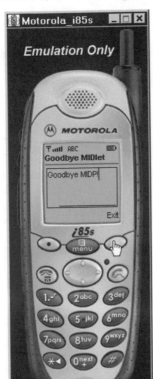

Including Images in a ChoiceGroup

The ChoiceGroup we included in the temperature conversion application in Chapter 5 was displayed as two radio buttons with no associated images. If you check the code, you will remember that the constructor we used was this:

```
ChoiceGroup tempChoice =
    new ChoiceGroup("Temp Type",Choice.EXCLUSIVE,tempType,null);
```

The third argument, tempType, was an array of Strings containing the names of the two temperature scales. The fourth argument, which was null, is described by the documentation as an array of images. We will now add an icon to each element of the `ChoiceGroup` by simply supplying a value other than `null` for the fourth argument. Here is the source code:

\OMH\com\paulsjavabooks\instantj2me\Chapter7\TempConv.java

```java
/*
 * TempConv.java
 *
 * Created on July 1, 2001, 2:58 PM
 */

package com.paulsjavabooks.instantj2me.Chapter7;

import javax.microedition.midlet.*;
import javax.microedition.lcdui.*;

import com.paulsjavabooks.instantj2me.Math.*;

/**
 *
 * @author  paul_tremblett
 * @version 1.0
 */
public class TempConv extends MIDlet implements CommandListener {

    private Display display;
    private Command cmdExit;
    private Command cmdConvert;
    private Command cmdOK;
    private Form form1;
    private Form form2;
    private TextField tempField;
    private ChoiceGroup tempChoice;
    private StringItem convertedTemp;

      public void startApp() {
        display = Display.getDisplay(this);

        cmdConvert = new Command("Convert",Command.SCREEN,1);
        cmdExit = new Command("Exit",Command.SCREEN,1);
        cmdOK = new Command("OK",Command.SCREEN,1);
```

```
form1 = new Form("TmpCnv");
tempField = new TextField("Temp:",null,10,TextField.ANY);
form1.addCommand(cmdConvert);
form1.addCommand(cmdExit);
form1.setCommandListener(this);
form1.append(tempField);
String[] tempType = {"Celsius","Farenheit"};
Image[] tempImages = null;
try {
  Image ctemp = Image.createImage("/Icons/ctemp.png");
  Image ftemp = Image.createImage("/Icons/ftemp.png");

  tempImages = new Image[] {ctemp, ftemp};
}
catch(java.io.IOException err) {
}
tempChoice =
  new ChoiceGroup("Temp Type",Choice.EXCLUSIVE,
                  tempType,tempImages);
form1.append(tempChoice);

form2 = new Form("Result");
convertedTemp = new StringItem(null, null);
form2.append(convertedTemp);
form2.addCommand(cmdOK);
form2.setCommandListener(this);

display.setCurrent(form1);
}

public void pauseApp() {
}

public void destroyApp(boolean unconditional) {
}

public void commandAction(Command cmd, Displayable d) {

  String displayString = null;

  if (cmd == cmdExit) {
    destroyApp(false);
    notifyDestroyed();
```

```
      }
    else if (cmd == cmdConvert) {
      String s = tempField.getString();
      displayString = convertTemp(s);
      convertedTemp.setText(displayString);
      display.setCurrent(form2);
    }
    else if (cmd == cmdOK) {
      tempField.setString(null);
      display.setCurrent(form1);
    }
  }

  private String convertTemp(String s) {
    char c = s.charAt(s.length() - 1);
    StringBuffer tsb = new StringBuffer();
    try {
      switch (tempChoice.getSelectedIndex()) {
        case 0:
          tsb.append(cToF(s));
          tsb.append('F');
          break;
        case 1:
          tsb.append(fToC(s));
          tsb.append('C');
          break;
        default:
          tsb.append("**ERROR**");
      }
    }
    catch(KMathException e) {
      tsb.append("**ERROR**");
    }
    finally {
      return tsb.toString();
    }
  }

  private String cToF(String c) throws KMathException {
    String cx9 = KMath.multiply(c,"9");
```

```
        String temp = KMath.divide(cx9,"5");
        String f = KMath.add(temp,"32");
        return f;
    }

    private String fToC(String f) throws KMathException {
        String fm32 = KMath.subtract(f,"32");
        String temp = KMath.multiply(fm32,"5");
        String c = KMath.divide(temp,"9");
        return c;
    }
}
```

This MIDlet differs from its counterpart in Chapter 5 in that the elements in the `ChoiceGroup` contain images. The images, which are contained in the instance variables `ctemp` and `ftemp`, are immutable. They are read from the files ctemp.png and ftemp.png by the following code:

```
Image[] tempImages = null;
try {
  Image ctemp = Image.createImage("/Icons/ctemp.png");
  Image ftemp = Image.createImage("/Icons/ftemp.png");

  tempImages = new Image[] {ctemp, ftemp};
}
catch(java.io.IOException err) {
}
```

The `catch` block can be empty because if an exception is thrown, it will be silently ignored and the elements of the `ChoiceGroup` will be displayed without the icons.

The variable `tempImages` containing the two images is passed as the fourth argument to the `ChoiceGroup`'s constructor.

Running the Modified MIDlet Suite

Add the new MIDlet to the MIDlet Suite as MIDlet-3. Assign it a display name of "Convert Temps" and specify c2f.png as the icon. Since the MIDlet uses the KMath library, you must also add the Math directory. Do this by selecting the Content tab and using the Add button.

Right-click the HelloGoodbye MIDlet suite icon and select Execute. When you do, this emulator window is displayed:

Notice the presence of the downward-pointing arrow indicating that this screen is scrollable. Use the scroll-down button to select Convert Temps. Now press Launch. When the application begins execution, the initial display looks like this:

As you can see, both elements of the `ChoiceGroup` no longer fit on the display, but the implementation supplies a down-arrow indicating that additional content can be viewed by scrolling. Press the scroll-down button and you will see that the remainder of the `ChoiceGroup` looks like this:

The implementation manages the display and provides an up-arrow indicating that scrolling up will reveal additional content. It also provides a horizontal line to delineate the two elements of the `ChoiceGroup`.

It's quite possible that you might find that the visual appeal offered by including icons in this case is not nearly as effective as including icons on the launch screen. In fact, you might even find they make the display look too busy or even confusing. Before you decide to eliminate the icons and revert to the original version of the application, try using the Blackberry-RIM-957 emulator. The initial display now looks like this:

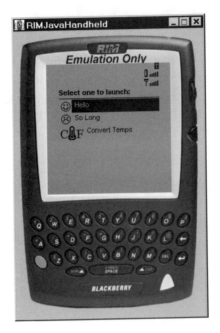

When you use the thumb-wheel to select Convert Temps and then launch it, a single screen with the `TextField` and both elements of the `ChoiceGroup` is displayed, as shown here:

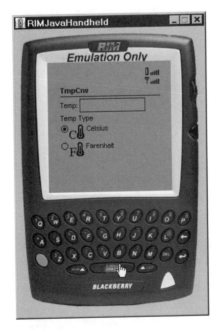

Now that you've seen the application running on two different devices, you can better decide whether you should eliminate the icons or seek an alternate solution such as using smaller icons. If you opt for the latter, you will discover that constructing a large quantity of unique icons is not an easy task when the size of the icons is severely restricted. The lesson you are learning here is that sometimes designing an interface for a MID that will be suitable for use across a wide variety of MIDs is more an artistic challenge than a technical one.

User Notification

IN THIS CHAPTER:

The Alert class

Alert types

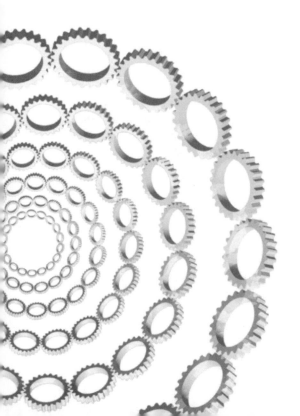

Your programming career was undoubtedly only in its infancy when you became aware of the fact that programs do not always execute in a perfect environment. Users make mistakes entering data, resources that a program needs become temporarily unavailable, and the list goes on. You quickly learn that prevention is beyond your control. You can and must, however, detect errors and exceptional conditions and inform the user. In this chapter, we will learn how to alert the user to conditions that affect an application.

The Alert Class

An alert is a screen that shows data to the user, waits for a specified period of time, and proceeds to the next screen. An alert can contain any or all of the following:

▶ A title

▶ A text String

▶ An image

▶ An alert type

The length of time that an alert is displayed before it proceeds to the next screen can be specified by the application. If this time is specified as infinity, the alert is considered to be *modal*. Like modal windows you already encountered in other GUIs such as Windows and X Windows, modal `Alerts` require the user to "dismiss" the alert. In Windows and X Windows, the applications programmer provides an OK or Cancel button that the user can click. In a MIDlet, the feature that allows the user to dismiss the alert is provided by the implementation. A timed alert can automatically become modal if it contains an amount of content that requires scrolling to view.

An alert can be assigned an alert type that indicates the nature of the alert. You will learn about alert types later in the chapter.

The `Alert` class is a subclass of `Screen`; but an instance of `Alert`, unlike an instance of `Screen`, does not accept application-defined commands. The `Alert` class provides its own implementation of the `addCommand` and `setCommandListener` methods. These methods do nothing more than throw an `IllegalStateException`.

If an alert is visible on the display and you make a change to its contents, the change takes place automatically. The application does not have to take any special action to refresh the display.

Using an Alert as a Splash Screen

\OMH\Icons\ca-proud.png

Many programs display a "splash screen" for a few seconds before presenting the main menu. This screen can contain a logo or text containing copyright, trademark, patent, or license information. The `Alert` class can be used to display such a splash screen.

Let's say you're a Canadian programmer and you want to present your software as "Proudly Canadian." An initial screen containing the following image might be appropriate:

The portion of your code that displays the initial screen and a dummy main menu would look something like this:

\OMH\com\paulsjavabooks\instantj2me\Chapter8\SplashExample.java

```
/*
 * SplashExample.java
 *
 * Created on July 5, 2001, 9:35 PM
 */

package com.paulsjavabooks.instantj2me.Chapter8;

import javax.microedition.midlet.*;
import javax.microedition.lcdui.*;


/**
 *
 * @author  paul_tremblett
 * @version 1.0
 */
```

```java
public class SplashExample extends MIDlet implements CommandListener
{

  private Display display;
  private Command cmdExit;
  private StringItem dummyMainMenu;

  private static final String menuText =
    "If this were an actual application, this " +
    "screen would contain the main menu and execution " +
    "would proceed from here.";

  public void startApp() {

    display = Display.getDisplay(this);

    Form f = new Form("Main Menu");
    cmdExit = new Command("Exit", Command.SCREEN,1);
    f.addCommand(cmdExit);
    dummyMainMenu = new StringItem(null, menuText);
    f.append(dummyMainMenu);
    f.setCommandListener(this);

    Image cflag = null;
    try {
      cflag = Image.createImage("/Icons/ca-proud.png");
    }
    catch(java.io.IOException err) {
    }

    Alert a = new Alert("Welcome!","Paul's Software",cflag,null);
    a.setTimeout(5000);

    display.setCurrent(a,f);
    }

  public void pauseApp() {
```

```
  }

  public void destroyApp(boolean unconditional) {
  }

  public void commandAction(Command cmd, Displayable d) {
    if (cmd == cmdExit) {
      destroyApp(false);
      notifyDestroyed();
    }
  }
}
```

The instance of `Alert` is created in the `startApp` method by the following code:

```
Alert a = new Alert("Welcome!","Paul's Software",cflag,null);
```

The constructor takes four arguments: the first is a title; the second is the content String; the third is an image; and the fourth specifies the alert type. We will discuss the alert type later in the chapter. You should make no assumptions about the layout of the contents. This depends on the implementation and can vary from device to device.

The newly created alert has a timeout value that is determined by the implementation. You can determine this value using the `getDefaultTimeout` method. To guarantee uniform behavior, most applications use the `setTimeout` method to specify a timeout value. The argument passed to `setTimeout` can either be a positive time value in milliseconds or the special value `Alert.FOREVER`, which represents infinity. In this example, a delay of five seconds was chosen, so the argument is 5000.

You have already learned that you display a screen by invoking the `setCurrent` method on the instance of `Display` that represents the manager of the display. You pass a single argument the `Displayable` object you want made visible. To display an alert, you use another form of the `setCurrent` method that takes two arguments. The first argument is the `Alert` object and the second is any displayable except another alert that will be made visible when the alert is dismissed. An alert can be dismissed in two ways. If the timeout is any value except `Alert.FOREVER`, the alert is dismissed when the timeout interval expires. If the alert is modal, either because a value of `Alert.FOREVER` was specified for the timeout or because the amount of content requires scrolling, the implementation provides a way for the user to dismiss the alert.

The alert is this example is made visible by

```
display.setCurrent(a,f);
```

Running *SplashExample*

Move ca-proud.png to the Icons directory and customize the KVM to specify the RIM-Blackberry-957 as the device to emulate. When you right-click the *SplashExample* MIDlet suite icon and then press the Launch button on the device, the following screen is displayed for five seconds:

After five seconds has elapsed, the alert is dismissed and the following screen is displayed:

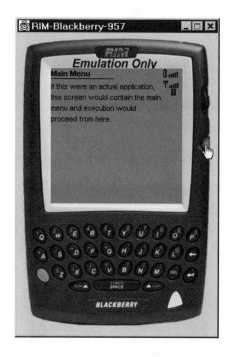

A Modal Alert

\OMH\Icons\ca-nf.png

Now that you have your application working, you decide that you want to show provincial as well as national pride, so you design a new image that looks like this:

Copy ca-nf.png to the Icons directory and modify *SplashExample.java* to create `cflag` as follows:

```
cflag = Image.createImage("/Icons/ca-nf.png");
```

Running the Modified *SplashExample*

This time, when you launch the application, you see a screen like this:

You wait five seconds, but the alert does not dismiss. Even though you specified a timeout of five seconds, the new, larger image requires scrolling so the alert is made modal. The presence of the down-arrow indicates that scrolling is in effect. If you use the thumbwheel to scroll down, you see the remainder of the image, as shown here:

When you press the button located beneath the thumbwheel, a menu like this appears:

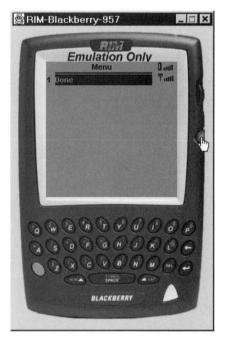

When you select Done, the main menu screen appears as it did in the first version of the example.

The AlertType Class

We mentioned earlier that you can assign an alert type to an alert. The type is indicated not by using a primitive like an int, but rather by using the `AlertType` object. There are five predefined `AlertTypes` that are static fields in the `AlertType` class. They are shown in Table 20-1.

You should take note that the `AlertType`'s constructor is protected so you would not use `new AlertType()`, but simply use one of the predefined types.

The `AlertType` class defines the single method `playSound`. This method alerts the user by playing a sound associated with the `AlertType`. You can use `playSound` to directly signal the user without switching to a new displayable. Before relying too heavily on this method, you should be aware of the following:

▶ Not all devices support sound. Some implementations might provide a visual substitute, but you should not make any assumptions.

▶ An `AlertType` instance is only a *hint* that the device should generate a sound. Even if the device is capable of producing sound, the hint can be ignored.

▶ There is no guarantee that a unique sound will be assigned to each `AlertType`. The device may use the same sound for two or more `AlertTypes`.

Field	Description	Example
ALARM	A hint to alert the user to an event for which the user had previously requested to be notified has occurred.	"It's 10:00 A.M.—call"
CONFIRMATION	A hint to confirm user actions.	"Database successfully updated!"
ERROR	A hint to notify the user that some error condition exists.	"Unable to contact host"
INFO	Provides nonthreatening information to the user.	The splash screen in the *SplashExample* MIDlet
WARNING	A hint to warn the user of a potentially dangerous operation.	"Warning: This erase cannot be undone!"

Table 8-1 *The Predefined Alert Types*

Example of Alert Types

\OMH\com\paulsjavabooks\instantj2me\Chapter8\AlertTypesDemo.java

Here is a MIDlet that displays each of the five predefined AlertTypes both modally and for a timed period.

```java
/*
 * AlertTypesDemo.java
 *
 * Created on July 5, 2001, 10:13 PM
 */

package com.paulsjavabooks.instantj2me.Chapter8;

import javax.microedition.midlet.*;
import javax.microedition.lcdui.*;


/**
 *
 * @author  paul_tremblett
 * @version 1.0
 */
public class AlertTypesDemo extends MIDlet implements CommandListener {

  private Display display;
  private List menu;

  private static final int TIMEOUT = 5;

  private AlertThread[] alerts = {

    new AlertThread("ALARM",
                    "Alert.ALARM",
                    "alarm",
                    AlertType.ALARM,
                    TIMEOUT),

    new AlertThread("ALARM (M)",
                    "Alert.ALARM",
```

```
                              "alarm",
                              AlertType.ALARM,
                              Alert.FOREVER),

          new AlertThread("CONFIRMATION",
                          "Alert.CONFIRMATION",
                          "confirmation",
                          AlertType.CONFIRMATION,
                          TIMEOUT),

          new AlertThread("CONFIRMATION (M)",
                          "Alert.CONFIRMATION",
                          "confirmation",
                          AlertType.CONFIRMATION,
                          Alert.FOREVER),

          new AlertThread("ERROR",
                          "Alert.ERROR",
                          "error",
                          AlertType.ERROR,
                          TIMEOUT),

          new AlertThread("ERROR (M)",
                          "Alert.ERROR",
                          "error",
                          AlertType.ERROR,
                          Alert.FOREVER),

          new AlertThread("INFO",
                          "Alert.INFO",
                          "information",
                          AlertType.INFO,
                          TIMEOUT),

          new AlertThread("INFO (M)",
                          "Alert.INFO",
                          "information",
                          AlertType.INFO,
                          Alert.FOREVER),

          new AlertThread("WARNING",
```

```
                    "Alert.WARNING",
                    "warning",
                    AlertType.WARNING,
                    TIMEOUT),

  new AlertThread("WARNING (M)",
                    "Alert.WARNING",
                    "warning",
                    AlertType.WARNING,
                    Alert.FOREVER)
  };

public void startApp() {
  display = Display.getDisplay(this);
  menu = new List("Alerts", List.IMPLICIT);
  for (int i = 0; i < alerts.length; ++i) {
    menu.append(alerts[i].title,null);
  }
  menu.append("Exit",null);
  menu.setCommandListener(this);
  display.setCurrent(menu);
}

public void pauseApp() {
}

public void destroyApp(boolean unconditional) {
}

public void commandAction(Command cmd, Displayable d) {
  if ((d == menu) && (cmd == List.SELECT_COMMAND) ) {
    int ix = ((List)d).getSelectedIndex();
    if ((ix >= 0) && (ix < alerts.length)) {
      alerts[ix].run();
      return;
    }
    else {
      destroyApp(false);
      notifyDestroyed();
    }
  }
```

```
        }

    class AlertThread implements Runnable {

      Alert alert;
      String title;

      public AlertThread(String title, String alertText,
                          String imageFile, AlertType type, int timeout) {
        this.title = title;

        Image alertImage = null;

        try {
          alertImage = Image.createImage("/Icons/" + imageFile + ".png");
        }
        catch(java.io.IOException err) {
        }
        alert = new Alert(title,alertText,alertImage,type);
        if (timeout != Alert.FOREVER) {
          alert.setTimeout(timeout * 1000);
        }
        else {
          alert.setTimeout(Alert.FOREVER);
        }
      }

      public void run() {
        display.setCurrent(alert,menu);
      }
    }
  }
}
```

The local variable `threads` holds an array of ten `AlertThread` objects, two (modal and timed) for each of the five predefined `AlertTypes`. The `AlertThread` class is an inner class that wraps an alert in a runnable. The `commandAction` method, which is invoked in response to selection of an alert type by the user, invokes the run method of the appropriate `AlertThread` object.

Of as much interest here as the `AlertTypes` we are studying is the main menu and how it is implemented. The `startApp` method creates a `List` to which it appends as many elements as there are `AlertThread` objects. The `List` class implements the `Choice` interface. We learned in Chapter 5 that there are three types of `Choice`, implicit choice, exclusive choice, and multiple choice, but the code we examined in that chapter did not include an example of implicit choice. Now we will see such an example. The code that creates the `List` looks like this:

```
menu = new List("Alerts", List.IMPLICIT);
```

When a list is IMPLICIT, selection of an item from the list takes places when the user presses the button dedicated to the "select" or "go" functionality of the device. When the button is pressed, the item that has the focus is implicitly selected and the application is notified via its `CommandListener`, if one is registered. The command that is sent as the first argument to the `commandAction` method is the special SELECT_COMMAND, which `commandAction` uses to recognize that the user performed the select operation on an IMPLICIT `List`.

One of the advantages of using the IMPLICIT `List` is that no application-defined commands have to be attached. Examine the code for `AlertTypesDemo` and you will see that this is true. So how does `commandAction` know which item was selected? It uses the `getSelectedIndex` or `getString` methods of the `Displayable` it receives as its second argument. In this case, the int returned by `getSelectedIndex` is used as the subscript to specify the element in the `threads` array whose `run` method should be invoked.

Running

alarm.png, confirmation.png, error.png, information.png, warning.png

Preparing the MIDlet to run consists of creating the MIDlet suite *AlertTypesDemo* and adding the `AlertTypesDemo` MIDlet class and the Icons directory to it. When that has been done, you must copy the alert images from the CD-ROM to the Icons directory. These images correspond to the alert types and look like this:

When you launch the MIDlet, a main menu screen like this is displayed:

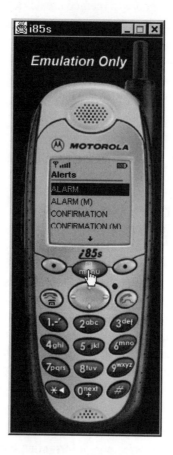

Notice the absence of labeled soft keys such as were present when you used application-defined commands. This is indicative of an IMPLICIT `List`. You still navigate the `List` using the scroll keys, but when you have navigated to the desired item, you press the select key pointed to by the hand icon. When you do, an alert like that shown next is displayed.

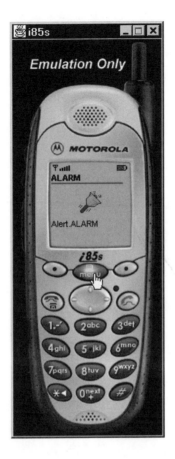

In the interest of space, we show only one of the ten possible alerts here. You should explore all of the others; and when you have finished, you can select the eleventh menu item, Exit, to terminate the application.

The Ticker Class

IN THIS CHAPTER:

A Simple Ticker
The Continuous Nature of a Ticker
The Shared Ticker Model
The Ticker-per-Screen Model
Changing a Ticker's Content

W

e have all seen data that scrolls across the bottom of a television screen. There's the stock ticker that's displayed as you watch your favorite financial show, the mini-headlines that are displayed while the news anchor reports full-length stories, and the local weather conditions that are displayed as you watch the national weather report. An interesting property of this "out-of-band" data is that it can for the most part be ignored, but it is always there if you need it or decide to use it. In this chapter, you will see how to use the `Ticker` class to incorporate this type of data into MIDlets.

A Simple Ticker

\OMH\com\paulsjavabooks\instantj2me\Chapter9\TickerExample1.java

The `Ticker` class implements what appears to the user as a ticker tape, a message string that runs continuously across the display. The exact behavior is determined by the implementation. The application cannot start or stop the animation. The scrolling is continuous, so when the last character in the String has been displayed, the String is displayed again starting at the first character. The implementation, on the other hand, can pause the Ticker if it decides that doing so will conserve power. It usually does so when the user does not interact with the application for a certain period of time. It should resume scrolling when the user resumes interaction with the device.

Let's start our exploration of the `Ticker` class with a very simple example. Here is the code:

```
/*
 * TickerExample1.java
 *
 * Created on July 5, 2001, 10:15 PM
 */


package com.paulsjavabooks.instantj2me.Chapter9;

import javax.microedition.midlet.*;
import javax.microedition.lcdui.*;


/**
 *
 * @author  paul_tremblett
 * @version 1.0
 */
```

```java
public class TickerExample1 extends MIDlet implements CommandListener {

  private Display display;
  private Form form;
  private Command cmdExit;
  private Ticker ticker;
  private String tickerText = "The time has come, the walrus said...";
  private String windowText =
    "If you have read the works of Lewis Carroll, the text that is " +
    "scrolling across the top of this window should be familiar. Lewis " +
    "Carroll was the pen name used by Charles Lutwidge Dodgson, a " +
    "clergyman who was also lectured in mathematics at Oxford. His two " +
    "most famous works are \"Alice's Adventures in Wonderland\" and " +
    "\"Through The Looking Glass\".";

  public void startApp() {

    display = Display.getDisplay(this);

    form = new Form("TickerExample 1");
    form.append(new StringItem(null,windowText));

    cmdExit = new Command("Exit",Command.SCREEN,1);
    form.addCommand(cmdExit);
    form.setCommandListener(this);

    ticker = new Ticker(tickerText);
    form.setTicker(ticker);

    display.setCurrent(form);
  }

  public void pauseApp() {
  }

  public void destroyApp(boolean unconditional) {
  }

  public void commandAction(Command cmd, Displayable d) {
      if (cmd == cmdExit) {
        destroyApp(true);
        notifyDestroyed();
      }
  }
}
```

This MIDlet does nothing more than display a form that contains a StringItem. The screen is displayed until the user presses the soft key labeled Exit. The only code you have not seen yet is this:

```
ticker = new Ticker(tickerText);
form.setTicker(ticker);
```

This code creates an instance of a Ticker. The constructor takes a single argument, a string that specifies the initial contents. The setTicker method binds the Ticker to the screen on which the method is invoked, replacing any Ticker that is already bound to the screen. You can also use this method remove a Ticker from a screen by using null as the argument.

Running TickerExample1

When you launch the MIDlet, you see a display like this:

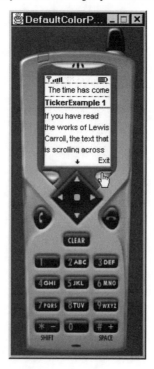

Whether you simply do nothing or use the scroll buttons to read the text in the main area of the display, the message "The time has come, the walrus said…" scrolls continuously across the top of the screen.

The Continuous Nature of a Ticker

\OMH\com\paulsjavabooks\instantj2me\Chapter9\TickerExample2.java

Here's a MIDlet that contains two screens, one with a Ticker and one without:

```java
/*
 * TickerExample2.java
 *
 * Created on July 5, 2001, 10:32 PM
 */


package com.paulsjavabooks.instantj2me.Chapter9;

import javax.microedition.midlet.*;
import javax.microedition.lcdui.*;


/**
 *
 * @author  paul_tremblett
 * @version 1.0
 */
public class TickerExample2 extends MIDlet implements CommandListener {

  private Display display;
  private Form menuForm;
  private Form textForm;
  private ChoiceGroup characterChoice;
  private StringItem prose;
  private Command cmdBack;
  private Command cmdExit;
  private Command cmdOK;
  private Ticker ticker;

  private String[] characters = {
    "Caterpillar",
    "Tweedledee",
    "Bellman"
  };
```

```java
private String fatherWilliam =
  "\"You are old, Father William,\" the young man said\n" +
  "\"And your hair has become very white;\n" +
  "And yet you incessantly stand on your head--\n" +
  "Do you think, at your age, it is right?\"";

private String walrus =
  "'The time has come,' the Walrus said,\n" +
  "To talk of many things:\n" +
  "Of shoes--and ships--and sealing wax--\n" +
  "Of cabbages--and--kings--\n" +
  "And why the sea is boiling hot--\n" +
  "And whether pigs have wings.'";

private String bellman =
  "\"What's the good of Mercator's North Poles and Equators,\n" +
  "Tropics, Zones and Meridian Lines?\"\n" +
  "So the Bellman would cry: and the crew would reply\n" +
  "\"They are merely conventional signs!\"";

private String tickerText = "Alice, White Rabbit, March Hare, " +
  "Mad Hatter, Cheshire Cat, Gryphon, Mock Turtle, Walrus";

public void startApp() {

  display = Display.getDisplay(this);

  menuForm = new Form("Menu");

  cmdBack = new Command("Back",Command.SCREEN,1);
  cmdExit = new Command("Exit",Command.SCREEN,1);
  cmdOK = new Command("OK",Command.SCREEN,1);

  menuForm.addCommand(cmdExit);
  menuForm.addCommand(cmdOK);

  characterChoice =
    new ChoiceGroup("Character",Choice.EXCLUSIVE,characters,null);
  menuForm.append(characterChoice);

  menuForm.setCommandListener(this);
```

```
    ticker = new Ticker(tickerText);
    menuForm.setTicker(ticker);

    textForm = new Form(null);
    textForm.addCommand(cmdBack);
    textForm.setCommandListener(this);
    prose = new StringItem(null,null);
    textForm.append(prose);

    display.setCurrent(menuForm);
  }

  public void pauseApp() {
  }

  public void destroyApp(boolean unconditional) {
  }

  public void commandAction(Command cmd, Displayable d) {
    if (cmd == cmdExit) {
      destroyApp(true);
      notifyDestroyed();
    }
    else if (cmd == cmdOK) {
      switch (characterChoice.getSelectedIndex()) {
          case 0:
          prose.setText(fatherWilliam);
          break;
          case 1:
          prose.setText(walrus);
          break;
          case 2:
          prose.setText(bellman);
          break;
      }
      display.setCurrent(textForm);
    }
    else if (cmd == cmdBack) {
      display.setCurrent(menuForm);
    }
  }
}
```

The MIDlet displays a form containing an EXCLUSIVE `ChoiceGroup` from which the user selects one of three characters from the works of Lewis Carroll. The form containing the `ChoiceGroup` has a Ticker attached that displays a list of characters that is much longer than the three contained in the `ChoiceGroup`. After the user makes the choice and presses the button labeled OK, a second form containing some words spoken by the selected character is displayed.

Running TickerExample2

When you launch the MIDlet, the first form that is displayed looks like this:

After you choose a character using the appropriate radio button, you press OK and another form like this is displayed:

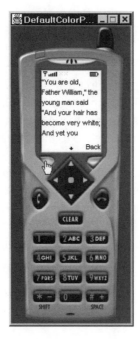

Notice that the scrolling message disappears because the second form does not have a Ticker. The animation in the Ticker bound to the first form, however, does not stop. When you have finished reading the text and press Back, the commandAction method sets the first form as current and one again you see the Ticker, as shown here:

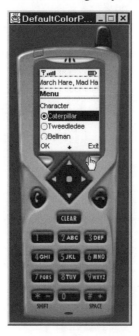

The Shared Ticker Model

\OMH\com\paulsjavabooks\instantj2me\Chapter9\TickerExample3.java

The application you just saw appears to the user as disjointed because the Ticker is attached to a single form and is visible only when that form is displayed. A more desirable behavior, and one that appears to the user as being much smoother, could be obtained by having the Ticker attached to the display. Unfortunately, it is not possible to do this directly. It is possible, however, to create an illusion that makes it appear to the user that such is the case. A single instance of `Ticker` can be attached to multiple forms and as the application switches between these forms, the Ticker is displayed at exactly the same location in each form and continues to scroll its contents at the same position. The overall effect is that the user perceives the Ticker as being attached to the display. Here's the code that shows how it's done:

```java
/*
 * TickerExample3.java
 *
 * Created on July 5, 2001, 11:04 PM
 */

package com.paulsjavabooks.instantj2me.Chapter9;

import javax.microedition.midlet.*;
import javax.microedition.lcdui.*;


/**
 *
 * @author  paul_tremblett
 * @version 1.0
 */
public class TickerExample3 extends MIDlet implements CommandListener {

    private Display display;
    private Form menuForm;
    private Form textForm;
    private ChoiceGroup characterChoice;
    private StringItem prose;
    private Command cmdBack;
    private Command cmdExit;
    private Command cmdOK;
```

```
private Ticker ticker;

private String[] characters = {
  "Caterpillar",
  "Tweedledee",
  "Bellman"
};

private String fatherWilliam =
  "\"You are old, Father William,\" the young man said\n" +
  "\"And your hair has become very white;\n" +
  "And yet you incessantly stand on your head--\n" +
  "Do you think, at your age, it is right?\"";

private String walrus =
  "'The time has come,' the Walrus said,\n" +
  "To talk of many things:\n" +
  "Of shoes--and ships--and sealing wax--\n" +
  "Of cabbages--and--kings--\n" +
  "And why the sea is boiling hot--\n" +
  "And whether pigs have wings.'";

private String bellman =
  "\"What's the good of Mercator's North Poles and Equators,\n" +
  "Tropics, Zones and Meridian Lines?\"\n" +
  "So the Bellman would cry: and the crew would reply\n" +
  "\"They are merely conventional signs!\"";

private String tickerText = "Alice, White Rabbit, March Hare, " +
  "Mad Hatter, Cheshire Cat, Gryphon, Mock Turtle, Walrus";

public void startApp() {

  display = Display.getDisplay(this);

  menuForm = new Form("Menu");

  cmdBack = new Command("Back",Command.SCREEN,1);
  cmdExit = new Command("Exit",Command.SCREEN,1);
  cmdOK = new Command("OK",Command.SCREEN,1);

  menuForm.addCommand(cmdExit);
  menuForm.addCommand(cmdOK);
```

```
  characterChoice =
    new ChoiceGroup("Character",Choice.EXCLUSIVE,characters,null);
  menuForm.append(characterChoice);

  menuForm.setCommandListener(this);

  ticker = new Ticker(tickerText);
  menuForm.setTicker(ticker);

  textForm = new Form(null);
  textForm.addCommand(cmdBack);
  textForm.setCommandListener(this);
  prose = new StringItem(null,null);
  textForm.append(prose);
  textForm.setTicker(ticker);

  display.setCurrent(menuForm);
}

public void pauseApp() {
}

public void destroyApp(boolean unconditional) {
}

public void commandAction(Command cmd, Displayable d) {
  if (cmd == cmdExit) {
    destroyApp(true);
    notifyDestroyed();
  }
  else if (cmd == cmdOK) {
    switch (characterChoice.getSelectedIndex()) {
        case 0:
        prose.setText(fatherWilliam);
        break;
        case 1:
        prose.setText(walrus);
        break;
        case 2:
```

```
                prose.setText(bellman);
                break;
        }
        display.setCurrent(textForm);
    }
    else if (cmd == cmdBack) {
        display.setCurrent(menuForm);
    }
  }
 }
}
```

Notice that setTicker is invoked on both menuForm and textForm and that the argument passed in each case is the same instance of Ticker.

Running TickerExample3

When you start the MIDlet, the initial display looks like this:

After you have selected the desired radio button, keep your eye on the contents of the Ticker as you press OK. The Ticker continues to scroll as the application switches to the second form. The display now looks like this:

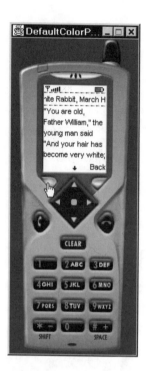

As you continue to use the application, you can see that whether you are navigating the `ChoiceGroup`, selecting the OK and Back buttons, or scrolling through text, the Ticker is always visible and always scrolling smoothly.

The Ticker-per-Screen Model

\OMH\com\paulsjavabooks\instantj2me\Chapter9\TickerExample4.java

The applications we have seen so far in this chapter have all used a single instance of `Ticker`. It's sometimes appropriate to have a different Ticker for each screen. Here's an example that demonstrates that scenario:

```
/*
 * TickerExample4.java
 *
 * Created on July 5, 2001, 11:21 PM
 */


package com.paulsjavabooks.instantj2me.Chapter9;
```

```java
import javax.microedition.midlet.*;
import javax.microedition.lcdui.*;


/**
 *
 * @author  paul_tremblett
 * @version 1.0
 */
public class TickerExample4 extends MIDlet implements CommandListener {

  private Display display;
  private Form menuForm;
  private Form textForm;
  private ChoiceGroup characterChoice;
  private StringItem prose;
  private Command cmdBack;
  private Command cmdExit;
  private Command cmdOK;
  private Ticker charactersTicker;
  private Ticker worksTicker;

  private String[] characters = {
    "Caterpillar",
    "Tweedledee",
    "Bellman"
  };

  private String fatherWilliam =
    "\"You are old, Father William,\" the young man said\n" +
    "\"And your hair has become very white;\n" +
    "And yet you incessantly stand on your head--\n" +
    "Do you think, at your age, it is right?\"";

  private String walrus =
    "'The time has come,' the Walrus said,\n" +
    "To talk of many things:\n" +
    "Of shoes--and ships--and sealing wax--\n" +
    "Of cabbages--and--kings--\n" +
    "And why the sea is boiling hot--\n" +
    "And whether pigs have wings.'";

  private String bellman =
```

```
    "\"What's the good of Mercator's North Poles and Equators,\n" +
    "Tropics, Zones and Meridian Lines?\"\n" +
    "So the Bellman would cry: and the crew would reply\n" +
    "\"They are merely conventional signs!\"";

  private String worksTickerText =
    "Alice's Adventures in Wonderland, Through The Looking Glass, " +
    "The Hunting of The Snark";

  private String charactersTickerText =
    "Alice, White Rabbit, March Hare, " +
    "Mad Hatter, Cheshire Cat, Gryphon, Mock Turtle, Walrus, Red Queen, " +
    "Bellman, Butcher, Barrister";

  public void startApp() {
    display = Display.getDisplay(this);

    menuForm = new Form("Menu");

    cmdBack = new Command("Back",Command.SCREEN,1);
    cmdExit = new Command("Exit",Command.SCREEN,1);
    cmdOK = new Command("OK",Command.SCREEN,1);

    menuForm.addCommand(cmdExit);
    menuForm.addCommand(cmdOK);

    characterChoice =
      new ChoiceGroup("Character",Choice.EXCLUSIVE,characters,null);
    menuForm.append(characterChoice);

    menuForm.setCommandListener(this);

    worksTicker = new Ticker(worksTickerText);
    menuForm.setTicker(worksTicker);

    textForm = new Form(null);
    textForm.addCommand(cmdBack);
    textForm.setCommandListener(this);

    prose = new StringItem(null,null);
    textForm.append(prose);
```

```
      charactersTicker = new Ticker(charactersTickerText);
      textForm.setTicker(charactersTicker);

      display.setCurrent(menuForm);
   }

   public void pauseApp() {
   }

   public void destroyApp(boolean unconditional) {
   }

   public void commandAction(Command cmd, Displayable d) {
      if (cmd == cmdExit) {
         destroyApp(true);
         notifyDestroyed();
      }
      else if (cmd == cmdOK) {
         switch (characterChoice.getSelectedIndex()) {
             case 0:
             prose.setText(fatherWilliam);
             break;
             case 1:
             prose.setText(walrus);
             break;
             case 2:
             prose.setText(bellman);
             break;
         }
         display.setCurrent(textForm);
      }
      else if (cmd == cmdBack) {
         display.setCurrent(menuForm);
      }
   }
}
```

The two lines of code that are of interest in this application are these:

```
   menuForm.setTicker(worksTicker);
   textForm.setTicker(charactersTicker);
```

Whenever the form containing the `ChoiceGroup` is visible, a Ticker containing the titles of some of Lewis Carroll's works scrolls across the display. When the form containing text is visible, a Ticker containing a list of characters scrolls across the display.

Running TickerExample4

This application presents the following initial screen:

Notice that the Ticker that is scrolling across the top of the display shows a list of some of Lewis Carroll's works. When you select a character and press OK, the display changes to this:

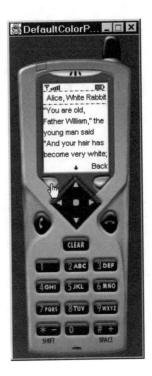

The Ticker at the top is now displaying a list of characters because a different Ticker is attached to the form.

Changing a Ticker's Content

\OMH\com\paulsjavabooks\instantj2me\Chapter9\TickerExample5.java

In the previous four examples, the contents of each Ticker remain constant for the life of the application. If you are a developer whose company is using the Ticker to present advertising, this might seem like an excellent idea. The user, on the other hand, will either completely ignore the Ticker after the first few iterations or might even find it a source of annoyance. The solution, of course, is to vary the contents of the Ticker.

If the application is connected to a host, you might use the Ticker to present corporate announcements obtained from the host. The Ticker might start out reading, "Barbara Hickey has been promoted to district manager" and might change to "The 2:00 sales meeting has been cancelled."

If you can tolerate one final visit from Lewis Carroll, we will now examine an application that changes the contents of a Ticker. Here is the code:

```java
/*
 * TickerExample5.java
 *
 * Created on July 5, 2001, 11:52 PM
 */


package com.paulsjavabooks.instantj2me.Chapter9;

import javax.microedition.midlet.*;
import javax.microedition.lcdui.*;


/**
 *
 * @author  paul_tremblett
 * @version 1.0
 */
public class TickerExample5 extends MIDlet implements CommandListener {

    private Display display;
    private Form menuForm;
    private Form textForm;
    private ChoiceGroup characterChoice;
    private StringItem prose;
    private Command cmdBack;
    private Command cmdExit;
    private Command cmdOK;
    private Ticker ticker;

    private String[] characters = {
        "Caterpillar",
        "Tweedledee",
        "Bellman"
    };

    private String fatherWilliam =
```

```java
    "\"You are old, Father William,\" the young man said\n" +
    "\"And your hair has become very white;\n" +
    "And yet you incessantly stand on your head--\n" +
    "Do you think, at your age, it is right?\"";

private String walrus =
    "'The time has come,' the Walrus said,\n" +
    "To talk of many things:\n" +
    "Of shoes--and ships--and sealing wax--\n" +
    "Of cabbages--and--kings--\n" +
    "And why the sea is boiling hot--\n" +
    "And whether pigs have wings.'";

private String bellman =
    "\"What's the good of Mercator's North Poles and Equators,\n" +
    "Tropics, Zones and Meridian Lines?\"\n" +
    "So the Bellman would cry: and the crew would reply\n" +
    "\"They are merely conventional signs!\"";

private String worksTickerText =
    "Alice's Adventures in Wonderland, Through The Looking Glass, " +
    "The Hunting of The Snark";

private String charactersTickerText = "Alice, White Rabbit, March Hare, " +
    "Mad Hatter, Cheshire Cat, Gryphon, Mock Turtle, Walrus Red Queen" +
    "Bellman, Butcher, Barrister";

private static final long SLEEP_TIME = 400001;

private boolean displayingWorks = true;

public void startApp() {

    new TickerTextSwitcher().start();

    display = Display.getDisplay(this);

    menuForm = new Form("Menu");

    cmdBack = new Command("Back",Command.SCREEN,1);
    cmdExit = new Command("Exit",Command.SCREEN,1);
    cmdOK = new Command("OK",Command.SCREEN,1);
```

```
menuForm.addCommand(cmdExit);
menuForm.addCommand(cmdOK);

characterChoice =
  new ChoiceGroup("Character",Choice.EXCLUSIVE,characters,null);
menuForm.append(characterChoice);

menuForm.setCommandListener(this);

textForm = new Form(null);
textForm.addCommand(cmdBack);
textForm.setCommandListener(this);
prose = new StringItem(null,null);
textForm.append(prose);

ticker = new Ticker(worksTickerText);
menuForm.setTicker(ticker);
textForm.setTicker(ticker);

display.setCurrent(menuForm);
}

public void pauseApp() {
}

public void destroyApp(boolean unconditional) {
}

public void commandAction(Command cmd, Displayable d) {
  if (cmd == cmdExit) {
    destroyApp(true);
    notifyDestroyed();
  }
  else if (cmd == cmdOK) {
    switch (characterChoice.getSelectedIndex()) {
        case 0:
        prose.setText(fatherWilliam);
        break;
        case 1:
        prose.setText(walrus);
        break;
        case 2:
        prose.setText(bellman);
```

```
          break;
      }
    display.setCurrent(textForm);
  }
  else if (cmd == cmdBack) {
    display.setCurrent(menuForm);
  }
}

class TickerTextSwitcher extends Thread {

  public TickerTextSwitcher() {
  }

  public void run() {
    while (true) {
      try {
        Thread.sleep(SLEEP_TIME);
      }
      catch (InterruptedException e) {
      }
      if (displayingWorks) {
        displayingWorks = false;
        ticker.setString(charactersTickerText);
      }
      else {
        ticker.setString(worksTickerText);
        displayingWorks = true;
      }
    }
  }
}
}
```

Notice that the application contains a single Ticker that is stored in the variable ticker. It is created in startApp and the String passed to the constructor is worksTickerText. The Ticker is attached to two forms.

Now locate the inner class TickerTextSwitcher that subclasses Thread. An instance of this class is created by startApp. Its run method consists of an endless loop in which the thread sleeps for the time specified by SLEEP_TIME, and each time it awakes it invokes setString on ticker to change the text.

Running TickerExample5

The initial screen is shown here. It looks exactly like the initial screen we saw in the previous example.

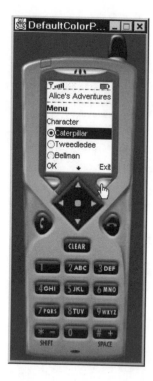

Now select the radio button labeled Bellman and press OK. Once again, the display looks quite familiar. So what's different? Just wait for a little over half a minute. You can scroll up and down through the text while you are waiting.

Suddenly, the contents of the Ticker change from a list of Lewis Carroll's works to a list of the characters who appear in these works. The display now looks like this:

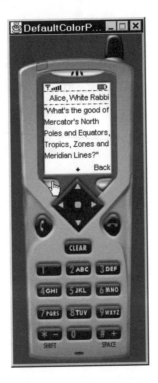

From the five examples, you can see that you can do a lot with the Ticker class.

Persistent Data

IN THIS CHAPTER:

The RecordStore Class
RecordStoreDemo Source Code

The MIDlets we have examined so far have all operated on data that was either defined in the application or input by the user at runtime. Displaying results obtained by performing calculations on or applying logic to such data is useful, but such results are unavailable after the program terminates. In many cases, a program needs to be able to obtain its input from a source other than the user—perhaps even from another program. There are also times when a program must pass its output to another program or save it for subsequent reuse hours, or even days or weeks, later. The resource the MIDP specification defines to meet such needs is the `RecordStore` class. In this chapter, you will develop a MIDlet that uses this class.

The RecordStore Class

The `RecordStore` class, as its name implies, represents a record store, which is a collection of records whose contents remain persistent across multiple invocations of a MIDlet. Maintaining persistence between invocations of the MIDlet is the responsibility of the platform, which should provide protection against such actions as reboots and battery changes. During the execution of a MIDlet, the application sometimes shares responsibility for maintaining persistence. You will see an illustration of this when you examine the example.

Record stores are created and maintained in locations that are platform dependent. The layout of records within the store and the logic that is used to store and retrieve records is also platform dependent. None of this is ever exposed to the MIDlet, which relies entirely on the API provided by the `RecordStore` class and four interfaces. These interfaces are `RecordComparator`, `RecordEnumerator`, `RecordFilter`, and `RecordListener`.

Each MIDlet suite has its own separate name space for record stores. To the application programmer, this means

▶ The record store named *rsname* referenced by MIDletA in a MIDlet suite is the same physical record store as the one named *rsname* referenced by MIDletB in the same MIDlet suite.

▶ All MIDlets in a MIDlet suite can share record stores.

▶ The record store named *rsname* in MIDlet suite A is not the same physical record store as the one named *rsname* in MIDlet suite B.

A record store's name consists of up to 32 unique Unicode characters and is case sensitive. A record store named *customercontacts* is not the same physical record store as one named *CustomerContacts*.

Each record in a store is identified by a unique recordId, which is an integer value. The first record added to the store is assigned a recordId of zero. Each record that is subsequently added is assigned a recordId that is one greater than the recordId of the record that was added before it. The recordId, which is used as a record's primary key, is permanently associated with the record. If a record is deleted, its recordId is never reused.

A record store maintains information about operations that are performed on it. One such piece of information is the version. This is an integer value that is incremented each time the contents of the record store are modified. A date/time stamp in the form of a long suitable for constructing an instance of Date is also maintained. This stamp is updated each time the store is modified.

The API does not provide a locking mechanism. Implementations of record stores protect individual records from corruption by ensuring that all individual record store operations are atomic, synchronous, and serialized. If a MIDlet accesses a record store from multiple threads, however, it must properly coordinate the activities of the threads. If, for example, ThreadA obtains a record from the store, applies an update to the record contents, and writes it back to the store, and ThreadB is performing a similar activity, data corruption is highly probable. The techniques you use to maintain data integrity in a MIDP application are the same as those you learned in the J2SE environment (i.e., intelligent use of synchronized, proper use of wait/notify, use of a well-written producer/consumer, implementation of mutex semaphores, etc.).

Using a Record Store to Implement a To-Do List

The best way to learn how to use the RecordStore class is to write an application that uses it. The application you will write is one that can be used to maintain a simple list of things to do or people to call. The size of the application (almost 1,000 lines of code) is testimony to the fact that small devices don't automatically mean trivial programs. Because of its size, the complete listing is presented at the end of the chapter. We will examine portions of the code as we discuss the API.

Running the *RecordStoreExample* Application

When you launch the *RecordStoreExample* MIDlet, you are presented with the menu shown here:

From the main menu screen, you can choose an action from the list and carry out that action by pressing OK. You can also obtain help for any item in the list by selecting the Help item from the menu. Help for the List Stores action looks like this:

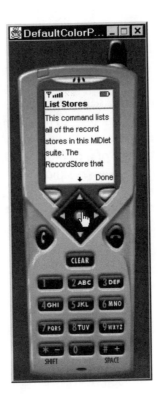

The `commandAction` method of `RecordStoreExample` stores all commands other than Help and Exit in the variable `currentCommand` and notifies an instance of the inner class `CommandThread` that a command is available for processing. Here is the code:

```
synchronized (this) {
  currentCommand = cmd;
  currentDisplayable = d;
  commandAvailable = true;
  notify();
}
```

The `run` method of `CommandThread` waits until a command is available to process. When it is notified by the main thread that a command is available, it determines the `Displayable` from which the command originated. If the command is from `mainMenuForm`, which is the form that contains the main menu `ChoiceGroup`, it invokes `processMainMenuItem`. If the command is from `dataForm`, which is the form used to obtain input data from the user, it invokes `processDataForm`. If the command is from `recordForm`, which is the form that displays the contents of a record from the record store, it invokes `processRecordForm`, which processes subcommands, as you will see later. Finally, if the command is from `statusForm`, which is used to display the status of the record store or of the program, it displays either the main menu or the contents of a record from the store, depending on what the last activity was. Here is the code for the `run` method:

```
public void run() {
  while (true) {
    synchronized(parent) {
      while(!commandAvailable) {
        try {
          parent.wait();
        }
        catch (InterruptedException e) {
        }
      }
    }
    commandAvailable = false;

    if (currentDisplayable == mainMenuForm) {
      processMainMenuItem();
    }
    else if (currentDisplayable == dataForm) {
      processDataForm();
    }
    else if (currentDisplayable == recordForm) {
      processRecordForm();
```

```
      }
    else if (currentDisplayable == statusForm) {
      if (state == ST_AFTER_DELETION) {
        state = ST_BROWSING_STORE;
        displayRecordData();
      }
      else {
        displayMainMenu();
      }
    }
  }
}
```

We will now see what happens when we carry out each of the actions listed in the main menu.

Listing a MIDlet Suite's Record Stores

You already know that each MIDlet in a MIDlet suite can create one or more record stores. To obtain a list of all of a MIDlet suite's record stores, you use the `listRecordStores` method. This is a static method that returns an array of Strings containing the names of the record stores owned by the MIDlet suite to which the invoking MIDlet belongs. If you examine the method `displayRecordStoreList` in `RecordStoreExample`, you will find the following line of code that uses the `listRecordStores` method:

```
String[] stores = RecordStore.listRecordStores();
```

NOTE

The skeleton code generated by Forte in all of the MIDlets in the preceding chapters included `import` statements for all classes in the Application Lifecycle Package; javax.microedition.midlet; and the User Interface Package, javax.microedition.lcdui. It does not automatically generate an `import` statement for the Persistence Package, javax.microedition.rms. You must hand code this `import` statement.

In this case, since we have just launched the MIDlet and have not yet created any record stores, listRecordStores returns null and the following screen is displayed:

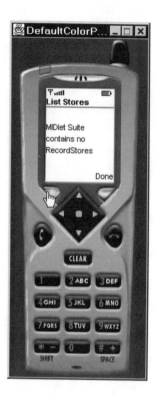

Creating a Record Store

Now, let's create a record store. You start by selecting Create Store from the main menu. When you do, a screen containing a TextField is displayed. Let's create a to-do by entering **TO-DO** into the TextField so that it looks like this:

When you press OK, the application creates the record store and confirms that it has been created by displaying a message like the one shown here:

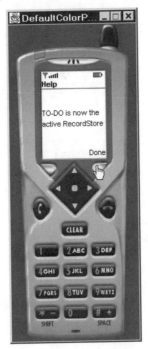

Now, you might be wondering about the meaning of the message "TO-DO is now the 'active' RecordStore." It is not only possible, but also perfectly OK for an application to have more than one record store open at a given time. It is also OK to open a record store even if it is already open. When you do so, the reference returned is to the store that is already open. Things get a little complicated, however, when you close the store. The store is not actually closed until the number of close operations is equal to the number of open operations. To avoid such complications, the *RecordStoreExample* application keeps one record store open at a time. The open store is referred to as the *active* store.

A record store is created by the openRecordStore method. This static method takes two arguments. The first is a String containing the name of the store to be opened. The second is a boolean that specifies whether the store should be created if it does not exist. Here is the code used by the *RecordStoreDemo* application:

```
private void createRecordStore() {
  RecordStore rs = null;
  String name = recordStoreNameTextField.getString();
  if ("".equals(name)) {
    displayAlert(errorAlert,"Name cannot be blank");
    return;
  }
  String[] stores = RecordStore.listRecordStores();
  if (stores != null) {
    for (int i = 0; i < stores.length; ++i) {
      if (stores[i].equals(name)) {
        displayAlert(errorAlert, name + " already exists");
        return;
      }
    }
  }
  try {
    rs = RecordStore.openRecordStore(name,true);
    if (currentRecordStore != null) {
      currentRecordStore.closeRecordStore();
    }
  }
  catch (RecordStoreException e) {
    displayAlert(errorAlert,msgRecordStoreException);
```

```
        return;
    }
    currentRecordStore = rs;
    displayAlert(infoAlert, name + " is now the active RecordStore");
}
```

Notice how the code first uses `listRecordStores` to determine whether the specified store already exists. This is simply to avoid multiple open operations against a single store, as mentioned before. Note also that if a record store is already open, as indicated by `currentRecordStore` having a value other than `null`, that record store is closed.

Before we move on, you should create a second record store called TO-CALL, which you will use later to store the names of persons you wish to call today. After you have created the second store, select List Stores from the main menu and the following screen will be displayed:

Notice that the active store is indicated by (*).

Opening a Record Store

The next item in the main menu that we have not used is Select Store. If you bring up the help screen for this option, it explains that this option is used to designate a store as the active store against which subsequent operations will be performed. When you select this option from the main menu, a `ChoiceGroup` that is constructed from the array returned by `listRecordStores` is presented, as shown here:

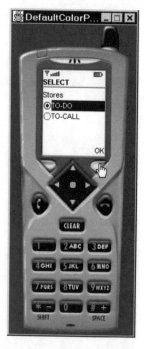

Select TO-DO and press OK. A confirmation screen is displayed, and, if you wish, you can use List Stores to verify that TO-DO is indeed the active store.

The code in the `processDataForm` method that carries out the Select Store action is as follows:

```
case ST_SELECTING_STORE_NAME:
  int i = recordStoreChoice.getSelectedIndex();
  sn = recordStoreChoice.getString(i);
  try {
    rs = RecordStore.openRecordStore(sn,false);
    if (currentRecordStore != null) {
      try {
        currentRecordStore.closeRecordStore();
      }
      catch (RecordStoreException e) {
      }
```

```
  }
  currentRecordStore = rs;
}
catch (RecordStoreException e) {
  displayAlert(errorAlert, msgRecordStoreException);
}
try {
  sn = currentRecordStore.getName();
}
catch (RecordStoreNotOpenException e) {
  displayAlert(errorAlert,msgRecordStoreNotOpenException);
}
displayAlert(infoAlert,sn +
  " is now the active RecordStore");
break;
```

Adding Records to the Record Store

Now that you have an open record store, you can start to add records to it. You start by selecting Add Record from the primary menu and entering data into the TextField that is displayed so that it looks like this:

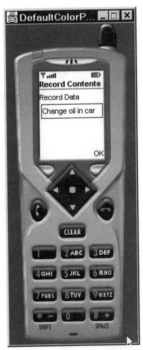

When you press OK, you receive confirmation that the record has been added.

The code in the `processDataForm` method that adds the record to the store looks like this:

```
case ST_GETTING_RECORD_DATA:
  if (currentRecordStore == null) {
   displayAlert(errorAlert,msgNoCurrentRecordStore);
  }
  recordData = recordDataTextField.getString().getBytes();
  try {
    currentRecordStore.addRecord(recordData,0,
      recordData.length);
    displayAlert(infoAlert,"Record added");
  }
  catch (RecordStoreNotOpenException e) {
    displayAlert(errorAlert,msgRecordStoreNotOpenException);
  }
  catch (RecordStoreException e) {
    displayAlert(errorAlert,msgRecordStoreException);
  }
  break;
```

The code gets the contents of `recordDataTextField`; converts it to a byte array using the `getBytes` method; and passes the byte array, the starting position, and the length to `addRecord`.

Obtaining Information About a Record Store

We mentioned earlier that the implementation maintains certain information about each record store. Let's see how to use the API to examine this information.

A Record Store's Version

Every record store has a current version that is initialized when the store is created. The initial value is implementation dependent. Each time the record store is modified, its version is incremented by some positive number greater than zero. The only assumption a MIDlet should make about the version is that the value will increase as the record store is modified. When you select Version from the main menu, the following screen is displayed:

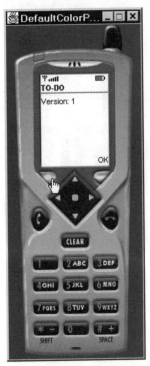

Here is the code in the `displayVersion` method that obtains the version:

```
int ver = currentRecordStore.getVersion();
```

The int that is returned is converted to a String using `Integer.toString` and is displayed as a `StringItem`.

A Record Store's Last Modification Date

When a record store is created, it is time stamped. The value used for the stamp is a long that is suitable for creating an instance of `Date`. Each time the store is modified, the stamp is updated. When you select Last Modified from the main menu, you see a display that looks like this:

The pertinent code from `displayLastModified` is as follows:

```
long lastModified = currentRecordStore.getLastModified();
Calendar cal = Calendar.getInstance();
cal.setTime(new Date(lastModified));
```

The instance of `Date` that is created using the value returned by `getLastModified` is used to set the time of an instance of `Calendar`, which is converted to a String and displayed.

A Record Store's Next RecordID

The primary key of each record in a record store is the recordID, which is an int that is incremented each time a record is added. In some situations, it is useful to know the recordID that will be assigned next. Let's say you are about to add a record to a store and you are maintaining your own index to the store. Having access to the recordID that will be assigned when you add the record enables you to include the recordID in your index when you add the record. If you select Get Next recID from the main menu, the next recordID is displayed, as shown here.

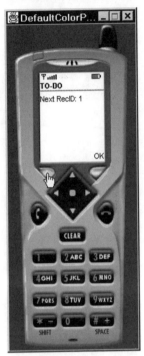

The code that gets the next recordID is

```
int next = currentRecordStore.getNextRecordID();
```

The value that is returned by getNextRecordID is converted to a String using Integer.toString and is displayed.

The Number of Records in a Record Store

Let's imagine a situation in which you are about to read every record in a record store and create an entry in a Hashtable for each record read. You can avoid the performance penalty associated with rehashing by instantiating the Hashtable using the form of the constructor that takes an initial capacity as an argument. To ensure an initial capacity that can hold an entry for each record, you need to know the number of records in the store. The `getNumRecords` method is used for this. To determine the number of records in the TO-DO store, select Get # Recs from the main menu. The record count is displayed, as shown here:

The code from method `displayNextRecID` that obtains the record count is

```
int nrecs = currentRecordStore.getNumRecords();
```

The int that is returned is converted to a String using `Integer.parseInt` and is displayed.

The Total Size of a Record Store

Another important statistic is the total number of bytes occupied by a record store. You can use the `getSize` method to obtain this value. If you select Get Size from the main menu, the total number of bytes occupied by TO-DO is displayed, as shown here:

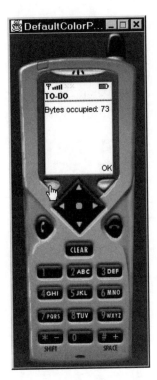

The code in the `displaySize` method that is used to obtain the total number of bytes is

```
int bytes = currentRecordStore.getSize();
```

As with the other statistics, the int that is returned is converted to a String and displayed.

Determining Room for Growth

The final statistic you can obtain is the number of bytes available for a record store to grow. You can use the `getSizeAvailable` method to obtain this number, but you should use it to make decisions related to storage. Let's say you determine that the number of bytes available for growth is *nba*, and you divide it by *rsz*, the size of an average record, to determine the number of records you can add to the store. You run the application on your wireless phone for months with no problems and find the application so useful that you install it on your PDA. After three days, the application fails when you try to add a record; and you discover that in order to facilitate synchronization with desktop applications, the implementation on the PDA appends an additional data structure to each record in the store—effectively rendering your calculation useless. The lesson here is that trying to correlate the number of bytes available for growth and the number of records that can be added is not wise.

To display the number of bytes available for TO-DO to grow, select Get Available from the main menu. The resulting display looks like this:

The code from the `displayAvailable` method that gets the available bytes is

```
int bytes = currentRecordStore.getSizeAvailable();
```

Navigating Through the Record Store

We will now see how to navigate through the record store; but since you've only added a single record so far, take a few minutes now to add the following:

▶ Pick up dry cleaning

▶ Drop off watch at jeweler

▶ Return book to library

Now select Browse Records from the main menu, and you will see this screen displayed:

The recordID is displayed at the top of the screen. When you press Menu, you see that you have the choices shown here:

Choose Next to navigate to the next record, and the following record is displayed:

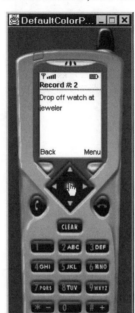

You might be somewhat surprised to see that the recordID is not 1, as you might have expected, but 2. Notice also that the menu contains the additional item Prev. When you select Next two more times, records 1 and 3 are displayed. Notice that the menu for record 3 does not contain Next.

Navigate through the records one more time and you can observe that they are presented in alphabetical order. We will now see why.

The RecordEnumeration Interface

When you want to iterate over the records in a record store, you do so with the help of the `RecordEnumerator` interface, which is a bidirectional enumerator that logically maintains a sequence of the recordIDs in the record store. The `enumerateRecords` method of `RecordStore` returns a `RecordEnumerator` object. The contents of the `RecordEnumerator` and the order in which they appear depend on two additional interfaces, `RecordComparator` and `RecordFilter`. The first two arguments passed to the `enumerateRecords` method are an instance of `RecordFilter` and an instance of `RecordComparator`, respectively. If you are interested only in efficiency, use `null` for both of these arguments, and the enumeration will traverse the records in the store in an undefined manner.

The first time you invoke the nextRecord method of RecordEnumeration, the record data from the first record in the enumeration is returned. Subsequent invocations return the next consecutive records in the enumeration. At any point in the enumeration, you can access the previous record, if one exists, by invoking previousRecord. If no record is available for nextRecord or previousRecord to return, the methods throw InvalidRecordIDException and continue to do so until you reset the enumeration by invoking the reset method. If you want to traverse the enumeration in reverse order, you start by invoking previousRecord. From the reset state, when previousRecord is the first method invoked, the record data of the last record in the enumeration is returned.

The RecordComparator Interface

The RecordComparator interface defines a comparator whose function is to compare two records in an implementation-defined manner and determine whether the first record in the pair precedes or follows the second in terms of search or sort order, or whether the two records are the same in terms of search or sort order.

As the enumerateRecords method of RecordStore builds the enumerator, if the second argument passed to the method was not null but an instance of RecordComparator, the enumerateRecords method passes pairs of candidate records as arguments to the compare method of the implementer of RecordComparator.

The *RecordStoreDemo* application uses an inner class to implement RecordComparator. The code looks like this:

```
class AlphaComparator implements RecordComparator {

  public AlphaComparator() {
  }

  public int compare(byte[] rec1, byte[] rec2) {
    String s1 = new String(rec1);
    String s2 = new String(rec2);
    int cr = s1.compareTo(s2);
    if (cr < 0) {
      return RecordComparator.PRECEDES;
    }
    else if (cr > 0) {
      return RecordComparator.FOLLOWS;
    }
    else {
```

```
        return RecordComparator.EQUIVALENT;
    }
  }
}
```

Now you know why the records were presented in alphabetical order. If you want to get an even clearer picture of what's happening, insert a `System.out.println()` statement before each of the three return statements in the `compare` method, launch the MIDlet, select TO-DO as the active store, and select Browse Records from the main menu. The Output Window will display the messages shown here:

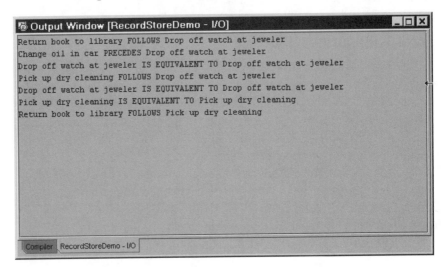

Deleting a Record

As each record in the record store is displayed, one of the menu options is Delete. When you select this option, it removes the record from the record store. Once the record is removed, any attempt to reference a record using the deleted record's recordID results in an InvalidRecordIDException. Since the recordID of the deleted record is contained in the enumeration being used to navigate through the record store, the application must refresh the contents of the enumeration. It uses the `rebuild` method to do this.

```
    private void deleteRecord() {
      int newRecordID = -1;
      try {
        if (enum.hasNextElement()) {
```

```
      newRecordID = enum.nextRecordId();
  }
  else if (enum.hasPreviousElement()) {
    newRecordID = enum.previousRecordId();
  }
}
catch (RecordStoreException e) {
  displayAlert(errorAlert, "Error while deleting record");
}
try {
  currentRecordStore.deleteRecord(currentRecordID);
}
catch (RecordStoreNotOpenException e) {
}
catch (InvalidRecordIDException e) {
}
catch (RecordStoreException e) {
}
enum.rebuild();
int nrecs = enum.numRecords();
if (nrecs == 0) {
  displayAlert(infoAlert,"No records in RecordStore");
  return;
}
clearForm(statusForm);
statusForm.setTitle("Record Deleted");
statusForm.append(new StringItem(null,"Record # " +
  Integer.toString(currentRecordID) + " deleted.\n" +
  "RecordStore now contains " + Integer.toString(nrecs) +
  Integer.toString(nrecs) + " records"));
while (enum.hasNextElement()) {
    try {
      if (enum.nextRecordId() == newRecordID) {
        currentRecordID = newRecordID;
        break;
      }
    }
    catch (InvalidRecordIDException e) {
    }
}
try {
  recordData = currentRecordStore.getRecord(currentRecordID);
}
```

```
        catch (RecordStoreNotOpenException e) {
        }
        catch (InvalidRecordIDException e) {
        }
        catch (RecordStoreException e) {
        }
        displayStatusForm(ST_AFTER_DELETION);
    }
```

In this code, we assume responsibility for determining when to invoke rebuild to refresh the enumeration. An alternative approach is to use the `RecordListener` interface. To do so, we would make the following modifications to the application:

▶ Include `implements RecordListener` in the `class` statement.

▶ Include our application-specific implementations of the `recordAdded`, `recordDeleted`, and `recordModified` methods.

▶ Invoke `addRecordListener` on the instance of `RecordStore` after it is created.

The advantage of taking this approach is that it relieves us of the responsibility of tracking changes. The `recordAdded`, `recordDeleted`, and `recordModified` methods will be called automatically. The downside is that these methods might be called more often than we wish. The nature of our application might be such that we can safely ignore certain modifications to the record store and make our own determination of when it is necessary to take action as the result of modifications.

Yet another approach to keeping an enumeration current with any changes to the record store is to set the third argument, `keepUpdated`, of the `enumerateRecords` method to `true`. You should be aware of the potential performance consequences.

Modifying a Record

Another item in the menu presented with each record is Modify. When you select this option, a `TextField` containing the contents of the current record is displayed. You can modify the contents, and when you press OK, the modified record is written back to the record store. The code from the `processDataForm` method is shown here:

```
case ST_MODIFYING_RECORD:
  recordData = recordDataTextField.getString().getBytes();;
  try {
    currentRecordStore.setRecord(currentRecordID, recordData,
      0, recordData.length);
```

```
  }
  catch (RecordStoreNotOpenException e) {
    displayAlert(errorAlert,"RecordStoreNotOpenException");
  }
  catch (InvalidRecordIDException e) {
    displayAlert(errorAlert,"InvalidRecordIDException");
  }
  catch (RecordStoreFullException e) {
    displayAlert(errorAlert,"RecordStoreFullException");
  }
  catch (RecordStoreException e) {
   displayAlert(errorAlert,"RecordStoreException");
  }
  displayRecordData();
```

The method that rewrites the modified record is `setRecord`.

The RecordFilter Interface

The `RecordFilter` interface defines a filter that examines a candidate record and determines whether it meets application-defined criteria. As the `enumerateRecords` method of `RecordStore` builds the enumerator, if the first argument passed to the method was not `null` but an instance of `RecordFilter`, the `enumerateRecords` method passes each candidate record as an argument to the `match` method of the implementer of `RecordFilter`.

The *RecordStoreDemo* application uses an inner class to implement `RecordFilter`. The code looks like this:

```
class FirstCharacterFilter implements RecordFilter {

  String startingCharacter;

  public FirstCharacterFilter(String startingCharacter)  {
    this.startingCharacter = startingCharacter.toLowerCase();
  }

  public boolean matches (byte[] candidate) {
    return new String(candidate).toLowerCase()
    .startsWith(startingCharacter);
  }
}
```

Now let's see how `RecordFilter` is used. Start by using Select Store to designate TO-CALL as the active record store. Then use Add Record to add the following names to the to-call list:

► Joe

► Tom

► Satish

► Steve

► Matt

► Paul T.

► Paul H.

After the names have been added, select Browse (filtered) from the main menu. Enter the letter **P** into the TextField so that it looks like this:

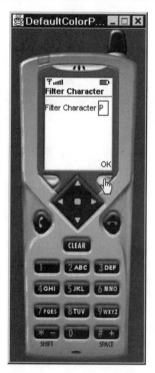

When you select Next, the following record is displayed:

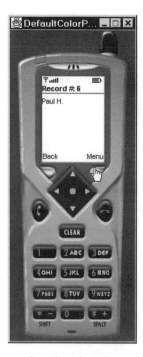

Now take a look at the menu and notice that the only navigational option is Prev, indicating that this is the last record in the enumeration. The only two records that were selected by `enumerateRecords` were those beginning with the letter *P*.

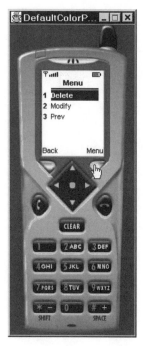

RecordStoreDemo Source Code

\OMH\com\paulsjavabooks\instantj2me\Chapter10\RecordStoreDemo.java

As we learned how to use the RecordStore API, we examined a number of isolated code segments. The complete application is shown here:

```java
/*
 * RecordStoreDemo.java
 *
 * Created on July 13, 2001, 10:16 PM
 */


package com.paulsjavabooks.instantj2me.Chapter10;

import java.util.*;

import javax.microedition.midlet.*;
import javax.microedition.lcdui.*;
import javax.microedition.rms.*;


/**
 *
 * @author  paul_tremblett
 * @version 1.0
 */
public class RecordStoreDemo extends MIDlet implements CommandListener {

    private Display display;

    private Form mainMenuForm;
    private Form dataForm;
    private Form recordForm;
    private Form statusForm;

    private TextField recordStoreNameTextField;
    private TextField filterCharacterTextField;
    private TextField recordDataTextField;

    private ChoiceGroup recordStoreChoice;

    private Alert errorAlert;
```

```java
private Alert infoAlert;

private Command cmdOK;
private Command cmdBack;
private Command cmdNext;
private Command cmdPrev;
private Command cmdDelete;
private Command cmdModify;
private Command cmdExit;
private Command cmdHelp;

private ChoiceGroup mainMenu;

private RecordStore currentRecordStore = null;
private String currentName = "";

private RecordEnumeration enum;
private RecordFilter filter;
private int currentRecordID;
private byte[] recordData;

private boolean commandAvailable;
private Command currentCommand;
private Displayable currentDisplayable;

private int state;

private static final int ST_MAIN_MENU =                          100;
private static final int ST_GETTING_RECORD_STORE_NAME =          101;
private static final int ST_SELECTING_STORE_NAME =               102;
private static final int ST_SELECTING_STORE_NAMES_FOR_DELETION = 103;
private static final int ST_GETTING_RECORD_DATA =                104;
private static final int ST_BROWSING_STORE =                     105;
private static final int ST_MODIFYING_RECORD =                   106;
private static final int ST_AFTER_DELETION =                     107;
private static final int ST_GETTING_FILTER_CHARACTER =           108;
private static final int ST_DISPLAYING_STATUS_FORM =             109;

private String[] actions = {
  "List Stores",        // 0
  "Create Store",       // 1
  "Select Store",       // 2
  "Delete Store(s)",    // 3
  "Add Record",         // 4
```

```
      "Browse Records",     //  5
      "Browse (filtered)",  //  6
      "Version",            //  7
      "Last Modified",      //  8
      "Get Next recID",     //  9
      "Get # Recs",         // 10
      "Get Size",           // 11
      "Get Available",      // 12
      "Close Store"         // 13
    };

    private static final int LIST_STORES =       0;
    private static final int CREATE_STORE =      1;
    private static final int SELECT_STORE =      2;
    private static final int DELETE_STORE =      3;
    private static final int ADD_RECORD =        4;
    private static final int BROWSE_RECORDS =    5;
    private static final int BROWSE_FILTERED =   6;
    private static final int GET_VERSION =       7;
    private static final int LAST_MODIFIED =     8;
    private static final int GET_NEXT_REC_ID =   9;
    private static final int GET_NUM_RECS =     10;
    private static final int GET_SIZE =         11;
    private static final int GET_AVAIL =        12;
    private static final int CLOSE_STORE =      13;

    private String[] recordSubCommands = {
      "Back",
      "Prev",
      "Next",
      "Delete",
      "Modify"
    };

    private static final int SUB_BACK =    0;
    private static final int SUB_PREV =    1;
    private static final int SUB_NEXT =    2;
    private static final int SUB_DELETE =  3;
    private static final int SUB_MODIFY =  4;

    private String msgNoRecordStores =
      "MIDlet Suite contains no RecordStores";

    private String msgNoCurrentRecordStore =
```

```
    "You must first select a RecordStore";

private String msgRecordStoreException =
    "RecordStoreException";

private String msgRecordStoreNotOpenException =
    "RecordStoreNotOpenException";

private String msgInvalidRecordIDException =
    "InvalidRecordIDException";

    private String[] helpText = {
        "This command lists all of the record stores in this " +
        "MIDlet suite. The RecordStore that has been designated as " +
        "'active' will be indicated by '(*)'",

        "This command is used to create a record store. " +
        "You will be prompted for the name of the record store. " +
        "After the store has been added, it will automatically " +
        "be made the 'active' RecordStore and the RecordStore " +
        "(if any) that had been the 'active' RecordStore is closed.",

        "This command is used to designate the 'active' RecordStore " +
        "(i.e. the one that is the target of subsequent commands " +
        "that operate on records or request information about the " +
        "RecordStore.",

        "This command is used to delete the designated RecordStore. " +
        "When a RecordStore is deleted, all of the records it " +
        "contains are also deleted.",

        "This command is used to add a record to the 'active' " +
        "RecordStore. You will be presented with a screen " +
        "containing a TextField into which you type the contents of " +
        "the record. You can create records whose contents are " +
        "identical.",

        "This command is used to initiate the process of iterating " +
        "over all of the records in the record store. For each " +
        "record that is presented, you have the option of deleting " +
        "or modifying the record or of navigating to the next or " +
        "previous record if such a record exists.",

        "This command is the same as the 'browse' command but it " +
        "uses a filter. You will be presented with a screen " +
```

```
          "containing a TextField into which you type a letter. Only " +
          "those names beginning with that letter will be displayed " +
          "during the browse operation.",

          "This command displays the version of the 'active' " +
          "RecordStore. The version number is incremented by 1 " +
          "each time the RecordStore is modified (i.e. a record is " +
          "added, modified or deleted).",

          "This command displays the date/time the 'active' " +
          "RecordStore was modified.",

          "This command displays the recordID that will be assigned " +
          "to the next record added to the 'active' RecordStore.",

          "This command displays the total number of records in the " +
          "'active' RecordStore.",

          "This command displays the amount of space, in bytes, that " +
          "the 'active' RecordStore occupies.",

          "This command displays the additional room (in bytes) " +
          "available for the 'active' RecordStore to grow. You should " +
          "NOT make any decision related to storage based on this number.",

          "This command is used to close the 'active' RecordStore."
       };



    public void startApp() {

       display = Display.getDisplay(this);

       cmdOK =     new Command("OK",Command.SCREEN,1);
       cmdBack =   new Command("Back",Command.SCREEN,1);
       cmdNext =   new Command("Next",Command.SCREEN,1);
       cmdPrev =   new Command("Prev",Command.SCREEN,1);
       cmdDelete = new Command("Delete",Command.SCREEN,1);
       cmdModify = new Command("Modify",Command.SCREEN,1);
       cmdHelp =   new Command("Help",Command.SCREEN,1);
       cmdExit =   new Command("Exit",Command.SCREEN,1);

       mainMenuForm = new Form("Menu");
```

```
mainMenu = new ChoiceGroup("Action",Choice.EXCLUSIVE,
  actions, null);
mainMenuForm.append(mainMenu);

recordForm = new Form("RECORD DATA");
recordForm.addCommand(cmdBack);
recordForm.addCommand(cmdDelete);
recordForm.addCommand(cmdModify);
recordForm.setCommandListener(this);

dataForm = new Form(null);
dataForm.setCommandListener(this);
dataForm.addCommand(cmdOK);

recordStoreNameTextField =
  new TextField("Store Name",null,32,TextField.ANY);
recordDataTextField =
  new TextField("Record Data",null,80,TextField.ANY);
filterCharacterTextField =
  new TextField("Filter Character",null,1,TextField.ANY);

statusForm = new Form(null);
statusForm.setCommandListener(this);
statusForm.addCommand(cmdOK);

mainMenuForm.addCommand(cmdOK);
mainMenuForm.addCommand(cmdHelp);
mainMenuForm.addCommand(cmdExit);

commandAvailable = false;
new CommandThread(this).start();

infoAlert = new Alert("Help");
infoAlert.setType(AlertType.INFO);
infoAlert.setTimeout(Alert.FOREVER);

errorAlert = new Alert("Error");
errorAlert.setType(AlertType.ERROR);
errorAlert.setTimeout(Alert.FOREVER);


mainMenuForm.setCommandListener(this);
```

```java
      display.setCurrent(mainMenuForm);
}

public void pauseApp() {
}

public void destroyApp(boolean unconditional) {
}

public void commandAction(Command cmd, Displayable d) {
  if (cmd == cmdExit) {
    destroyApp(true);
    notifyDestroyed();
  }
  else if (cmd == cmdHelp) {
    int index = mainMenu.getSelectedIndex();
    infoAlert.setTitle(mainMenu.getString(index));
    infoAlert.setString(helpText[mainMenu.getSelectedIndex()]);
    display.setCurrent(infoAlert, mainMenuForm);
  }
  else {
    synchronized (this) {
      currentCommand = cmd;
      currentDisplayable = d;
      commandAvailable = true;
      notify();
    }
  }
}

class CommandThread extends Thread {
  MIDlet parent;

  public CommandThread(MIDlet parent) {
    this.parent = parent;
  }

  public void run() {
    while (true) {
      synchronized(parent) {
        while(!commandAvailable) {
          try {
            parent.wait();
```

```
          }
          catch (InterruptedException e) {
          }
        }
      }
    commandAvailable = false;

    if (currentDisplayable == mainMenuForm) {
      processMainMenuItem();
    }
    else if (currentDisplayable == dataForm) {
      processDataForm();
    }
    else if (currentDisplayable == recordForm) {
      processRecordForm();
    }
    else if (currentDisplayable == statusForm) {
      if (state == ST_AFTER_DELETION) {
        state = ST_BROWSING_STORE;
        displayRecordData();
      }
      else {
        displayMainMenu();
      }
    }
  }
}

private void displayDataForm(int st) {
  state = st;
  display.setCurrent(dataForm);
}

private void displayStatusForm(int st) {
  state = st;
  display.setCurrent(statusForm);
}

private void displayMainMenu() {
  mainMenu.setSelectedIndex(0,true);
  state = ST_MAIN_MENU;
  display.setCurrent(mainMenuForm);
}
```

```java
private void processMainMenuItem() {
  int commandIndex = mainMenu.getSelectedIndex();
  if (commandRequiresOpenStore(commandIndex))
    if (!storeOpen()) {
      displayAlert(errorAlert, msgNoCurrentRecordStore);
      return;
    }
  switch (commandIndex) {
    case LIST_STORES:
      displayRecordStoreList();
      break;
    case CREATE_STORE:
      requestRecordStoreName();
      break;
    case SELECT_STORE:
      requestRecordStoreFromList("SELECT", ChoiceGroup.EXCLUSIVE);
      break;
    case DELETE_STORE:
      requestRecordStoreFromList("DELETE", ChoiceGroup.MULTIPLE);
      break;
    case ADD_RECORD:
      requestRecordData();
      break;
    case BROWSE_RECORDS:
      filter = null;
      startIteration();
      break;
    case BROWSE_FILTERED:
      requestFilterCharacter();
      break;
    case GET_VERSION:
      displayVersion();
      break;
    case LAST_MODIFIED:
      displayLastModified();
      break;
    case GET_NEXT_REC_ID:
      displayNextRecID();
      break;
    case GET_NUM_RECS:
      displayRecordCount();
      break;
    case GET_SIZE:
```

```
        displaySize();
        break;
    case GET_AVAIL:
        displayAvailable();
        break;
      case CLOSE_STORE:
        closeRecordStore();
        break;
    default:
        break;
    }
}

private boolean commandRequiresOpenStore(int index) {
  if ((index == ADD_RECORD) ||
      (index == BROWSE_RECORDS) ||
      (index == BROWSE_FILTERED) ||
      (index == GET_VERSION) ||
      (index == LAST_MODIFIED) ||
      (index == GET_NEXT_REC_ID) ||
      (index == GET_NUM_RECS) ||
      (index == GET_SIZE) ||
      (index == GET_AVAIL) ||
      (index == CLOSE_STORE)) {
    return true;
  }
  else {
   return false;
  }
}

private boolean storeOpen() {
  boolean open = true;
  try {
    getCurrentStoreName();
  }
  catch (RecordStoreNotOpenException e) {
    open = false;
  }
  finally {
    return open;
  }
}
```

```java
    private void displayAlert(Alert alert, String message) {
      alert.setString(message);
      mainMenu.setSelectedIndex(0,true);
      state = ST_MAIN_MENU;
      display.setCurrent(alert,mainMenuForm);
    }

    private void displayNextRecord() {
      try {
        currentRecordID = enum.nextRecordId();
        recordData = currentRecordStore.getRecord(currentRecordID);
        displayRecordData();
      }
      catch (InvalidRecordIDException e) {
        displayAlert(errorAlert,"Invalid RecordID");
      }
      catch (RecordStoreNotOpenException e) {
        displayAlert(errorAlert,"RecordStore not open");
      }
      catch (RecordStoreException e) {
        displayAlert(errorAlert,"RecordStoreException");
      }
    }

    private void displayPreviousRecord() {
      try {
        currentRecordID = enum.previousRecordId();
        recordData = currentRecordStore.getRecord(currentRecordID);
        displayRecordData();
      }
      catch (InvalidRecordIDException e) {
        displayAlert(errorAlert,"Invalid RecordID");
      }
      catch (RecordStoreNotOpenException e) {
        displayAlert(errorAlert,"RecordStore not open");
      }
      catch (RecordStoreException e) {
        displayAlert(errorAlert,"RecordStoreException");
      }
    }

    private void displayRecordData() {
      clearForm(recordForm);
```

```java
      recordForm.removeCommand(cmdPrev);
      recordForm.removeCommand(cmdNext);
      if (enum.hasNextElement()) {
        recordForm.addCommand(cmdNext);
      }
      if (enum.hasPreviousElement()) {
        recordForm.addCommand(cmdPrev);
      }
      recordForm.setTitle("Record #: " +
        Integer.toString(currentRecordID));
      recordForm.append(new StringItem(null,new String(recordData)));
      state = ST_BROWSING_STORE;
      display.setCurrent(recordForm);
  }

  private void processRecordForm() {
    int subCommandIndex = 0;
    String label = currentCommand.getLabel();
    for (int i = 0; i < recordSubCommands.length; ++i) {
      if (recordSubCommands[i].equals(label)) {
        subCommandIndex = i;
        break;
      }
    }
    switch (subCommandIndex) {
      case SUB_BACK:
        displayMainMenu();
        break;
      case SUB_PREV:
        displayPreviousRecord();
        break;
      case SUB_NEXT:
        displayNextRecord();
        break;
      case SUB_DELETE:
        deleteRecord();
        break;
      case SUB_MODIFY:
        modifyRecord();
        break;
    }
  }
```

```java
private void modifyRecord() {
  clearForm(dataForm);
  dataForm.setTitle("Modify Record");
  recordDataTextField.setString(new String(recordData));
  dataForm.append(recordDataTextField);
  state = ST_MODIFYING_RECORD;
  display.setCurrent(dataForm);
}

private void deleteRecord() {
  int newRecordID = -1;
  try {
    if (enum.hasNextElement()) {
      newRecordID = enum.nextRecordId();
    }
    else if (enum.hasPreviousElement()) {
      newRecordID = enum.previousRecordId();
    }
  }
  catch (RecordStoreException e) {
    displayAlert(errorAlert, "Error while deleting record");
  }
  try {
    currentRecordStore.deleteRecord(currentRecordID);
  }
  catch (RecordStoreNotOpenException e) {
  }
  catch (InvalidRecordIDException e) {
  }
  catch (RecordStoreException e) {
  }
  enum.rebuild();
  int nrecs = enum.numRecords();
  if (nrecs == 0) {
    displayAlert(infoAlert,"No records in RecordStore");
    return;
  }
  clearForm(statusForm);
  statusForm.setTitle("Record Deleted");
  statusForm.append(new StringItem(null,"Record # " +
    Integer.toString(currentRecordID) + " deleted.\n" +
    "RecordStore now contains " + Integer.toString(nrecs) +
    Integer.toString(nrecs) + " records"));
```

```
    while (enum.hasNextElement()) {
        try {
          if (enum.nextRecordId() == newRecordID) {
            currentRecordID = newRecordID;
            break;
          }
        }
        catch (InvalidRecordIDException e) {
        }
    }
    try {
      recordData = currentRecordStore.getRecord(currentRecordID);
    }
    catch (RecordStoreNotOpenException e) {
    }
    catch (InvalidRecordIDException e) {
    }
    catch (RecordStoreException e) {
    }
    displayStatusForm(ST_AFTER_DELETION);
}

private void startIteration() {
  try {
    AlphaComparator ac = new AlphaComparator();
    enum = currentRecordStore.enumerateRecords(filter,ac,false);
    if (enum.numRecords() == 0) {
      displayAlert(infoAlert,"Store contains no records!");
      return;
    }
    displayNextRecord();
  }
  catch (RecordStoreNotOpenException e) {
    displayAlert(errorAlert,msgRecordStoreNotOpenException);
    return;
  }
}

private void requestRecordData() {
  clearForm(dataForm);
  dataForm.setTitle("Record Contents");
  recordDataTextField.setString("");
  dataForm.append(recordDataTextField);
```

```
    displayDataForm(ST_GETTING_RECORD_DATA);
  }

  private void requestRecordStoreName() {
    clearForm(dataForm);
    dataForm.setTitle("STORE NAME");
    recordStoreNameTextField.setString("");
    dataForm.append(recordStoreNameTextField);
    displayDataForm(ST_GETTING_RECORD_STORE_NAME);
  }

  private void requestFilterCharacter() {
    clearForm(dataForm);
    dataForm.setTitle("Filter Character");
    filterCharacterTextField.setString("");
    dataForm.append(filterCharacterTextField);
    displayDataForm(ST_GETTING_FILTER_CHARACTER);
  }

  private void requestRecordStoreFromList(String title,
        int choiceType) {
    String[] storeNames = RecordStore.listRecordStores();
    if (storeNames == null) {
      displayAlert(errorAlert,msgNoRecordStores);
      return;
    }
    else {
      dataForm.setTitle(title);
      clearForm(dataForm);
      recordStoreChoice = new ChoiceGroup("Stores",choiceType,
        storeNames,null);
      dataForm.append(recordStoreChoice);
      int state;
      if (title.equals("SELECT")) {
        state = ST_SELECTING_STORE_NAME;
      }
      else {
        state = ST_SELECTING_STORE_NAMES_FOR_DELETION;
      }
      displayDataForm(state);
    }
  }
```

```java
private void clearForm(Form f) {
  int sz = f.size();
  while (sz > 0) {
    f.delete(-sz);
  }
}

private void closeRecordStore() {
  if (currentRecordStore == null) {
    displayAlert(errorAlert,msgNoCurrentRecordStore);
    return;
  }
  try {
    currentRecordStore.closeRecordStore();
    currentRecordStore = null;
    displayAlert(infoAlert,"RecordStore closed");
  }
  catch (RecordStoreNotOpenException e) {
    displayAlert(errorAlert,msgRecordStoreNotOpenException);
  }
  catch (RecordStoreException e) {
    displayAlert(errorAlert,msgRecordStoreException);
  }
}

private String getCurrentStoreName()
    throws RecordStoreNotOpenException {
  if (currentRecordStore == null) {
    throw new RecordStoreNotOpenException();
  }
  else {
    return currentRecordStore.getName();
  }
}

private void displayRecordCount() {
  clearForm(statusForm);
  try {
    statusForm.setTitle(getCurrentStoreName());
    int nrecs = currentRecordStore.getNumRecords();
    statusForm.append(new StringItem(null,"# recs: " +
      Integer.toString(nrecs)));
  }
```

```java
      catch (RecordStoreNotOpenException e) {
        displayAlert(errorAlert,msgRecordStoreNotOpenException);
        return;
      }
      displayStatusForm(ST_DISPLAYING_STATUS_FORM);
  }

  private void displayAvailable() {
    clearForm(statusForm);
    try {
      statusForm.setTitle(getCurrentStoreName());
      int bytes = currentRecordStore.getSizeAvailable();
      statusForm.append(new StringItem(null,"Bytes Available: " +
        Integer.toString(bytes)));
    }
    catch (RecordStoreNotOpenException e) {
      displayAlert(errorAlert,msgRecordStoreNotOpenException);
      return;
    }
    displayStatusForm(ST_DISPLAYING_STATUS_FORM);
  }

  private void displaySize() {
    clearForm(statusForm);
    try {
      statusForm.setTitle(getCurrentStoreName());
      int bytes = currentRecordStore.getSize();
      statusForm.append(new StringItem(null,"Bytes occupied: " +
        Integer.toString(bytes)));
    }
    catch (RecordStoreNotOpenException e) {
      displayAlert(errorAlert,msgRecordStoreNotOpenException);
      return;
    }
    displayStatusForm(ST_DISPLAYING_STATUS_FORM);
  }

  private void displayNextRecID() {
    clearForm(statusForm);
    try {
      statusForm.setTitle(getCurrentStoreName());
      int next = currentRecordStore.getNextRecordID();
      statusForm.append(new StringItem(null, "Next RecID: " +
```

```
      Integer.toString(next)));
   }
  catch (RecordStoreNotOpenException e) {
    displayAlert(errorAlert,msgRecordStoreNotOpenException);
    return;
  }
  catch (RecordStoreException e) {
    displayAlert(errorAlert,msgRecordStoreException);
    return;
  }
  displayStatusForm(ST_DISPLAYING_STATUS_FORM);
}

private void displayLastModified() {
  clearForm(statusForm);
  try {
    statusForm.setTitle(getCurrentStoreName());
    long lastModified = currentRecordStore.getLastModified();
    Calendar cal = Calendar.getInstance();
    cal.setTime(new Date(lastModified));
    statusForm.append(new StringItem(null, "Last modified: " +
      cal.toString()));
   }
  catch (RecordStoreNotOpenException e) {
    displayAlert(errorAlert,msgRecordStoreNotOpenException);
    return;
  }
  displayStatusForm(ST_DISPLAYING_STATUS_FORM);
}

private void displayVersion() {
  clearForm(statusForm);
  try {
    statusForm.setTitle(getCurrentStoreName());
    int ver = currentRecordStore.getVersion();
    statusForm.append(new StringItem(null,
      "Version: " + Integer.toString(ver)));
  }
  catch (RecordStoreNotOpenException e) {
    displayAlert(errorAlert,msgRecordStoreNotOpenException);
    return;
  }
  displayStatusForm(ST_DISPLAYING_STATUS_FORM);
```

```
    }

    private void displayRecordStoreList() {
      String[] stores = RecordStore.listRecordStores();
      if (stores == null) {
        displayAlert(infoAlert,msgNoRecordStores);
        return;
      }
      clearForm(statusForm);
      statusForm.setTitle("Store List");
      String csn = "";
      try {
        if (currentRecordStore != null) {
          csn = currentRecordStore.getName();
        }
      }
      catch (RecordStoreNotOpenException e) {
      }
      for (int i = 0; i < stores.length; ++i) {
        if (!stores[i].equals(csn)) {
        statusForm.append(new StringItem(null,stores[i]));
        }
        else {
        statusForm.append(new StringItem(null,stores[i] + " (*)"));
        }
        statusForm.append(new StringItem(null,"\n"));
      }
    displayStatusForm(ST_DISPLAYING_STATUS_FORM);
  }

    private void createRecordStore() {
      RecordStore rs = null;
      String name = recordStoreNameTextField.getString();
      if ("".equals(name)) {
        displayAlert(errorAlert,"Name cannot be blank");
        return;
      }
      String[] stores = RecordStore.listRecordStores();
      if (stores != null) {
        for (int i = 0; i < stores.length; ++i) {
          if (stores[i].equals(name)) {
            displayAlert(errorAlert, name + " already exists");
            return;
          }
```

```
      }
    }
    try {
      rs = RecordStore.openRecordStore(name,true);
      if (currentRecordStore != null) {
        currentRecordStore.closeRecordStore();
      }
    }
    catch (RecordStoreException e) {
      displayAlert(errorAlert,msgRecordStoreException);
      return;
    }
    currentRecordStore = rs;
    displayAlert(infoAlert, name + " is now the active RecordStore");
  }

  private void processDataForm() {
    RecordStore rs = null;
    String sn = null;
    switch (state) {
      case ST_GETTING_RECORD_STORE_NAME:
        createRecordStore();
        break;

      case ST_SELECTING_STORE_NAME:
        int i = recordStoreChoice.getSelectedIndex();
        sn = recordStoreChoice.getString(i);
        try {
          rs = RecordStore.openRecordStore(sn,false);
          if (currentRecordStore != null) {
            try {
              currentRecordStore.closeRecordStore();
            }
            catch (RecordStoreException e) {
            }
          }
          currentRecordStore = rs;
        }
        catch (RecordStoreException e) {
          displayAlert(errorAlert, msgRecordStoreException);
        }
        try {
          sn = currentRecordStore.getName();
        }
```

```
      catch (RecordStoreNotOpenException e) {
        displayAlert(errorAlert,msgRecordStoreNotOpenException);
      }
      displayAlert(infoAlert,sn +
        " is now the active RecordStore");
      break;

  case ST_SELECTING_STORE_NAMES_FOR_DELETION:
    int ndel = 0;
    for (int ix = 0; ix < recordStoreChoice.size(); ++ix) {
      if (!recordStoreChoice.isSelected(ix)) {
        continue;
      }
      sn = recordStoreChoice.getString(ix);
      if (currentRecordStore != null) {
        try {
          if (currentRecordStore.getName().equals(sn)) {
            currentRecordStore.closeRecordStore();
          }
        }
        catch (RecordStoreException e) {
        }
        finally {
          currentRecordStore = null;
        }
      }
      try {
        rs.closeRecordStore();
      }
      catch (RecordStoreNotOpenException e) {
      }
      catch (RecordStoreException e) {
      }
      try {
        RecordStore.deleteRecordStore(sn);
        ++ndel;
      }
      catch (RecordStoreException e) {
      }
    }
    displayAlert(infoAlert, Integer.toString(ndel) +
      " RecordStores deleted");
    break;

  case ST_GETTING_FILTER_CHARACTER:
```

```
    if (currentRecordStore == null) {
      displayAlert(errorAlert,msgNoCurrentRecordStore);
    }
    String filterCharacter =
      filterCharacterTextField.getString();
    filter = new FirstCharacterFilter(filterCharacter);
    startIteration();
    break;

case ST_GETTING_RECORD_DATA:
    if (currentRecordStore == null) {
      displayAlert(errorAlert,msgNoCurrentRecordStore);
    }
    recordData = recordDataTextField.getString().getBytes();
    try {
      currentRecordStore.addRecord(recordData,0,
        recordData.length);
      displayAlert(infoAlert,"Record added");
    }
    catch (RecordStoreNotOpenException e) {
      displayAlert(errorAlert,msgRecordStoreNotOpenException);
    }
    catch (RecordStoreException e) {
      displayAlert(errorAlert,msgRecordStoreException);
    }
    break;

case ST_MODIFYING_RECORD:
    recordData = recordDataTextField.getString().getBytes();;
    try {
      currentRecordStore.setRecord(currentRecordID, recordData,
        0, recordData.length);
    }
    catch (RecordStoreNotOpenException e) {
      displayAlert(errorAlert,"RecordStoreNotOpenException");
    }
    catch (InvalidRecordIDException e) {
      displayAlert(errorAlert,"InvalidRecordIDException");
    }
    catch (RecordStoreFullException e) {
      displayAlert(errorAlert,"RecordStoreFullException");
    }
    catch (RecordStoreException e) {
      displayAlert(errorAlert,"RecordStoreException");
    }
```

```
            displayRecordData();
        }
      }
    }

  class AlphaComparator implements RecordComparator {

    public AlphaComparator() {
    }

    public int compare(byte[] rec1, byte[] rec2) {
      String s1 = new String(rec1);
      String s2 = new String(rec2);
      int cr = s1.compareTo(s2);
      if (cr < 0) {
        return RecordComparator.PRECEDES;
      }
      else if (cr > 0) {
        return RecordComparator.FOLLOWS;
      }
      else {
        return RecordComparator.EQUIVALENT;
      }
    }
  }

  class FirstCharacterFilter implements RecordFilter {

    String startingCharacter;

    public FirstCharacterFilter(String startingCharacter)  {
      this.startingCharacter = startingCharacter.toLowerCase();
    }

    public boolean matches (byte[] candidate) {
      return new String(candidate).toLowerCase()
      .startsWith(startingCharacter);
    }
  }
}
```

The Record Store as a Portable Log

IN THIS CHAPTER:

Recording data in a record store
Adapting a MIDlet to a specific country
Sorting a record store by date

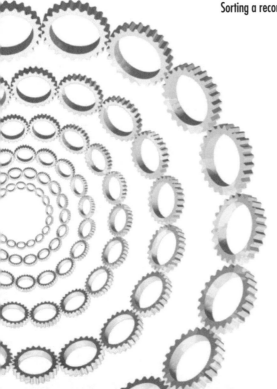

Now that you have learned to use a record store, you can undoubtedly imagine any number of ways in which you might use it. One use for a record store is accumulative logging of events or data. In this chapter, we will examine an application that records data. You will see an example of how a MIDlet can dynamically adapt itself to use units of measurement appropriate for the country in which the user lives.

Tracking Fuel Consumption

\OMH\com\paulsjavabooks\instantj2me\Chapter11\FuelTracker.java

Whenever you purchase a new automobile, you go through a period of a few months where you pay a great deal of attention to how efficiently the vehicle uses fuel. Typically, each time you purchase gasoline, you record the odometer's current reading and the amount of gasoline you purchased. Here's a MIDlet that can help you record such data:

```java
/*
 * FuelTracker.java
 *
 * Created on November 8, 2001, 6:07 PM
 */


package com.paulsjavabooks.instantj2me.Chapter11;


import javax.microedition.midlet.*;
import javax.microedition.lcdui.*;
import javax.microedition.rms.*;


import com.paulsjavabooks.instantj2me.Math.*;


/**
 *
 * @author  Paul Tremblett
 * @version 1.0
 */
public class FuelTracker extends javax.microedition.midlet.MIDlet
    implements CommandListener {
```

```
Display display;


boolean commandAvailable;
Command command;
Displayable displayable;
CommandThread commandThread;


List menu;


Form inputForm;
TextField distance;
TextField amount;


Form outputForm;
StringItem displayDistance;
StringItem displayVolume;
StringItem result;


Command cmdExit;
Command cmdOK;

public void startApp() {
  display = Display.getDisplay(this);


  String volumeType = getAppProperty("VOLUME_TYPE");
  String distanceType = getAppProperty("DISTANCE_TYPE");


  menu = new List("Main Menu",List.IMPLICIT);
  menu.append("Record Purchase",null);
  menu.append("View Log",null);
  menu.append("View Statistics",null);
  menu.append("Exit",null);
  menu.setCommandListener(this);


  inputForm = new Form("Record Purchase");
  distance =
```

```
            new TextField(distanceType.substring(0,1).toUpperCase() +
                     distanceType.substring(1),null,9,
                     TextField.NUMERIC);
      inputForm.append(distance);
      amount =
         new TextField(volumeType.substring(0,1).toUpperCase() +
                     volumeType.substring(1) ,null,3,
                     TextField.NUMERIC);
      inputForm.append(amount);
      cmdOK = new Command("OK",Command.EXIT,1);
      cmdExit = new Command("Exit",Command.EXIT,1);
      inputForm.addCommand(cmdOK);
      inputForm.addCommand(cmdExit);
      inputForm.setCommandListener(this);


      outputForm = new Form("Performance");
      displayDistance = new StringItem(distanceType + ":",null);
      outputForm.append(displayDistance);
      displayVolume = new StringItem(volumeType, null);
      outputForm.append(displayVolume);
      int vlen = volumeType.length() - 1;
      result = new StringItem(distanceType + " per " +
         volumeType.substring(0,vlen) + ": ", null);
      outputForm.append(result);
      outputForm.addCommand(cmdOK);
      outputForm.addCommand(cmdExit);
      outputForm.setCommandListener(this);


      commandAvailable = false;
      commandThread = new CommandThread(this);
      commandThread.start();


      display.setCurrent(menu);
   }


   public void pauseApp() {
   }


   public void destroyApp(boolean unconditional) {
   }


   public void commandAction(Command cmd, Displayable d) {
```

```
  if (cmd == cmdExit) {
    destroyApp(false);
    notifyDestroyed();
  }
  else {
    synchronized (this) {
    command = cmd;
    displayable = d;
    commandAvailable = true;
    notify();
    }
  }
}


class CommandThread extends Thread {

  MIDlet parent;

  boolean exit = false;


  public CommandThread(MIDlet parent) {
    this.parent = parent;
  }


  public void run() {
    while (!exit) {
      synchronized(parent) {
        while(!commandAvailable) {
          try {
            parent.wait();
          }
          catch (InterruptedException e) {
          }
        }
        commandAvailable = false;
      }


      if (command == cmdOK) {
        if (displayable == inputForm) {
          recordData();
        }
        else if (displayable == outputForm) {
          display.setCurrent(menu);
        }
      }
```

```java
    else if ((displayable == menu) &&
            (command == List.SELECT_COMMAND)) {
      switch (menu.getSelectedIndex()) {
        case 0:
          distance.setString(null);
          amount.setString(null);
          display.setCurrent(inputForm);
          break;
        case 1:
          Alert alert = new Alert("Missing Feature",
            "This feature has not yet been implemented",
            null, AlertType.INFO);
          alert.setTimeout(Alert.FOREVER);
          display.setCurrent(alert, menu);
          break;
        case 2:
          displayStatistics();
          break;
        case 3:
          exit = true;
          break;
      }
    }
  }
  destroyApp(false);
  notifyDestroyed();
}


private void recordData() {
  try {
    RecordStore rs = RecordStore.openRecordStore("FUEL_LOG", true);

    long dateNow = System.currentTimeMillis();
    String record = Long.toString(dateNow) + "\t" +
      distance.getString() + "\t" +
      amount.getString();

    rs.addRecord(record.getBytes(),0,record.length());

    rs.closeRecordStore();


    Alert alert = new Alert("Confirmation", "Data Recorded",
      null, AlertType.INFO);
    alert.setTimeout(Alert.FOREVER);
    display.setCurrent(alert, menu);
  }
  catch (RecordStoreNotOpenException e) {
```

```
      displayError(e);
    }
    catch (RecordStoreException e) {
      displayError(e);
    }
  }


private void displayStatistics() {
  try {
    RecordStore rs = RecordStore.openRecordStore("FUEL_LOG",false);
    RecordEnumeration enum =
      rs.enumerateRecords(null,new DateComparator(),false);
    if (enum.numRecords() == 0) {
      displayError(new Exception("Log is empty"));
    }
    else if (enum.numRecords() ==1) {
      displayError(new Exception("Log has only one entry"));
    }
    String rec = new String(enum.nextRecord());
    int tabix = rec.indexOf("\t");
    rec = rec.substring(tabix+1);
    tabix = rec.indexOf("\t");
    int startDistance = Integer.parseInt(rec.substring(0,tabix));
    enum.reset();
    rec = new String(enum.previousRecord());
    tabix = rec.indexOf("\t");
    rec = rec.substring(tabix+1);
    tabix = rec.indexOf("\t");
    int endDistance = Integer.parseInt(rec.substring(0,tabix));
    rec = rec.substring(tabix+1);
    int volumeSum = 0;
    int totalDistance = endDistance - startDistance;
    while (enum.hasPreviousElement()) {
      rec = new String(enum.previousRecord());
      tabix = rec.indexOf("\t");
      rec = rec.substring(tabix+1);
      tabix = rec.indexOf("\t");
      rec = rec.substring(tabix+1);
      volumeSum += Integer.parseInt(rec);
    }
    String ds = Integer.toString(totalDistance);
    String vs = Integer.toString(volumeSum);
    try {
      displayDistance.setText(ds);
      displayVolume.setText(vs);
      result.setText(KMath.divide(ds,vs));
      display.setCurrent(outputForm);
    }
```

```java
      catch (KMathException e) {
        displayError(e);
      }
    }
    catch (RecordStoreNotFoundException e) {
      displayError(e);
    }
    catch (RecordStoreException e) {
      displayError(e);
    }
  }

  private void displayError(Exception e) {
    String msg = e.getMessage();
    if (msg == null) {
      msg = "No error message available";
    }
    Alert alert = new Alert("Error", "Error: " + msg, null,
      AlertType.ERROR);
    alert.setTimeout(Alert.FOREVER);
    display.setCurrent(alert,menu);
  }
}


class DateComparator implements RecordComparator {

  public int compare(byte[] rec1, byte[] rec2) {


    String s1 = new String(rec1);
    String s2 = new String(rec2);


    int tabix = s1.indexOf("\t");
    long d1 = Long.parseLong(s1.substring(0,tabix));
    tabix = s2.indexOf("\t");
    long d2 = Long.parseLong(s2.substring(0,tabix));

    if (d1 < d2) {
      return RecordComparator.PRECEDES;
    }
    else if (d1 > d2) {
      return RecordComparator.FOLLOWS;
    }
    else {
      return RecordComparator.EQUIVALENT;
    }
```

```
        }
    }
}
```

The MIDlet first uses the `getAppProperty` method to read the values that are to be used to measure distance and volume of fuel. It then displays a menu containing four choices presented as an IMPLICIT `List`. When the user selects Record Purchase, a form containing two `TextField`s is displayed. After the user enters the odometer reading and the amount of fuel purchased into these fields, the MIDlet uses `System.getCurrentTimeMillis` to obtain a `long` corresponding to the current time. It then converts this `long`, the distance, and the amount of fuel to strings and creates a record consisting of these three strings separated by the tab character. Next, it writes this record to an instance of `RecordStore`.

NOTE

As you explore the application, you might want to add code that checks whether the odometer reading that the user enters is greater than the last reading the user recorded and displays an alert if it is not.

When the user selects View Statistics from the menu, the MIDlet uses the `enumerateRecords` method to obtain an enumeration of all records in the store. The second argument it passes to `enumerateRecords` is an instance of `DateComparator`. This class implements `RecordComparator` and so has a `matches` method. Successive call-ins to the `matches` method by the `enumerateRecords` method result in the list of records being returned in ascending date order. The application invokes the `nextRecord` method to get the first record in the enumeration and extracts the distance field from the record. Since the records are sorted in ascending date order, this distance is the first one that the user recorded. After invoking `reset` to return the enumeration to its initial state, the application invokes `getPrevious`. Whenever `getPrevious` is the first method invoked against an instance of `RecordEnumeration`, it returns the last record. In this case, because of the sort order, this record is the last one the user recorded. The application extracts the distance field from this record and performs a simple subtraction to compute the total distance traveled. The MIDlet then iterates backward through the enumeration, extracting from each record the field containing the volume of fuel. It accumulates all of these values except the latest, which has not been used to operate the vehicle yet. The final step consists of performing a simple division to compute the fuel efficiency, which it displays.

Running the Application

Before you run the application, you must customize it by specifying values for application properties. The first such property is the unit you use to measure distance. If you live in the United States, this would be miles. If you live elsewhere, you might use kilometers. The second application property is the unit you use to measure the amount of fuel you purchase. In the United States, you would use gallons, and elsewhere you might use liters. You specify these properties by double-clicking on the MIDlet Suite icon and then selecting the Descriptor tab. You use the text entry field at the bottom of the window to enter the name of a tag and then use the New Tag button to add a new row containing the tag to the descriptor. Next, you double-click on the blank field to the right of the new tag and enter a value. When the MIDlet has been customized for use in the United States, the descriptor looks like this:

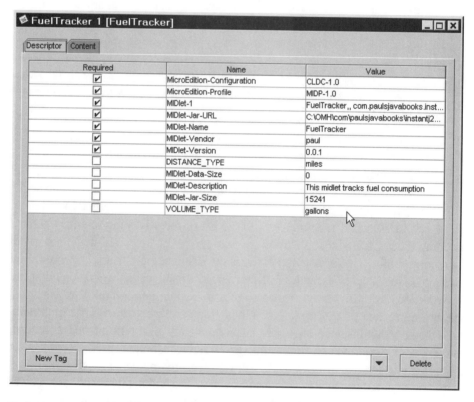

Before you close the MIDlet Suite window, you must perform one additional task. Since computing miles per gallon or kilometers per liter involves floating point math, you must make sure that the class file containing the floating point math library from Chapter 5 is available at runtime. You do this by selecting the Content tab and using the Add> button to add the Math package. When you do so, the Contents window looks like this:

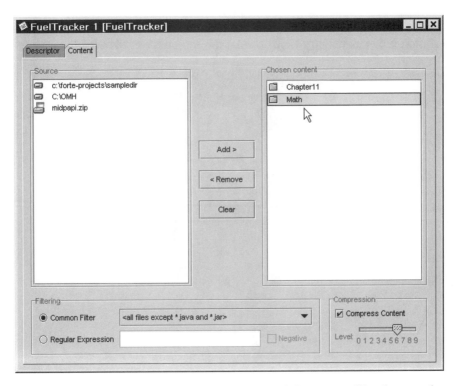

The MIDlet is now ready to run. When you launch it, a menu like the one shown here is displayed:

To record an entry, select Record Purchase from the menu. Enter the appropriate values into the two data entry fields so that the screen looks like this:

When you press OK, the MIDlet creates a record and writes it to the record store. It provides positive feedback that the data has been recorded by displaying the following screen:

After you have refueled several times, you might want to see just how efficiently your new car is using fuel, so you start the MIDlet and select View Statistics from the main menu. If you do so before you have entered any data, an error message will be displayed indicating that no log file has been created. If you attempt to view the data after you have recorded only a single entry, the MIDlet will display an error message since it cannot calculate total distance using a single value. Assuming that neither of these is the case, the MIDlet retrieves the data from the store, calculates the total distance traveled, accumulates the total volume of fuel consumed and displays the results on a screen like the one shown here:

If you select View Log from the main menu, you will see a message informing you that this feature has not yet been implemented. If you wish to implement this feature, you would use a RecordEnumerator like the one used to iterate over the log to generate fuel utilization and use a Next/Prev technique like the one you saw in Chapter 10. The DateComparator ensures that the RecordEnumeration is sorted chronologically.

Simple Networking

IN THIS CHAPTER:

The Generic Connection Framework

Querying a Daytime Server

I n the examples we have developed up to this point, input has been either from the user or from a record store, and output has been limited to the display or a record store. To realize the full power Java can bring to small devices, we need to explore network I/O. We will begin our exploration in this chapter and continue it in the next few chapters.

The Generic Connection Framework

You already know from experience with J2SE and J2EE that the number of interfaces, regular classes, and exception classes found in the packages java.io.* and java.net.* is in excess of 100. You also know that the rich functionality delivered by the combination of these two packages provides you with the tools to handle almost any kind of I/O you can expect to encounter. As desirable as you might think it would be to have all that power at your fingertips as you write programs in the MIDP environment, it just isn't practical. First of all, the total static size of the classes in the two packages is in the neighborhood of 200K. Second, the traditional I/O addressed by the two packages is for the most part not applicable to small devices, which often use such nontraditional connectivity as infrared, Bluetooth, or radio packets.

The challenge of providing a suitable facility capable of providing I/O functionality on small devices was met by the designers of the CLDC. Their goal, as described in the CLDC specification, was to provide a precise functional subset of J2SE classes, which can easily map to common low-level hardware or to any J2SE implementation, but with better extensibility, flexibility, and coherence in supporting new devices and protocols. Their solution was the Generic Connection Framework.

If you compare the approach taken by the Generic Connection Framework to that taken by J2SE and J2EE, you will see that the latter two achieve their goal by providing a number of totally different abstractions for different kinds of communication. The Generic Connection Framework provides a set of closely related abstractions at the application programming level.

Regardless of the type of connection the applications programmer wants to create, he or she creates it by invoking the static method `open` in the `Connector` class. There are three forms of the `open` method and they all have one argument in common, a String containing data that takes the form `<protocol>:<address>;`

<parameters>. The syntax follows the Uniform Resource Indicator (URI) syntax. This syntax is discussed in detail in RFC 2396, which is available at http://www.ietf.org/rfc/rfc2396.txt.

The CLDC specification clearly states: "The Generic Connection Framework included in CLDC does not specify the actual supported protocols or include implementations of specific protocols. The actual implementations and decisions regarding supported protocols must be made at the profile level." In the next several chapters, we will use some of the supported protocols as implemented in the MID Profile.

The framework is implemented using a hierarchy of Connection interfaces that become progressively more capable at levels further from the root Connection interface. This hierarchy is illustrated in Figure 12-1.

Much of the power of the Generic Connection Framework comes from late binding. The binding of a protocol to a J2ME application is done at runtime. The implementation uses the first portion of the URI up to the colon (:) to instruct the system to obtain a protocol implementation from a collection of protocol implementations. This permits a program to dynamically adapt to use a different protocol at runtime.

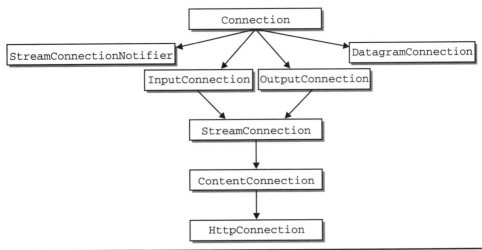

Figure 12-1 *The Connection hierarchy*

Querying a Daytime Server

Now it's time to write a simple application that uses the Generic Connection Framework. Since you've undoubtedly already used sockets in J2SE, we'll start with a program that establishes a socket connection to a server, reads data from the socket, and displays it. The server we'll choose is the daytime server, which is probably already running or can be easily installed on the system you're using to run the examples in this book.

The Server

\OMH\DayTimeServer.java

If you already have a daytime server running, you can skip this section. If you do not wish to permanently install a daytime server or if you simply want to get a clearer picture of everything that's happening, you can use the following code:

```java
import java.io.BufferedOutputStream;
import java.io.DataOutputStream;
import java.io.IOException;
import java.net.Socket;
import java.net.ServerSocket;
import java.util.Date;


public class DayTimeServer {


  public static void main(String args[]) {


    int dayTimePort = 13;


    if (args.length == 1) {
      try {
        dayTimePort = Integer.parseInt(args[0]);
      }
      catch (NumberFormatException e) {
        System.out.println("invalid port number");
        System.exit(0);
      }
```

```
    }


    ServerSocket serverSocket = null;
    Socket sock;


    DataOutputStream dataout;


    try {
      serverSocket = new ServerSocket(dayTimePort);
    }
    catch (IOException e) {
      System.out.println(e.getMessage());
      e.printStackTrace();
      System.exit(0);
    }


    while (true) {
      try {
        sock = serverSocket.accept();
        dataout = new DataOutputStream(new BufferedOutputStream
          (sock.getOutputStream()));
        String dateString = new Date().toString();
        dataout.write(dateString.getBytes(),0,dateString.length());
        dataout.flush();
        sock.close();
        }
      catch (IOException e) {
        System.out.println(e.getMessage());
        e.printStackTrace();
      }
    }
  }
}
```

If no command-line argument is specified, the program uses the default,
well-known port 13. Otherwise, it uses the first argument as the port number on
which it will listen for connections. This permits you to use this test server even
if you already have a daytime server using the well-known port.

When the program accepts an incoming connection, it simply returns the current date and time to the client that initiated the connection.

The Client

OMH\com\paulsjavabooks\instantj2me\Chapter12\DayTimeClient.java

The code for the client looks like this:

```
/*
 * DayTimeClient.java
 *
 * Created on September 18, 2001, 9:49 PM
 */


package com.paulsjavabooks.instantj2me.Chapter12;


import javax.microedition.midlet.*;
import javax.microedition.lcdui.*;


import java.io.*;
import javax.microedition.io.*;


/**
 *
 * @author  paul
 * @version
 */
public class DayTimeClient extends javax.microedition.midlet.MIDlet
    implements CommandListener {


  Display display;


  private boolean commandAvailable;
  CommandThread commandThread;

  List menu;
```

```
Form outputForm;
StringItem dt;

Command cmdBack;
Command cmdExit;


private static final String PROTOCOL = "socket:";

private String dayTimeURL;


public void startApp() {
  String host = getAppProperty("HOST");
  String port = getAppProperty("DAYTIME_PORT");
  try {
    (Integer.parseInt(port));
  }
  catch (NumberFormatException e) {
    destroyApp(false);
    notifyDestroyed();
  }

  dayTimeURL = PROTOCOL + "//" + host + ":" + port;
  display = Display.getDisplay(this);
  outputForm = new Form("Date/Time");
  dt = new StringItem(null,null);
  outputForm.append(dt);
  cmdBack = new Command("Back",Command.BACK,1);
  outputForm.addCommand(cmdBack);
  cmdExit = new Command("Exit",Command.EXIT,1);
  outputForm.addCommand(cmdExit);
  outputForm.setCommandListener(this);


  menu = new List("Menu",List.IMPLICIT);
  menu.append("Get Date/Time",null);
  menu.append("Exit",null);
  menu.setCommandListener(this);
  display.setCurrent(menu);


  commandAvailable = false;
```

```
    commandThread = new CommandThread(this);
    commandThread.start();
  }


  public void pauseApp() {
  }


  public void destroyApp(boolean unconditional) {
  }


  public void commandAction(Command cmd, Displayable d) {
    if (cmd == cmdExit) {
      destroyApp(false);
      notifyDestroyed();
    }
    else if (cmd == cmdBack) {
      display.setCurrent(menu);
    }
    else if ((d == menu) && (cmd == List.SELECT_COMMAND)) {
      synchronized (this) {
        commandAvailable = true;
        notify();
      }
    }
  }
}


class CommandThread extends Thread {
  MIDlet parent;


  StreamConnection socket = null;
  InputStream is = null;


  boolean exit = false;


  public CommandThread(MIDlet parent) {
    this.parent = parent;
```

```
  }


    public void run() {
      boolean stop = false;
      while (!exit) {
        synchronized(parent) {
          while(!commandAvailable) {
            try {
              parent.wait();
            }
            catch (InterruptedException e) {
            }
          }
        }
        commandAvailable = false;

        switch (menu.getSelectedIndex()) {
          case 0:
            getDate();
            break;
          case 1:
            stop = true;
        }
      }
      destroyApp(false);
      notifyDestroyed();
    }


  public void getDate() {
    try {
      socket =
        (StreamConnection)Connector.open(dayTimeURL,
          Connector.READ, true);


      is = socket.openInputStream();
    }
    catch (Exception e) {
    }


    try {
```

```
      int b;
      StringBuffer sb = new StringBuffer();
      while ( (b = is.read()) != -1) {
        sb.append((char)b);
      }
      socket.close();
      dt.setText(sb.toString());
      display.setCurrent(outputForm);
    }
    catch (Exception e) {
    }
  }
 }
}
```

The MIDlet reads the properties HOST and DAYTIME_PORT, which contain the name of the host on which the daytime server is running and the port on which it is listening. You must specify these properties in the descriptor, as shown here:

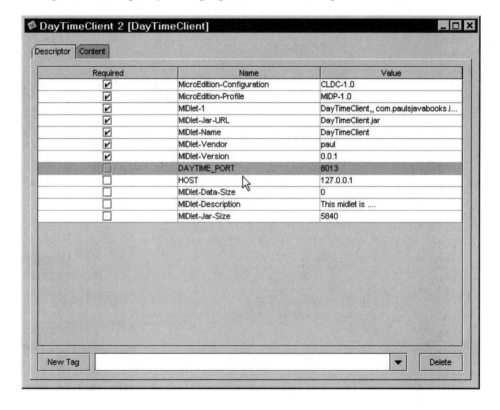

The MIDlet constructs a URL using the protocol contained in the static variable PROTOCOL, the host, and the port. In the present case, the URL String is socket://127.0.0.1:8013. When the user selects Get Date/Time, the MIDlet invokes `getDate`. This method passes the String containing the URL to the static `open` method of `Connector`. It casts the `Connection` object that is returned to `StreamConnection` and then invokes the `openInputStream` method on the stream. Next, it uses the `read` method of `InputStream` to retrieve data 1 byte at a time and appends each byte received to a `StringBuffer`. When a value of –1 is received, indicating that no more data is available, `getDate` closes the connection, converts the `StringBuffer` to a String, and displays it.

Running the Example

Before you run the MIDlet, you must first make sure a daytime server is running. In a Command Prompt window, type **netstat -a**. You will see a display that looks like this:

```
C:\OMH>netstat -a


Active Connections


   Proto   Local Address           Foreign Address         State
   TCP     paul-t:echo             paul-t:0                LISTENING
   TCP     paul-t:discard          paul-t:0                LISTENING
   TCP     paul-t:daytime          paul-t:0                LISTENING
   TCP     paul-t:qotd             paul-t:0                LISTENING
   TCP     paul-t:chargen          paul-t:0                LISTENING
```

In this case, the third entry in the Local Address column indicates that a daytime server is listening. If you see no such entry, you have the choice of installing simple TCP/IP services or compiling and starting the DayTimeServer application that was presented earlier in the chapter.

When you launch the MIDlet, it looks like this:

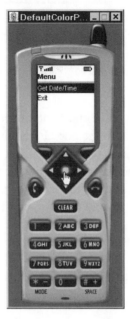

When you select Get Date/Time, the date and time are retrieved from the server and the display looks like this:

You can now either select Back to retrieve the date and time again, or Exit to terminate the MIDlet.

Communicating Over a Socket

IN THIS CHAPTER:

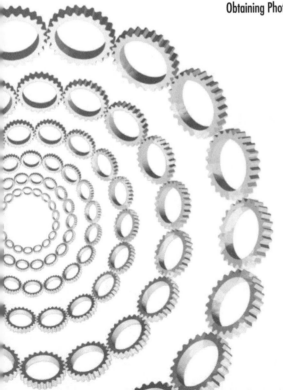

I n Chapter 12, we used a socket connection to receive data from a server. In this chapter, we will present several examples that go beyond simple one-way transfer of data and conduct conversations with servers. The servers use JDBC to access databases and send the results of queries back to the MIDlets that originated the queries. By the end of this chapter, it should be clear to you that using a high-end server as an extension of a handheld device packs quite a punch.

Checking the Status of an Order
\OMH\com\paulsjavabooks\instantj2me\Chapter13\OrderStatusClient.java

Let's imagine you are a salesperson who spends a significant amount of time visiting customers who almost always ask you the status of one or more orders they have placed. In ancient times, you carried a report you hoped was not too badly outdated. Then came the laptop and before you started your daily rounds you created your own report containing the status of all the customers you planned to visit that day. This was much better than leafing through a stack of fanfold paper, but you had no way of knowing if the status of an order had changed a few seconds after you generated the report. One solution was to find a phone at the customer location and dial in to access the order database, but that meant imposing on the customer. Finally, you are lucky enough to get your hands on a handheld wireless device. Let's see how that helps matters.

NOTE

Before you start this chapter, you should make sure you have installed the MySQL RDBMS as described in Appendix A.

Here is the code for a MIDlet that obtains the status of an order from a remote host:

```
/*
* OrderStatusClient.java
*
* Created on October 1, 2001, 9:08 PM
*/


package com.paulsjavabooks.instantj2me.Chapter13;


import javax.microedition.midlet.*;
```

```java
import javax.microedition.lcdui.*;


import javax.microedition.io.Connector;
import javax.microedition.io.StreamConnection;


import java.io.DataInputStream;
import java.io.DataOutputStream;
import java.io.InputStream;
import java.io.IOException;
import java.io.OutputStream;


/**
 *
 * @author  paul tremblett
 * @version 1.0
 */
public class OrderStatusClient extends javax.microedition.midlet.MIDlet
     implements CommandListener {


  Display display;


  private boolean commandAvailable;
  private byte[] xmit;
  CommandThread commandThread;

  List menu;
  Form inputForm;
  Form outputForm;
  TextField orderNumber;
  StringItem orderStatus;

  Command cmdBack;
  Command cmdExit;
  Command cmdOK;


  private static final String URL =
```

```
    "socket://127.0.0.1:1921";


StreamConnection conn = null;
InputStream is = null;
OutputStream os = null;


public void startApp() {
  display = Display.getDisplay(this);


  inputForm = new Form("Order Status");
  orderNumber = new TextField("Order #",null,
     6, TextField.NUMERIC);
  inputForm.append(orderNumber);
  cmdOK = new Command("OK",Command.SCREEN,1);
  cmdExit = new Command("Exit",Command.EXIT,1);
  inputForm.addCommand(cmdOK);
  inputForm.addCommand(cmdExit);
  inputForm.setCommandListener(this);


  outputForm = new Form("Order Status");
  orderStatus = new StringItem(null,null);
  outputForm.append(orderStatus);
  cmdBack = new Command("Back",Command.BACK,1);
  outputForm.addCommand(cmdBack);
  outputForm.addCommand(cmdExit);
  outputForm.setCommandListener(this);


  try {
    conn =
      (StreamConnection)Connector.open(URL,
        Connector.READ_WRITE, true);
    os = conn.openOutputStream();
    is = conn.openInputStream();


  }
  catch (Exception e) {
    destroyApp(false);
    notifyDestroyed();
```

```
    }


    commandAvailable = false;
    commandThread = new CommandThread(this);
    commandThread.start();


    display.setCurrent(inputForm);
  }


  public void pauseApp() {
  }


  public void destroyApp(boolean unconditional) {
    try {
      os.write("Q".getBytes());
      conn.close();
    }
    catch (IOException e) {
    }
  }


  public void commandAction(Command cmd, Displayable d) {
    if (cmd == cmdExit) {
      destroyApp(false);
      notifyDestroyed();
    }
    else if (cmd == cmdBack) {
      orderNumber.setString(null);
      display.setCurrent(inputForm);
    }
    else if (cmd == cmdOK)
      synchronized (this) {
        xmit = orderNumber.getString().getBytes();
        commandAvailable = true;
        notify();
      }
  }


  class CommandThread extends Thread {
```

```java
    MIDlet parent;


    boolean exit = false;


    public CommandThread(MIDlet parent) {
      this.parent = parent;
    }


    public void run() {
      while (true) {
        synchronized(parent) {
          while(!commandAvailable) {
            try {
              parent.wait();
            }
            catch (InterruptedException e) {
            }
          }
          commandAvailable = false;
        }

        getStatus();
      }
    }


    public void getStatus() {
      try {
        os.write(xmit);
        os.flush();


        int ch;
        StringBuffer sb = new StringBuffer();
        while ((ch = is.read()) != -1) {
          sb.append((char)ch);
          if ((char)ch == '\n') {
            break;
          }
        }
        orderStatus.setText(sb.toString());
```

```
      display.setCurrent(outputForm);
      //yield();
    }
    catch (Exception e) {
    }
  }
 }
}
```

The `startApp` method uses `Connector.open()` to obtain a
`StreamConnection` object that is an implementation of a socket. It uses
`getInputStream` and `getOutputStream` to get the streams required for
two-way communication.

The `getStatus` method transmits an order number entered by the user to the
host, reads the reply, and displays it.

The Server

\OMH\OrderStatusServer.java

Here is the code for the simple server from which the *OrderStatusClient* MIDlet
obtains the status of an order:

```java
import java.io.BufferedInputStream;
import java.io.BufferedOutputStream;
import java.io.DataInputStream;
import java.io.DataOutputStream;
import java.io.IOException;
import java.net.Socket;
import java.net.ServerSocket;


import java.sql.*;


public class OrderStatusServer {


  private int port = 1921;


  private ServerSocket serverSocket;


  static final String dbURL =
```

```java
        "jdbc:mysql://localhost/j2mebook?" +
        "user=j2meapps&password=bigsecret";


    public OrderStatusServer() throws ClassNotFoundException {
        Class.forName("org.gjt.mm.mysql.Driver");
    }


    public void acceptConnections() {


        try {
            serverSocket = new ServerSocket(1921);
        }
        catch (IOException e) {
            System.err.println("ServerSocket instantiation failure");
            e.printStackTrace();
            System.exit(0);
        }


        while (true) {
            try {
                Socket newConnection = serverSocket.accept();
                System.out.println("accepted connection");
                ServerThread st = new ServerThread(newConnection);
                new Thread(st).start();
            }
            catch (IOException ioe) {
                System.err.println("server accept failed");
            }
        }
    }

    public static void main(String args[]) {


        OrderStatusServer server = null;
        try {
            server = new OrderStatusServer();
        }
        catch (ClassNotFoundException e) {
            System.out.println("unable to load JDBC driver");
            e.printStackTrace();
```

```
      System.exit(1);
  }



  server.acceptConnections();
}


class ServerThread implements Runnable {


  private Socket socket;
  private DataInputStream datain;
  private DataOutputStream dataout;


  public ServerThread(Socket socket) {
    this.socket = socket;
  }


  public void run() {
    try {
      datain = new DataInputStream(new BufferedInputStream
        (socket.getInputStream()));
      dataout = new DataOutputStream(new BufferedOutputStream
        (socket.getOutputStream()));
    }
    catch (IOException e) {
      return;
    }
    byte[] ba = new byte[6];
    boolean conversationActive = true;
    while(conversationActive) {
      String orderNumber = null;
      try {
        datain.read(ba,0,6);
        orderNumber = new String(ba);
        if (orderNumber.toUpperCase().charAt(0) == 'Q') {
          conversationActive = false;
        }
        else {
          System.out.println("order number = " + orderNumber);
          String status = getStatus(orderNumber);
          System.out.println("status: " + status);
```

```
                dataout.write(status.getBytes(),0,status.length());
                dataout.write("\n".getBytes(),0,1);
                dataout.flush();
              }
            }
            catch (IOException ioe) {
              conversationActive = false;
            }
          }
          try {
            System.out.println("closing socket");
            datain.close();
            dataout.close();
            socket.close();
          }
          catch (IOException e) {
          }
        }


    private String getStatus(String orderNumber) {
      String status = "Not on file";
      Connection conn = null;
      try {
        conn = DriverManager.getConnection(dbURL);


        Statement stmt = conn.createStatement();
        String query = "SELECT status FROM orders " +
                       "WHERE ordernumber = " + orderNumber;
        ResultSet rs = stmt.executeQuery(query);
        if (rs.next()) {
          status = rs.getString(1);
        }
      }
      catch (SQLException e) {
        status = "server error";
      }
      finally {
        if (conn != null) {
          try {
            conn.close();
```

```
        }
        catch (SQLException e) {
        }
      }
    }
    return status;
  }
}
}
```

This server does the following:

▶ Listens on a port

▶ Accepts an incoming connection

▶ Reads an order number

▶ Uses JDBC to execute the appropriate SQL SELECT statement to obtain the order status

▶ Sends the status back to the requestor

Running the Example

Before you run the example, you must make sure that the database server and the order status server are both running. To determine whether the database server is running, type the command **mysqladmin status**. Since you have not yet started the database, you will observe output that looks like this:

```
Command Prompt                                                      _ □ x

C:\OMH>mysqladmin status
mysqladmin: connect to server at 'localhost' failed
error: 'Can't connect to MySQL server on 'localhost' (10061)'
Check that mysqld is running on localhost and that the port is 3306.
You can check this by doing 'telnet localhost 3306'

C:\OMH>
```

Start the database by typing the command **mysqld-nt --standalone**.

NOTE

The MySQL database server can also be run as a service.

After the database server has been started, bring up a second command prompt window and create the database we will be using by typing the command **mysqladmin create j2mebook**.

Minimize this second window for later use and start a third command prompt window. Start the MySQL Client by typing the command **mysql**. You will see the following introductory message displayed:

```
Command Prompt - mysql                                        _ □ ×

C:\OMH>mysql
Welcome to the MySQL monitor.  Commands end with ; or \g.
Your MySQL connection id is 2 to server version: 3.23.42-nt

Type 'help;' or '\h' for help. Type '\c' to clear the buffer.

mysql> _
```

Now connect to the database by typing the command **connect j2mebook**, as shown here:

```
Command Prompt - mysql                                        _ □ ×

C:\OMH>mysql
Welcome to the MySQL monitor.  Commands end with ; or \g.
Your MySQL connection id is 5 to server version: 3.23.42-nt

Type 'help;' or '\h' for help. Type '\c' to clear the buffer.

mysql> connect j2mebook
Connection id:    6
Current database: j2mebook

mysql> _
```

When you installed the software from the CD, you saved three files with .sql extensions in C:\OMH. These files contain the SQL commands that create the tables you will be using. Create the first table by typing the command \. **cr_orders.sql**. Type **describe orders;** to display the description of the columns in the table. To display the contents of the table, type the command **select * from orders;**. The output from the last three commands is shown here:

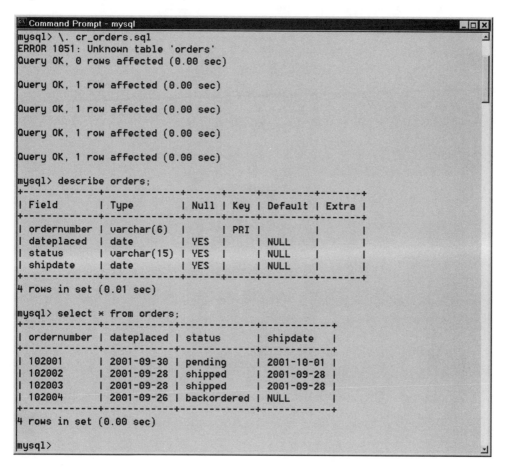

```
Command Prompt - mysql                                          _ □ X
mysql> \. cr_orders.sql
ERROR 1051: Unknown table 'orders'
Query OK, 0 rows affected (0.00 sec)

Query OK, 1 row affected (0.00 sec)

Query OK, 1 row affected (0.00 sec)

Query OK, 1 row affected (0.00 sec)

Query OK, 1 row affected (0.00 sec)

mysql> describe orders;
+-------------+-------------+------+-----+---------+-------+
| Field       | Type        | Null | Key | Default | Extra |
+-------------+-------------+------+-----+---------+-------+
| ordernumber | varchar(6)  |      | PRI |         |       |
| dateplaced  | date        | YES  |     | NULL    |       |
| status      | varchar(15) | YES  |     | NULL    |       |
| shipdate    | date        | YES  |     | NULL    |       |
+-------------+-------------+------+-----+---------+-------+
4 rows in set (0.01 sec)

mysql> select × from orders;
+-------------+------------+-------------+------------+
| ordernumber | dateplaced | status      | shipdate   |
+-------------+------------+-------------+------------+
| 102001      | 2001-09-30 | pending     | 2001-10-01 |
| 102002      | 2001-09-28 | shipped     | 2001-09-28 |
| 102003      | 2001-09-28 | shipped     | 2001-09-28 |
| 102004      | 2001-09-26 | backordered | NULL       |
+-------------+------------+-------------+------------+
4 rows in set (0.00 sec)

mysql>
```

NOTE

The Error 1051 you see is perfectly okay. The first SQL statement in cr_orders.sql is a DROP statement that removes an existing instance of the table. Since you have not created such an instance, you receive the error.

The order status server will be connecting to the database as user *j2meapps*. The password for this user is *bigsecret*. To establish this user, type the command **grant all privileges on *.* to j2meapps identified by 'bigsecret';**.

Now open yet another command prompt window and start the order status server by typing **java OrderStatusServer**.

Finally, you can launch the MIDlet by right-clicking on the MIDlet Suite icon and selecting Execute. Enter an order number, as shown here:

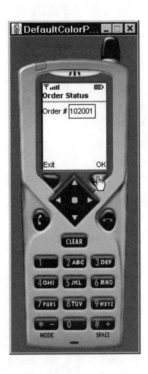

When you press OK, the MIDlet sends the order number to the server, retrieves the status, and displays it, as shown here:

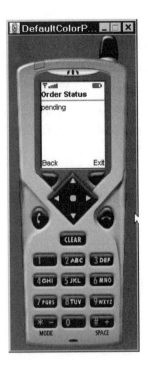

The order status server contains some debugging statements that were deliberately left in so that you can observe what the server does. If you look at the window in which the server is running, you see the following display:

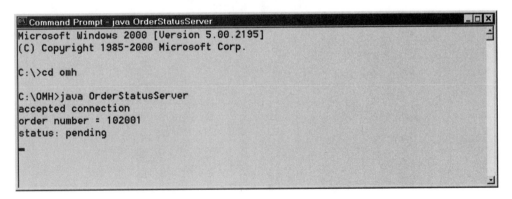

Querying a Skills Database

\OMH\com\paulsjavabooks\instantj2me\Chapter13\SkillsClient.java

In the next scenario, imagine you are a customer representative from a consulting firm. You are at a meeting with one of your clients where the topic of discussion is whether you can provide personnel who are qualified to staff an upcoming project. You might find this MIDlet useful:

```java
/*
 * SkillsClient.java
 *
 * Created on October 1, 2001, 10:09 PM
 */


package com.paulsjavabooks.instantj2me.Chapter13;


import javax.microedition.midlet.*;
import javax.microedition.lcdui.*;


import javax.microedition.io.Connector;
import javax.microedition.io.StreamConnection;


import java.io.DataInputStream;
import java.io.DataOutputStream;
import java.io.InputStream;
import java.io.IOException;
import java.io.OutputStream;


/**
 *
 * @author  paul tremblett
 * @version 1.0
 */
public class SkillsClient extends javax.microedition.midlet.MIDlet
```

```
    implements CommandListener {


Display display;


private boolean commandAvailable;
private byte[] xmit;
CommandThread commandThread;

List menu;
Form inputForm;
Form outputForm;
TextField skill;
StringItem results;

Command cmdBack;
Command cmdExit;
Command cmdOK;


private static final String URL =
  "socket://127.0.0.1:1927";


StreamConnection conn = null;
InputStream is = null;
OutputStream os = null;


public void startApp() {
  display = Display.getDisplay(this);


  inputForm = new Form("Skills");
  skill = new TextField("Skill",null,
    10, TextField.ANY);
  inputForm.append(skill);
  cmdOK = new Command("OK",Command.SCREEN,1);
  cmdExit = new Command("Exit",Command.EXIT,1);
```

```
      inputForm.addCommand(cmdOK);
      inputForm.addCommand(cmdExit);
      inputForm.setCommandListener(this);


      outputForm = new Form("Candidates");
      results = new StringItem(null,null);
      outputForm.append(results);
      cmdBack = new Command("Back",Command.BACK,1);
      outputForm.addCommand(cmdBack);
      outputForm.addCommand(cmdExit);
      outputForm.setCommandListener(this);


      try {
        conn =
          (StreamConnection)Connector.open(URL,
            Connector.READ_WRITE, true);
        os = conn.openOutputStream();
        is = conn.openInputStream();


      }
      catch (Exception e) {
        destroyApp(false);
        notifyDestroyed();
      }


      commandAvailable = false;
      commandThread = new CommandThread(this);
      commandThread.start();


      display.setCurrent(inputForm);
  }


  public void pauseApp() {
  }


  public void destroyApp(boolean unconditional) {
```

```
    try {
      os.write("Q".getBytes());
      conn.close();
    }
    catch (IOException e) {
    }
  }


public void commandAction(Command cmd, Displayable d) {
  if (cmd == cmdExit) {
    destroyApp(false);
    notifyDestroyed();
  }
  else if (cmd == cmdBack) {
    skill.setString(null);
    display.setCurrent(inputForm);
  }
  else if (cmd == cmdOK)
    synchronized (this) {
      xmit = skill.getString().getBytes();
      commandAvailable = true;
      notify();
    }
  }


class CommandThread extends Thread {
  MIDlet parent;


  boolean exit = false;


  public CommandThread(MIDlet parent) {
    this.parent = parent;
  }


  public void run() {
    while (true) {
      synchronized(parent) {
        while(!commandAvailable) {
```

```
                    try {
                      parent.wait();
                    }
                    catch (InterruptedException e) {
                    }
                  }
                  commandAvailable = false;
                }

              getSkills();
            }
          }


      public void getSkills() {
        try {
          os.write(xmit);
          os.flush();


          int ch;
          StringBuffer sb = new StringBuffer();
          while ((ch = is.read()) != -1) {
            if (ch == '\n') {
              break;
            }
            if (ch == '$') {
              ch = '\n';
            }
            sb.append((char)ch);
          }
          results.setText(sb.toString());
          display.setCurrent(outputForm);
          //yield();
        }
        catch (Exception e) {
        }
      }
    }
  }
```

This client is functionally similar to the order status client.

The Server
\OMH\SkillsServer.java

The server code looks like this:

```java
import java.io.BufferedInputStream;
import java.io.BufferedOutputStream;
import java.io.DataInputStream;
import java.io.DataOutputStream;
import java.io.IOException;
import java.net.Socket;
import java.net.ServerSocket;


import java.sql.*;


public class SkillsServer {


  private int port = 1927;


  private ServerSocket serverSocket;


  static final String dbURL =
    "jdbc:mysql://localhost/j2mebook?" +
    "user=j2meapps&password=bigsecret";


  public SkillsServer() throws ClassNotFoundException {
    Class.forName("org.gjt.mm.mysql.Driver");
  }


  public void acceptConnections() {


    try {
      serverSocket = new ServerSocket(port);
    }
```

```java
      catch (IOException e) {
        System.err.println("ServerSocket instantiation failure");
        e.printStackTrace();
        System.exit(0);
      }


    while (true) {
      try {
        Socket newConnection = serverSocket.accept();
        System.out.println("accepted connection");
        ServerThread st = new ServerThread(newConnection);
        new Thread(st).start();
      }
      catch (IOException ioe) {
        System.err.println("server accept failed");
      }
    }
  }

  public static void main(String args[]) {


    SkillsServer server = null;
    try {
      server = new SkillsServer();
    }
    catch (ClassNotFoundException e) {
      System.out.println("unable to load JDBC driver");
      e.printStackTrace();
      System.exit(1);
    }


    server.acceptConnections();
  }


class ServerThread implements Runnable {


  private Socket socket;
  private DataInputStream datain;
```

```java
    private DataOutputStream dataout;


    public ServerThread(Socket socket) {
      this.socket = socket;
    }


    public void run() {
      try {
        datain = new DataInputStream(new BufferedInputStream
          (socket.getInputStream()));
        dataout = new DataOutputStream(new BufferedOutputStream
          (socket.getOutputStream()));
      }
      catch (IOException e) {
        return;
      }
      byte[] ba = new byte[6];
      boolean conversationActive = true;
      while(conversationActive) {
        String skill = null;
        try {
          datain.read(ba,0,6);
          skill = new String(ba);
          if ((skill.length() == 1) &&
              (skill.toUpperCase().charAt(0) == 'Q')) {
            conversationActive = false;
          }
          else {
            System.out.println("requested skill = " + skill);
            String names = getNames(skill);
            System.out.println("names: " + names);
            System.out.println("writing " + names.length() + " bytes");
            dataout.write(names.getBytes(),0,names.length());
            dataout.write("\n".getBytes(),0,1);
            dataout.flush();
          }
        }
        catch (IOException ioe) {
          conversationActive = false;
        }
      }
      try {
```

```java
        System.out.println("closing socket");
        datain.close();
        dataout.close();
        socket.close();
      }
      catch (IOException e) {
      }
    }


  private String getNames(String skill) {
    String result = "None available";
    Connection conn = null;
    try {
      conn = DriverManager.getConnection(dbURL);


      Statement stmt = conn.createStatement();
      String query = "SELECT lastname, firstname " +
                     "FROM skills " + "WHERE skill = " +
                     "'" + skill.trim() + "'" +
                     " ORDER BY lastname";
      System.out.println("query = " + query);
      ResultSet rs = stmt.executeQuery(query);
      StringBuffer sb = new StringBuffer();
      while (rs.next()) {
        sb.append(rs.getString(1));
        sb.append(", ");
        sb.append(rs.getString(2));
        sb.append('$');
      }
      result = sb.toString();
    }
    catch (SQLException e) {
      System.out.println(e.getMessage());
      result = "server error";
    }
    finally {
      if (conn != null) {
        try {
          conn.close();
        }
        catch (SQLException e) {
        }
```

```
        }
      }
      return result;
    }
  }
}
```

Running the Second Skills Example

This example uses yet another database table, which you create by typing the command **\. cr_skills.sql** in the window in which the MySQL client is running. You can display a description of the table by typing **describe skills**. Type **select * from skills** to display the contents of the table. The table description and contents are shown here:

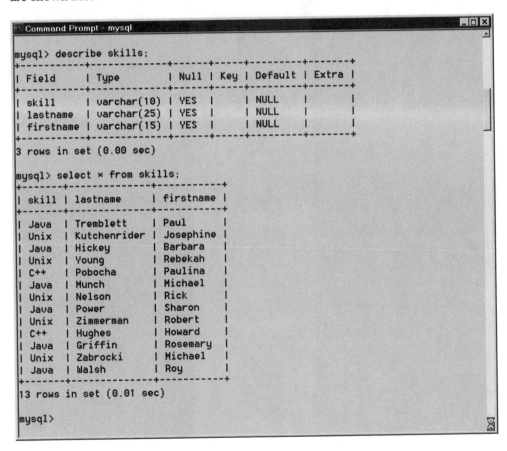

In a separate command prompt window, start the skills server by typing **java SkillsServer**.

Launch the MIDlet and enter a request for all employees who know the Java programming language. The request looks like this:

When you press OK, the MIDlet sends the request to the server, retrieves the list of candidates and displays it, as shown here:

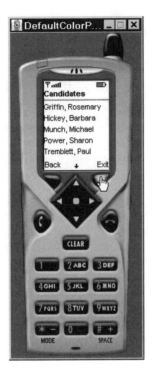

As in the previous example, you can observe the behavior of the server, as shown here:

```
Command Prompt - java SkillsServer

C:\OMH>java SkillsServer
accepted connection
requested skill = Java
query = SELECT lastname, firstname FROM skills WHERE skill = 'Java' ORDER BY las
tname
names: Griffin, Rosemary$Hickey, Barbara$Munch, Michael$Power, Sharon$Tremblett,
 Paul$Walsh, Roy$
writing 90 bytes
```

Obtaining Photos from a Server
\OMH\com\paulsjavabooks\instantj2me\Chapter13\PhotoClient.java

In this final scenario, put yourself in a position that finds you working in the Human Resources department of a very large company. As part of your job, you visit branch offices around the country and you find that it makes a good impression if you know ahead of time what people look like. You can't very well carry around an album containing tens of thousands of photos. Here's a solution that lets you spend a few minutes in the parking lot learning faces before going into the branch office. If you were discreet, you could even sneak a glance at a sign-in sheet being passed around at a meeting and match names to faces even if you have not met any of the attendees.

The MIDlet code looks like this:

```
/*
 * PhotoClient.java
 *
 * Created on October 1, 2001, 9:10 PM
 */


package com.paulsjavabooks.instantj2me.Chapter13;


import javax.microedition.midlet.*;
import javax.microedition.lcdui.*;


import javax.microedition.io.Connector;
import javax.microedition.io.StreamConnection;


import java.io.DataInputStream;
import java.io.DataOutputStream;
import java.io.InputStream;
import java.io.IOException;
import java.io.OutputStream;
/**
 *
 * @author  paul
 * @version
 */
public class PhotoClient extends javax.microedition.midlet.MIDlet
```

```
    implements CommandListener {


Display display;


private boolean commandAvailable;
private byte[] xmit;
CommandThread commandThread;

List menu;
Form inputForm;
Form outputForm;
TextField lastName;
TextField firstName;
ImageItem photo;

Command cmdBack;
Command cmdExit;
Command cmdOK;


private static final String URL =
  "socket://127.0.0.1:1929";


StreamConnection conn = null;
InputStream is = null;
OutputStream os = null;


public void startApp() {
  display = Display.getDisplay(this);


  inputForm = new Form(null);
  lastName = new TextField("Last Name",null,
    25, TextField.ANY);
  inputForm.append(lastName);
  firstName = new TextField("First Name",null,
    15, TextField.ANY);
  inputForm.append(firstName);
  cmdOK = new Command("OK",Command.SCREEN,1);
```

```java
    cmdExit = new Command("Exit",Command.EXIT,1);
    inputForm.addCommand(cmdOK);
    inputForm.addCommand(cmdExit);
    inputForm.setCommandListener(this);


    outputForm = new Form(null);
    photo = new ImageItem(null,null,ImageItem.LAYOUT_CENTER,"x");
    outputForm.append(photo);
    cmdBack = new Command("Back",Command.BACK,1);
    outputForm.addCommand(cmdBack);
    outputForm.addCommand(cmdExit);
    outputForm.setCommandListener(this);


    try {
      conn =
        (StreamConnection)Connector.open(URL,
          Connector.READ_WRITE, true);
      os = conn.openOutputStream();
      is = conn.openInputStream();


    }
    catch (Exception e) {
      //ALERT GOES HERE
      destroyApp(false);
      notifyDestroyed();
    }


    commandAvailable = false;
    commandThread = new CommandThread(this);
    commandThread.start();


    display.setCurrent(inputForm);
  }


  public void pauseApp() {
  }


  public void destroyApp(boolean unconditional) {
```

```
  try {
    os.write("Q".getBytes());
    conn.close();
  }
  catch (IOException e) {
  }
}


public void commandAction(Command cmd, Displayable d) {
  if (cmd == cmdExit) {
    destroyApp(false);
    notifyDestroyed();
  }
  else if (cmd == cmdBack) {
    lastName.setString(null);
    firstName.setString(null);
    display.setCurrent(inputForm);
  }
  else if (cmd == cmdOK)
    synchronized (this) {
      StringBuffer sb = new StringBuffer();
      sb.append(lastName.getString());
      sb.append(',');
      sb.append(firstName.getString());
      xmit = sb.toString().getBytes();
      commandAvailable = true;
      notify();
    }
}


class CommandThread extends Thread {
  MIDlet parent;


  boolean exit = false;


  public CommandThread(MIDlet parent) {
    this.parent = parent;
  }


  public void run() {
```

```java
      while (true) {
        synchronized(parent) {
          while(!commandAvailable) {
            try {
              parent.wait();
            }
            catch (InterruptedException e) {
            }
          }
          commandAvailable = false;
        }

        getImage();
      }
}


public void getImage() {
  try {
    os.write(xmit);
    os.flush();


    StringBuffer sb = new StringBuffer();
    int ch;
    while ((ch = is.read()) != -1) {
      if ((char)ch == '\n') {
        break;
      }
      sb.append((char)ch);
    }
    int len = Integer.parseInt(sb.toString());
    byte[] image = new byte[len];
    is.read(image,0,len);
    Image im = Image.createImage(image,0,len);
    photo.setImage(im);
    display.setCurrent(outputForm);
    //yield();
  }
  catch (NumberFormatException e) {
    System.out.println("nfe " + e.getMessage());
  }
  catch (Exception e) {
```

```
                System.out.println("exception " + e.getMessage());
        }
    }
  }
}
```

This client is functionally similar to the previous two, but instead of reading character data, it reads binary data into a byte array. It passes this byte array to the static `createImage` method of the `Image` class and displays the resulting image.

The Server
\OMH\PhotoServer.java

Here is the server code:

```
import java.io.BufferedInputStream;
import java.io.BufferedOutputStream;
import java.io.DataInputStream;
import java.io.DataOutputStream;
import java.io.File;
import java.io.FileInputStream;
import java.io.IOException;
import java.net.Socket;
import java.net.ServerSocket;


import java.sql.*;


public class PhotoServer {

  private int port = 1929;


  private ServerSocket serverSocket;


  static final String dbURL =
    "jdbc:mysql://localhost/j2mebook?" +
```

```java
    "user=j2meapps&password=bigsecret";


  public PhotoServer() throws ClassNotFoundException {
    Class.forName("org.gjt.mm.mysql.Driver");
  }


  public void acceptConnections() {


    try {
      serverSocket = new ServerSocket(port);
    }
    catch (IOException e) {
      System.err.println("ServerSocket instantiation failure");
      e.printStackTrace();
      System.exit(0);
    }


    while (true) {
      try {
        Socket newConnection = serverSocket.accept();
        System.out.println("accepted connection");
        ServerThread st = new ServerThread(newConnection);
        new Thread(st).start();
      }
      catch (IOException ioe) {
        System.err.println("server accept failed");
      }
    }
  }

  public static void main(String args[]) {


    PhotoServer server = null;
    try {
      server = new PhotoServer();
    }
```

```
    catch (ClassNotFoundException e) {
      System.out.println("unable to load JDBC driver");
      e.printStackTrace();
      System.exit(1);
    }


    server.acceptConnections();
}


class ServerThread implements Runnable {


  private Socket socket;
  private DataInputStream datain;
  private DataOutputStream dataout;


  public ServerThread(Socket socket) {
    this.socket = socket;
  }


  public void run() {
    try {
      datain = new DataInputStream(new BufferedInputStream
        (socket.getInputStream()));
      dataout = new DataOutputStream(new BufferedOutputStream
        (socket.getOutputStream()));
    }
    catch (IOException e) {
      return;
    }
    byte[] ba = new byte[50];
    boolean conversationActive = true;
    while(conversationActive) {
      String name = null;
      try {
        datain.read(ba,0,50);
```

```
        name = new String(ba);
        if ((name.length() == 1) &&
            (name.toUpperCase().charAt(0) == 'Q')) {
          conversationActive = false;
        }
        else {
          String fileName = getFileName(name.trim());
          byte[] ia = getImage(fileName);
          String sl = Integer.toString(ia.length) + "\n";
          System.out.println("sending length = " + sl);
          dataout.write(sl.getBytes(),0,sl.length());
          dataout.flush();
          System.out.println("sending " + ia.length + " bytes");
          dataout.write(ia,0,ia.length);
          dataout.flush();
          System.out.println("photo sent");
        }
      }
      catch (IOException ioe) {
        conversationActive = false;
      }
    }
    try {
      System.out.println("closing socket");
      datain.close();
      dataout.close();
      socket.close();
    }
    catch (IOException e) {
    }
  }


  private String getFileName(String name) {
    String fileName = "nophoto";
    Connection conn = null;
    try {
```

```java
            conn = DriverManager.getConnection(dbURL);


            Statement stmt = conn.createStatement();
            int ix = name.indexOf(",");
            String first = name.substring(ix + 1);
            String last = name.substring(0,ix);
            String query = "SELECT filename FROM photos " +
                           "WHERE lastname = '" + last + "'" +
                           " AND " +
                           "firstname = '" + first  + "'";
            System.out.println("query = " + query);
            ResultSet rs = stmt.executeQuery(query);
            if (rs.next()) {
              fileName = rs.getString(1);
            }
          }
        catch (SQLException e) {
          System.out.println("ERROR: " + e.getMessage());
          fileName = "error";
        }
        finally {
          if (conn != null) {
            try {
              conn.close();
            }
            catch (SQLException e) {
            }
          }
        }
        return fileName + ".png";
      }


    private byte[] getImage(String fname) {
      byte[] ba = new byte[0];
```

```
    try {
      File f = new File("c:\\OMH\\photos\\" + fname);
      ba = new byte[(int)f.length()];
      BufferedInputStream bis =
        new BufferedInputStream(new FileInputStream(f));
      int nb = bis.read(ba,0,ba.length);
      System.out.println("nb = " + nb);
      bis.close();
    }
    catch (IOException e) {
      System.out.println(e.getMessage());
    }
    finally {
      return ba;
    }
  }
}



  }
}
```

The server does the following:

▶   Listens on a port

▶   Accepts a connection

▶   Reads an employee name

▶   Uses JDBC to execute a SQL statement to retrieve the name of the file in which the employee's photo is stored

▶   Reads the contents of the file and transmits them to the client

Running the Photo Retrieval Example

Create the appropriate database table as you did in the two previous examples. The SQL is contained in file *cr_photos.sql*. The description and contents of the table look like this:

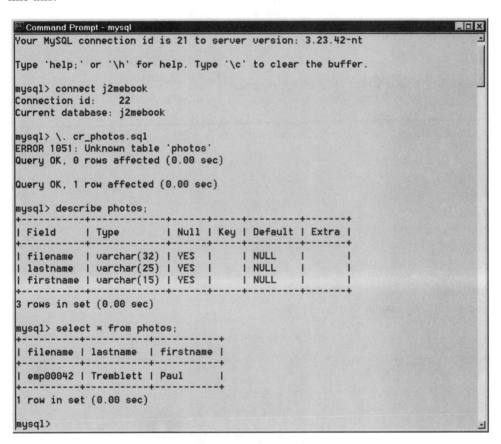

```
Command Prompt - mysql
Your MySQL connection id is 21 to server version: 3.23.42-nt

Type 'help;' or '\h' for help. Type '\c' to clear the buffer.

mysql> connect j2mebook
Connection id:    22
Current database: j2mebook

mysql> \. cr_photos.sql
ERROR 1051: Unknown table 'photos'
Query OK, 0 rows affected (0.00 sec)

Query OK, 1 row affected (0.00 sec)

mysql> describe photos;
+-----------+-------------+------+-----+---------+-------+
| Field     | Type        | Null | Key | Default | Extra |
+-----------+-------------+------+-----+---------+-------+
| filename  | varchar(32) | YES  |     | NULL    |       |
| lastname  | varchar(25) | YES  |     | NULL    |       |
| firstname | varchar(15) | YES  |     | NULL    |       |
+-----------+-------------+------+-----+---------+-------+
3 rows in set (0.00 sec)

mysql> select * from photos;
+----------+-----------+-----------+
| filename | lastname  | firstname |
+----------+-----------+-----------+
| emp00042 | Tremblett | Paul      |
+----------+-----------+-----------+
1 row in set (0.00 sec)

mysql>
```

Start the photo server by typing **java PhotoServer**.

Now start the MIDlet and enter an employee name, as shown here:

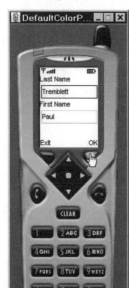

When you press OK, the MIDlet transmits the employee name to the server, retrieves the contents of the .PNG file containing the photo, creates an image and displays it. The display looks like this:

If you watch the window in which the server is running, you will see the following output:

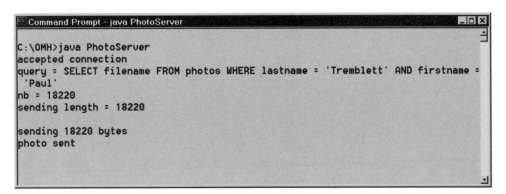

```
Command Prompt - java PhotoServer                                    _ □ ✕

C:\OMH>java PhotoServer
accepted connection
query = SELECT filename FROM photos WHERE lastname = 'Tremblett' AND firstname =
 'Paul'
nb = 18220
sending length = 18220

sending 18220 bytes
photo sent
```

The Detached Office

IN THIS CHAPTER:

A record store as a subset of a relational database

A practical use of a socket connection

A practical use of filters and comparators

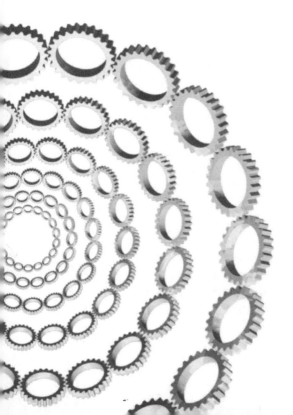

I n this chapter, we'll begin to combine some of the techniques we learned in the last chapter and in Chapter 10. We will use a socket connection to download a subset of a relational database from a server to a handheld device. After we have applied updates to the data, we will upload it to the server, which will update the database.

Taking Part of the Office with You

Imagine that your company is conducting a fundraiser for charity, and you have been assigned the task of visiting every branch office in each division to solicit contributions. As you receive contributions, you would like to update a database on one of the corporate servers, but you are concerned that you might not have adequate connectivity. We will now examine a MIDlet that might prove helpful. The source code is presented at the end of the chapter.

The MIDlet presents a menu that is an IMPLICIT List. If you select Download, the MIDlet displays a form containing a TextField into which you enter the number of the division you will be visiting next. The application opens a socket connection to a server and sends a request for all records from that division. The program running on the server uses the division number to construct a SQL query that selects the appropriate records from the database and sends these records over the socket connection to the MIDlet, which writes them to a RecordStore. It adds a single blank character to the beginning of each record.

If you select Update, the MIDlet reads each record from the RecordStore, extracts the branch number, and adds it to a list of branch office numbers that it displays as an IMPLICIT List. The enumerateRecords method used to obtain the records from the store takes as its second argument an instance of AlphaComparator, which implements RecordComparator. We have already discussed the RecordComparator interface in Chapter 10. This implementation sorts records into ascending alphabetical sequence. When you select a branch office from the list that is displayed, the MIDlet retrieves the record for that branch office from the store. The enumerateRecords method it uses to do this takes as its first argument an instance of BranchFilter. This inner class implements RecordFilter. Its constructor takes as an argument the branch office to be extracted. The matches method accepts a record only if it is for that branch office. When the record has been obtained from the store, a TextField containing the amount of the contributions from the branch office is displayed. You can update this amount and, when you dismiss the Form, the MIDlet uses the new amount from the `TextField` to update the record store. It changes the first character in the record to U to indicate that the record has been updated.

When you select Synchronize, the MIDlet uses the `enumerateRecords` method in conjunction with an instance of `AlteredFilter` to obtain all records that have been updated. It establishes a socket connection to the server and sends these records. The application on the server uses the information from the records to update the database.

The server application is also presented at the end of this chapter.

Running the Example

\OMH\cr_fundraiser.sql

Before running the example, you must create and populate the *fundraiser* database table using the file *cr_fundraiser.sql*.

The description of the *fundraiser* table and its contents are shown here:

```
Command Prompt - mysql                                               _ □ ×
+----------+----------+------+-----+---------+-------+
| Field    | Type     | Null | Key | Default | Extra |
+----------+----------+------+-----+---------+-------+
| division | char(5)  | YES  |     | NULL    |       |
| branch   | char(5)  | YES  |     | NULL    |       |
| amount   | int(11)  | YES  |     | NULL    |       |
+----------+----------+------+-----+---------+-------+
3 rows in set (0.00 sec)

mysql> select * from fundraiser;
+----------+--------+--------+
| division | branch | amount |
+----------+--------+--------+
| 10001    | 10201  |   1004 |
| 10001    | 20567  |   2304 |
| 10001    | 32324  |   1080 |
| 10001    | 30221  |   1220 |
| 20002    | 44546  |   2005 |
| 20002    | 55001  |   2430 |
| 20002    | 61198  |   2002 |
| 20002    | 77497  |   2800 |
+----------+--------+--------+
8 rows in set (0.00 sec)

mysql>
```

The next step is to start the server application by typing the command **java DB2RS**.

You can now launch the MIDlet. When you do so, the main menu is displayed as follows:

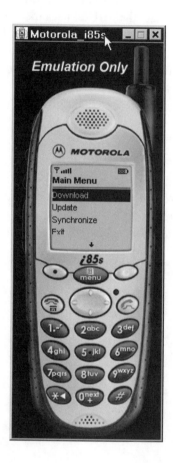

Select Download, and the MIDlet displays a request for the division number. Enter **10001** as shown here. Then press OK, and records for each branch office in Division 10001 are obtained from the database on the server.

Next, select Update from the main menu, and a list of branch offices like the one shown here is displayed:

Now select branch office 10201, and the current amount for the branch office is displayed. It looks like this:

Update the amount so that it now looks like this:

Finally, when you return to the office, start the MIDlet and select Synchronize. The MIDlet sends all updated records to the server, which updates the fundraiser table so that it now looks like this:

```
Command Prompt - mysql                                          _ □ X
mysql> select × from fundraiser;
+----------+--------+--------+
| division | branch | amount |
+----------+--------+--------+
| 10001    | 10201  | 1080   |
| 10001    | 20567  | 2304   |
| 10001    | 32324  | 1080   |
| 10001    | 30221  | 1220   |
| 20002    | 44546  | 2005   |
| 20002    | 55001  | 2430   |
| 20002    | 61198  | 2002   |
| 20002    | 77497  | 2800   |
+----------+--------+--------+
8 rows in set (0.00 sec)

mysql>
```

The above example is rather trivial, but could easily expanded to offload a greater variety of records containing a larger number of fields that you could carry with you. You can see that the concept of a detached office is quite feasible.

Code for the Detached Office

This section contains the listings for the MIDlet and the server application with which it communicates.

The Detached Office MIDlet

\OMH\com\paulsjavabooks\Chapter14\DetachedOffice.java

The code for the MIDlet component of the detached office application is shown here:

```
/*
 * DetachedOffice.java
 *
 * Created on November 2, 2001, 7:39 PM
 */
```

```
package com.paulsjavabooks.instantj2me.Chapter14;


import javax.microedition.midlet.*;
import javax.microedition.lcdui.*;
import javax.microedition.io.*;
import javax.microedition.rms.*;
import java.io.*;


/**
 *
 * @author  Paul Tremblett
 * @version 1.0
 */
public class DetachedOffice extends javax.microedition.midlet.MIDlet
    implements CommandListener {


  Display display;


  List mainMenu;
  List branchMenu;


  Form getDivision;
  TextField division;


  Form getAmount;
  StringItem branch;
  TextField amount;


  Form outputForm;

  Command cmdExit;
  Command cmdOK;


  Alert alert;

  private Command cmd;
```

```
    private Displayable displayable;


    private boolean commandAvailable;
    CommandThread commandThread;


    String uri = "socket://localhost:4004";

    RecordStore rs;


    int recID;
    String divisionValue;
    String branchValue;
    String amountValue;


    private static final int ID_DOWNLOAD    = 0;
    private static final int ID_UPDATE      = 1;
    private static final int ID_SYNCHRONIZE = 2;
    private static final int ID_EXIT        = 3;


    private final String RECORD_STORE_NAME = "DetachedOffice";

    public void startApp() {

      display = Display.getDisplay(this);


      mainMenu = new List("Main Menu",List.IMPLICIT);
      mainMenu.append("Download",null);
      mainMenu.append("Update",null);
      mainMenu.append("Synchronize",null);
      mainMenu.append("Exit",null);
      mainMenu.setCommandListener(this);


      getDivision = new Form("Input Division");
      division = new TextField("Division",null,5,TextField.NUMERIC);
      getDivision.append(division);
      cmdOK = new Command("OK",Command.SCREEN,1);
```

```
      getDivision.addCommand(cmdOK);
      cmdExit = new Command("Exit",Command.EXIT,1);
      getDivision.addCommand(cmdExit);
      getDivision.setCommandListener(this);


      getAmount = new Form("Input Amount");
      branch = new StringItem("Branch:",null);
      amount = new TextField("Amount",null,5,TextField.NUMERIC);
      getAmount.append(branch);
      getAmount.append(amount);
      getAmount.addCommand(cmdOK);
      getAmount.addCommand(cmdExit);
      getAmount.setCommandListener(this);


      outputForm = new Form("Date/Time");
      cmdExit = new Command("Exit",Command.EXIT,1);
      outputForm.addCommand(cmdExit);
      outputForm.setCommandListener(this);


      alert = new Alert(null);
      alert.setTimeout(Alert.FOREVER);

      commandAvailable = false;
      commandThread = new CommandThread(this);
      commandThread.start();


      display.setCurrent(mainMenu);
   }


public void pauseApp() {
}


public void destroyApp(boolean unconditional) {
}


public void commandAction(Command cmd, Displayable d) {
```

```
    if (cmd == cmdExit) {
      destroyApp(false);
      notifyDestroyed();
    }
    else {
      synchronized (this) {
        this.cmd = cmd;
        this.displayable = d;
        commandAvailable = true;
        notify();
      }
    }
}


class CommandThread extends Thread implements CommandListener {
  MIDlet parent;


  boolean exit = false;


  public CommandThread(MIDlet parent) {
    this.parent = parent;
  }


  public void run() {
    while (!exit) {
      synchronized(parent) {
        while(!commandAvailable) {
          try {
            parent.wait();
          }
          catch (InterruptedException e) {
          }
        }
        commandAvailable = false;
      }

      if (cmd == cmdOK) {
        if (displayable == getDivision) {
          download(division.getString());
```

```
        }
        else if (displayable == getAmount) {
          updateRecordStore(amount.getString());
        }
      }
      else if ((displayable == mainMenu) &&
               (cmd == List.SELECT_COMMAND)) {
        switch (mainMenu.getSelectedIndex()) {
          case ID_DOWNLOAD:
            display.setCurrent(getDivision);
            break;
          case ID_UPDATE:
            update();
            break;
          case ID_SYNCHRONIZE:
            upload();
            break;
          case ID_EXIT:
            exit = true;
        }
      }
    }
    destroyApp(false);
    notifyDestroyed();
  }

  public void commandAction(Command cmd, Displayable d) {
    if ((d == branchMenu) && (cmd == List.SELECT_COMMAND)) {
      displayBranchRecord(branchMenu.getSelectedIndex());
    }
  }


  public void download(String division) {
    StreamConnection conn = null;
    InputStreamReader reader = null;
    OutputStreamWriter writer = null;
    RecordStore rs = null;
    String alertText = null;
    try {
      conn = (StreamConnection)Connector.open(uri);
```

```
      reader = new InputStreamReader(conn.openInputStream());
      writer = new OutputStreamWriter(conn.openOutputStream());


      writer.write(Integer.toString(ID_DOWNLOAD) + "\n");
      writer.write(division + "\n");
      writer.flush();
      rs = loadTable(reader);
      if (rs == null) {
        alertText = "Table Load Failed";
      }
      else {
        alertText = "Table Loaded";
      }
    }
    catch (IOException e) {
    }
    finally {
      try {
        if (reader != null) {
          reader.close();
        }
        if (writer != null) {
          writer.close();
        }
        if (conn != null) {
          conn.close();
        }
      }
      catch (IOException e) {
      }
      if (rs != null) {
        try {
          rs.closeRecordStore();
        }
        catch (RecordStoreNotOpenException e) {
        }
        catch (RecordStoreException e) {
        }
      }
    }
    displayAlert(AlertType.INFO,"Table Loaded");
```

```java
    }


    private void displayBranchRecord(int index) {
      branchValue = branchMenu.getString(index);
      try {
        rs = RecordStore.openRecordStore(RECORD_STORE_NAME, false);
        BranchFilter filter = new BranchFilter(branchValue);
        RecordEnumeration enum =
          rs.enumerateRecords(filter,null,false);
        if (enum.hasNextElement()) {
          recID = enum.nextRecordId();
          String rec = new String(rs.getRecord(recID));
          int ix = rec.indexOf("\t");
          rec = rec.substring(ix+1);
          ix = rec.indexOf("\t");
          branch.setText(rec.substring(0,ix));
          amountValue = rec.substring(ix+1);
          amount.setString(amountValue);
          display.setCurrent(getAmount);
        }
      }
      catch (RecordStoreNotFoundException e) {
        displayAlert(AlertType.ERROR,"no local copy of database");
      }
      catch (RecordStoreException e) {
        displayAlert(AlertType.ERROR,"Error");
      }
      finally {
        try {
          if (rs != null) {
            rs.closeRecordStore();
          }
        }
        catch (RecordStoreNotOpenException e) {
        }
        catch (RecordStoreException e) {
        }
      }
    }


    private byte[] getReply(InputStreamReader rdr)
```

```
      throws IOException {
  StringBuffer sb = new StringBuffer();
  while (true) {
    int ch = rdr.read();
    if (ch == '\n') {
      break;
    }
    sb.append((char)ch);
  }
  return new String(sb).getBytes();
}

private String readLine(InputStreamReader rdr)
    throws IOException {
  StringBuffer sb = new StringBuffer();
  while (true) {
    int ch = rdr.read();
    if ((ch < 0) || (ch == '\n')) {
      break;
    }
    sb.append((char)ch);
  }
  return sb.toString();
}

private void displayAlert(AlertType t, String s) {
  alert.setType(t);
  alert.setString(s);
  display.setCurrent(alert, mainMenu);
}

public void update() {
  branchMenu = new List("Branches",List.IMPLICIT);
  branchMenu.setCommandListener(this);


  try {
    rs = RecordStore.openRecordStore(RECORD_STORE_NAME, false);
  }
  catch (RecordStoreNotFoundException e) {
    displayAlert(AlertType.ERROR,"No local database copy");
  }
  catch (RecordStoreException e) {
```

```java
      displayAlert(AlertType.ERROR,"Error");
    }
    try {
      AlphaComparator comparator = new AlphaComparator();
      RecordEnumeration enum =
        rs.enumerateRecords(null,comparator,false);
      while (enum.hasNextElement()) {
        String rec = new String(enum.nextRecord());
        int ix = rec.indexOf("\t");
        rec = rec.substring(ix+1);
        ix = rec.indexOf("\t");
        branchMenu.append(rec.substring(0,ix),null);
      }
      display.setCurrent(branchMenu);
    }
    catch (RecordStoreNotOpenException e) {
      displayAlert(AlertType.ERROR,"Error");
    }
    catch (InvalidRecordIDException e) {
      displayAlert(AlertType.ERROR,"Error");
    }
    catch (RecordStoreException e) {
      displayAlert(AlertType.ERROR,"Error");
    }
    finally {
      try {
        if (rs != null) {
          rs.closeRecordStore();
        }
      }
      catch (RecordStoreNotOpenException e) {
      }
      catch (RecordStoreException e) {
      }
    }
  }


  public void upload() {
    try {
      rs = RecordStore.openRecordStore(RECORD_STORE_NAME,false);
    }
    catch (RecordStoreNotFoundException e) {
```

```
      displayAlert(AlertType.ERROR,"No local copy of database");
  }
  catch (RecordStoreException e) {
    displayAlert(AlertType.ERROR,"Error");
  }
  StreamConnection conn = null;
  OutputStreamWriter writer = null;


  try {
    conn = (StreamConnection)Connector.open(uri);
    writer = new OutputStreamWriter(conn.openOutputStream());
    writer.write(Integer.toString(ID_SYNCHRONIZE) + "\n");
    AlteredFilter alteredFilter = new AlteredFilter();
    RecordEnumeration enum =
      rs.enumerateRecords(alteredFilter, null, false);
    while(enum.hasNextElement()) {
      String rec = new String(enum.nextRecord());
      writer.write(rec.substring(1) + "\n");
    }
    writer.write("\n");
    displayAlert(AlertType.INFO,"Table Synchronized");
  }
  catch (RecordStoreNotFoundException e) {
    displayAlert(AlertType.ERROR,"No Table");
  }
  catch (RecordStoreNotOpenException e) {
  }
  catch (InvalidRecordIDException e) {
  }
  catch (RecordStoreException e) {
  }
  catch (IOException e) {
  }
  finally {
    if (rs != null) {
      try {
        rs.closeRecordStore();
      }
      catch (RecordStoreNotOpenException e) {
      }
      catch (RecordStoreException e) {
      }
```

```
        }
      try {
        if (writer != null) {
          writer.close();
        }
        if (conn != null) {
          conn.close();
        }
      }
      catch (IOException e) {
      }
    }
  }


  private void updateRecordStore(String amount) {
    try {
      rs = RecordStore.openRecordStore(RECORD_STORE_NAME,false);
      String oldRec = new String(rs.getRecord(recID));
      int ix = oldRec.indexOf("\t");
      divisionValue = oldRec.substring(1,ix);
      String s = "U" + divisionValue + "\t" +
        branchValue + "\t" + amount;
      byte[] rec = s.getBytes();
      rs.setRecord(recID, rec,0,rec.length);
      display.setCurrent(mainMenu);
    }
    catch (RecordStoreNotOpenException e) {
      displayAlert(AlertType.ERROR,"Error");
    }
    catch (InvalidRecordIDException e) {
      displayAlert(AlertType.ERROR,"Error");
    }
    catch (RecordStoreException e) {
      displayAlert(AlertType.ERROR,"Error");
    }
    finally {
      try {
        if (rs != null) {
          rs.closeRecordStore();
        }
      }
```

```java
        catch (RecordStoreNotOpenException e) {
        }
        catch (RecordStoreException e) {
        }
      }
    }


    private RecordStore loadTable(InputStreamReader rdr)
        throws IOException {
      RecordStore rs = null;
      try {
        RecordStore.deleteRecordStore(RECORD_STORE_NAME);
      }
      catch (RecordStoreNotFoundException e) {
      }
      catch (RecordStoreException e) {
      }
      try {
        rs = RecordStore.openRecordStore(RECORD_STORE_NAME, true);
        while (true) {
          String record = readLine(rdr);
          if (record.length() == 0) {
            break;
          }
          StringBuffer sb = new StringBuffer(" ");
          sb.append(record);
          rs.addRecord(sb.toString().getBytes(),0,sb.length());
        }
      }
      catch (RecordStoreNotFoundException e) {
      }
      catch (RecordStoreFullException e) {
      }
      catch (RecordStoreException e) {
      }
      finally {
        return rs;
      }
    }
  }
```

```java
class BranchFilter implements RecordFilter {

  private String branch;

  public BranchFilter(String branch) {
    this.branch = branch;
  }

  public boolean matches(byte[] candidate) {
    String rec = new String(candidate);
    int ix = rec.indexOf("\t");
    rec = rec.substring(ix+1);
    ix = rec.indexOf("\t");
    return rec.substring(0,ix).equals(branch);
  }
}


class AlteredFilter implements RecordFilter {

  public boolean matches(byte[] candidate) {
    return ((char)candidate[0] == 'U');
  }
}


class AlphaComparator implements RecordComparator {
  public int compare(byte[] rec1, byte[] rec2) {
    int result;
    String s1 = new String(rec1);
    int ix = s1.indexOf("\t");
    s1 = s1.substring(ix+1);
    ix = s1.indexOf("\t");
    s1 = s1.substring(0,ix);
    String s2 = new String(rec2);
    ix = s2.indexOf("\t");
    s2 = s2.substring(ix+1);
    ix = s2.indexOf("\t");
    s2 = s2.substring(0,ix);
```

```
      int cr = s1.compareTo(s2);
      if (cr < 0)
        result = PRECEDES;
      else if (cr > 0)
        result = FOLLOWS;
      else result = EQUIVALENT;


      return result;
    }
  }
}
```

The Detached Office Server

\OMH\DB2RS.java

The server component of the detached office application is as follows:

```java
import java.io.InputStreamReader;
import java.io.OutputStreamWriter;
import java.io.BufferedReader;
import java.io.BufferedWriter;
import java.io.DataInputStream;
import java.io.DataOutputStream;
import java.io.IOException;
import java.net.Socket;
import java.net.ServerSocket;


import java.sql.*;


public class DB2RS {

  private int port = 4004;


  private ServerSocket serverSocket;


  static final String dbURL =
```

```java
    "jdbc:mysql://localhost/j2mebook?" +
    "user=j2meapps&password=bigsecret";


  private static final int ID_DOWNLOAD    = 0;
  private static final int ID_SYNCHRONIZE = 2;
  private static final int ID_EXIT        = 3;


  public DB2RS() throws ClassNotFoundException {
    Class.forName("org.gjt.mm.mysql.Driver");
  }


  public void acceptConnections() {


    try {
      serverSocket = new ServerSocket(port);
    }
    catch (IOException e) {
      System.err.println("ServerSocket instantiation failure");
      e.printStackTrace();
      System.exit(0);
    }


    while (true) {
      try {
        Socket newConnection = serverSocket.accept();
        ServerThread st = new ServerThread(newConnection);
        new Thread(st).start();
      }
      catch (IOException ioe) {
        System.err.println("server accept failed");
      }
    }
  }

  public static void main(String args[]) {


    DB2RS server = null;
```

```java
  try {
    server = new DB2RS();
  }
  catch (ClassNotFoundException e) {
    System.out.println("unable to load JDBC driver");
    e.printStackTrace();
    System.exit(1);
  }


  server.acceptConnections();
}


class ServerThread implements Runnable {


  private Socket socket;
  private BufferedReader datain;
  private BufferedWriter dataout;


  public ServerThread(Socket socket) {
    this.socket = socket;
  }


  public void run() {
    String line = null;
    try {
      datain = new BufferedReader(new InputStreamReader
        (socket.getInputStream()));
      dataout = new BufferedWriter(new OutputStreamWriter
        (socket.getOutputStream()));
    }
    catch (IOException e) {
      return;
    }
    byte[] ba = new byte[1024];
    int op = -1;
    try {
      line = datain.readLine();
      op = Integer.parseInt(line);
```

```
          switch (op) {
            case ID_DOWNLOAD:
              String division = datain.readLine();
              download(dataout, division);
              break;
            case ID_SYNCHRONIZE:
              synchronize(datain);
              break;
            default:
              break;
          }
          socket.close();
        }
      catch (IOException ioe) {
        }
    }


  private void synchronize(BufferedReader br)
      throws IOException {
    Connection dbConn = null;
    try {
        dbConn = DriverManager.getConnection(dbURL);


        String update = "UPDATE fundraiser SET amount =  " +
                        " ? WHERE division = ? AND " +
                        " branch = ?";
        PreparedStatement stmt =
          dbConn.prepareStatement(update);
        while (true) {
          String line = br.readLine();
          if (line.length() == 0) {
            break;
          }
          int ix = line.indexOf("\t");
          String division = line.substring(0,ix);
          line = line.substring(ix+1);
          ix = line.indexOf("\t");
          String branch = line.substring(0,ix);
          int amount = Integer.parseInt(line.substring(ix+1));
          stmt.setInt(1,amount);
          stmt.setString(2,division);
```

```java
        stmt.setString(3,branch);
        stmt.executeUpdate();
      }
    }
    catch (SQLException e) {
      System.out.println(e);
    }
    finally {
      if (dbConn != null) {
        try {
          dbConn.close();
        }
        catch (SQLException e) {
        }
      }
    }
  }
}


private void download(BufferedWriter bw, String division)
    throws IOException {
  Connection dbConn = null;
  try {
    dbConn = DriverManager.getConnection(dbURL);


    Statement stmt = dbConn.createStatement();
    String query = "SELECT * " +
                   "FROM fundraiser " + "WHERE division = " +
                   "'" + division + "'";
    ResultSet rs = stmt.executeQuery(query);
    while (rs.next()) {
      StringBuffer sb = new StringBuffer();
      sb.append(rs.getString(1));
      sb.append("\t");
      sb.append(rs.getString(2));
      sb.append("\t");
      sb.append(rs.getString(3));
      sb.append('\n');
      dataout.write(sb.toString());
    }
    dataout.write("\n");
    dataout.flush();
```

```
      }
      catch (SQLException e) {
        System.out.println(e.getMessage());
      }
      finally {
        if (dbConn != null) {
          try {
            dbConn.close();
          }
          catch (SQLException e) {
          }
        }
      }
    }
  }
}
```

Advanced Networking

IN THIS CHAPTER:

The HttpConnection interface

A GET request

URL encoding

ContentConnection

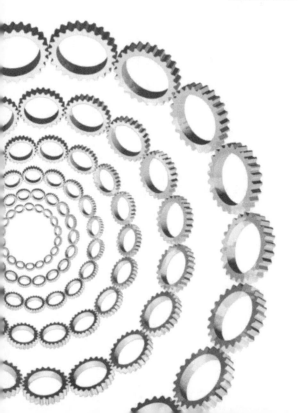

You now know how to use the *Connection* interface to write MIDlets that can act as clients to server applications that use the socket mechanism. Unfortunately, the server applications that use this mechanism are for the most part legacy applications. When you set out to develop a client application these days, you almost assume it will be HTTP-based. As a matter of fact, HTTP is so dominant that designers of the MID profile decided that this would be the only protocol that is mandated. The specification states "MIDP implementations MUST provide support for accessing HTTP 1.1 servers and services."

The Generic Connection Framework from the CLDC provides the base stream and content interfaces. The interface *HttpConnection* provides the additional functionality needed to set request headers, parse response headers, and perform other HTTP-specific functions.

In this chapter, we will develop several applications that use the *HttpConnection* interface.

The *HttpConnection* Interface

The *HttpConnection* interface provides the methods and constants required for an HTTP connection. HTTP is a request/response protocol in which the parameters of the request must be set before the request is sent. An HTTP connection can exist in one of the following three states:

▶ **Setup**   A connection to the server has not yet been made.
▶ **Connected**   A connection has been made, request parameters have been sent, and a response is expected.
▶ **Closed**   The connection has been closed.

The state of the connection defines the methods that may be invoked. If a method is invoked that is not valid according to the present state, an exception is thrown. Certain methods cause a transition to another state. Table 15-1 shows each state, the methods permitted in that state, and whether they cause a transition to another state.

State	Allowable Method	State After Call
Setup	setRequestMethod	Setup
Setup	setRequestProperty	Setup
Setup	openInputStream	Connected
Setup, Connected	openOutputStream	Connected
Setup	openDataInputStream	Connected
Setup, Connected	openDataOutputStream	Connected
Setup, Connected	getLength	Connected
Setup, Connected	getType	Connected
Setup, Connected	getEncoding	Connected
Setup, Connected	getHeaderField	Connected
Setup, Connected	getResponseCode	Connected
Setup, Connected	getResponseMessage	Connected
Setup, Connected	getHeaderFieldInt	Connected
Setup, Connected	getHeaderFieldDate	Connected
Setup, Connected	getExpiration	Connected
Setup, Connected	getDate	Connected
Setup, Connected	getLastModified	Connected
Setup, Connected	getHeaderField	Connected
Setup, Connected	getHeaderFieldKey	Connected
Connected	close	Closed
Connected	getRequestMethod	Connected
Connected	getRequestProperty	Connected
Connected	getURL	Connected
Connected	getProtocol	Connected
Connected	getHost	Connected
Connected	getFile	Connected
Connected	getRef	Connected
Connected	getPort	Connected
Connected	getQuery	Connected
Closed	No methods permitted. All methods will throw IOException.	Closed

Table 15-1   *HttpConnection States and Methods*

Local Weather

If you have a web-enabled cellular phone, chances are you've already used it to check the weather. Most likely, it used the Wireless Application Protocol (WAP). Let's see how to do the same using a MIDlet.

The Client

\OMH\com\paulsjavabooks\instantj2me\Chapter15\LocalWeather.java

Here is the code for the MIDlet that acts as a client:

```
/*
 * LocalWeather.java
 *
 * Created on October 15, 2001, 6:16 PM
 */

package com.paulsjavabooks.instantj2me.Chapter15;

import javax.microedition.midlet.*;
import javax.microedition.lcdui.*;

import javax.microedition.io.Connector;
import javax.microedition.io.StreamConnection;
import javax.microedition.io.HttpConnection;

import java.io.DataInputStream;
import java.io.DataOutputStream;
import java.io.InputStream;
import java.io.IOException;
import java.io.OutputStream;

/**
 *
 * @author  paul tremblett
 * @version 1.0
 */
public class LocalWeather extends javax.microedition.midlet.MIDlet
    implements CommandListener {

  Display display;
```

```
private boolean commandAvailable;
CommandThread commandThread;

Form inputForm;
Form outputForm;
TextField postalCode;
StringItem localWeather;

Command cmdBack;
Command cmdExit;
Command cmdOK;

private static final String URL =
  "http://localhost/J2MEBOOK/servlet/WeatherServlet?postalCode=";

public void startApp() {
  display = Display.getDisplay(this);

  inputForm = new Form("Postal Code");
  postalCode = new TextField("Postal Code",null,
    7, TextField.ANY);
  inputForm.append(postalCode);
  cmdOK = new Command("OK",Command.SCREEN,1);
  cmdExit = new Command("Exit",Command.EXIT,1);
  inputForm.addCommand(cmdOK);
  inputForm.addCommand(cmdExit);
  inputForm.setCommandListener(this);

  outputForm = new Form("Local Weather");
  localWeather = new StringItem(null,null);
  outputForm.append(localWeather);
  cmdBack = new Command("Back",Command.BACK,1);
  outputForm.addCommand(cmdBack);
  outputForm.addCommand(cmdExit);
  outputForm.setCommandListener(this);

  commandAvailable = false;
  commandThread = new CommandThread(this);
  commandThread.start();

  display.setCurrent(inputForm);
}
```

```
public void pauseApp() {
}

public void destroyApp(boolean unconditional) {
}

public void commandAction(Command cmd, Displayable d) {
  if (cmd == cmdExit) {
    destroyApp(false);
    notifyDestroyed();
  }
  else if (cmd == cmdBack) {
    postalCode.setString(null);
    display.setCurrent(inputForm);
    localWeather.setText(null);
  }
  else if (cmd == cmdOK)
    synchronized (this) {
      commandAvailable = true;
      notify();
    }
}

class CommandThread extends Thread {
  MIDlet parent;

  boolean exit = false;

  public CommandThread(MIDlet parent) {
    this.parent = parent;
  }

  public void run() {
    while (true) {
      synchronized(parent) {
        while(!commandAvailable) {
          try {
            parent.wait();
          }
          catch (InterruptedException e) {
          }
        }
        commandAvailable = false;
```

```
      }
      getWeather();
    }
  }

  public void getWeather() {
    HttpConnection conn = null;
    InputStream is = null;
    OutputStream os = null;
    byte[] receivedData = null;
    try {
      StringBuffer sb = new StringBuffer(URL);
      sb.append(urlEncode(postalCode.getString()));
      conn =
        (HttpConnection)Connector.open(sb.toString());
      conn.setRequestMethod(HttpConnection.GET);
      conn.setRequestProperty("User-Agent",
        "Profile/MIDP-1.0 Configuration/CLDC-1.0");
      conn.setRequestProperty("Content-type",
        "application/x-www-form-urlencoded");
      is = conn.openInputStream();
      String contentType = conn.getType();
      int len = (int)conn.getLength();
      if (len > 0) {
        receivedData = new byte[len];
        int nb = is.read(receivedData);
      }
      else {
        receivedData = new byte[1024];
        int ch;
        len = 0;
        while ((ch = is.read()) != -1) {
          receivedData[len++] = (byte)ch;
        }
      }
      localWeather.setText(new String(receivedData,0,len));
      display.setCurrent(outputForm);
    }
    catch (IOException e) {
      System.out.println(e.getMessage());
      e.printStackTrace();
    }
    finally {
```

```java
      try {
        if (is != null) {
          is.close();
        }
        if (os != null) {
          os.close();
        }
        if (conn != null) {
          conn.close();
        }
      }
      catch (IOException e) {
      }
    }
  }

  private String urlEncode(String s) {
    StringBuffer sb = new StringBuffer();

    for (int i = 0; i < s.length(); ++i) {
      switch (s.charAt(i)) {
        case ' ':
          sb.append("%20");
          break;
        case '+':
          sb.append("%2b");
          break;
        case '\'':
          sb.append("%27");
          break;
        case '<':
          sb.append("%3c");
          break;
        case '>':
          sb.append("%3e");
          break;
        case '#':
          sb.append("%23");
          break;
        case '%':
          sb.append("%25");
          break;
        case '{':
```

```
            sb.append("%7b");
            break;
        case '}':
            sb.append("%7d");
            break;
        case '\\':
            sb.append("%5c");
            break;
        case '^':
            sb.append("%5e");
            break;
        case '~':
            sb.append("%73");
            break;
        case '[':
            sb.append("%5b");
            break;
        case ']':
            sb.append("%5d");
            break;
        default:
            sb.append(s.charAt(i));
            break;
        }
      }
    return sb.toString();
    }
  }
}
```

This example sends the equivalent of an HTML form. Forms are sent using either the GET, POST, or HEAD request. In this chapter, we will use GET. Data in a GET request is sent as NAME=VALUE pairs and is concatenated to the URL following a ? delimiter.

In response to the user pressing OK, the MIDlet invokes the getWeather method. This method constructs the complete URL by concatenating the value it extracts from the TextField named postalCode.

If this URL were used exactly as is, it could be problematic. The rules for writing a URL state restrict the allowable characters in the URL to a subset of the ASCII character set. The blank character is not one of the valid characters, so if postalCode held a Canadian postal code such as A2A 1M7, the blank in the fourth position would not be allowed. The solution consists of replacing all characters outside the subset with a sequence consisting of the % character followed by a two-character hexadecimal representation of the character to be transmitted. The urlEncode method, inefficient as it might be, performs this substitution. You can see that A2A 1M7 becomes A2A%201M7.

After the URL has been encoded, it is passed to the open method of the Connector class. The Connection that is returned is cast to an HttpConnection object.

At this point, the connection is in the setup state. The setRequestMethod is invoked to set the request type to GET. Next, a call to setRequestProperty sets the User-Agent field in the request header to "Profile/MIDP-1.0 Configuration/CLDC-1.0." Server-side applications often use this field to determine capabilities of a browser. Even though you are not likely to find any applications that look for values other than those that identify Internet Explorer or Netscape, you can expect that this will change, so even though the value you specify for User-Agent is free form, it is wise to use a String like the one used in this example. A second call to setRequestProperty sets the Content-type header field to "application/x-www- form-urlencoded."

Next, the openInputStream method is invoked. As shown in Table 15-1, this causes the HttpConnection to transition to the connected state. The request is sent to the server and a response is sent back. The getLength method, which is inherited from ContentConnection, is then called. If the response header contains a content-length field, this method returns its value as an integer; otherwise, it returns –1. If the length is available, it is used to read the response data using a single call to the read method. If the length is not available, the read method is called repetitively to retrieve one byte at a time from the input stream until the method returns –1, indicating that no more data is available.

After the response data has been retrieved from the input stream, it is converted to a String, which is used to set the value of a StringItem, which is displayed.

The Server

\OMH\WeatherServlet.java

You already know from J2EE that server-side processing of HTTP requests is done using servlets and/or Java Server Pages. The MIDP specification clearly states that the Internet server *must not* be required to know either that non-IP networks are being used or the characteristics of these networks. In other words, on the server side, it should be business as usual. The following servlet, which is indistinguishable from others you have already seen, proves that:

```java
import java.io.*;
import java.text.*;
import java.util.*;
import javax.servlet.*;
import javax.servlet.http.*;

import java.sql.*;

public class WeatherServlet extends HttpServlet {

  static final String dbURL =
    "jdbc:mysql://localhost/j2mebook?" +
    "user=j2meapps&password=bigsecret";

  public void doGet(HttpServletRequest request,
                    HttpServletResponse response)
      throws IOException, ServletException {

    Connection conn = null;

    String nextJSP = null;

    try {
      Class.forName("org.gjt.mm.mysql.Driver");
    }
    catch (ClassNotFoundException e) {
      throw new ServletException("Unable to load JDBC driver");
    }

    try {
      String postalCode =
        (String)request.getParameter("postalCode");

      conn = DriverManager.getConnection(dbURL);

      Statement stmt = conn.createStatement();
      String query = "SELECT city, stateprovince, weather " +
                     "FROM localweather " + "WHERE postalcode = '" +
                     postalCode + "'";
      ResultSet rs = stmt.executeQuery(query);
      if (rs.next()) {
        request.setAttribute ("city", rs.getString(1));
        request.setAttribute ("stateprovince", rs.getString(2));
```

```
      request.setAttribute ("weather", rs.getString(3));
      nextJSP = "/ReportWeather.jsp";
    }
    else {
      nextJSP = "/NoWeatherAvailable.jsp";
    }
    conn.close();
    ServletConfig config = getServletConfig();
    ServletContext context = config.getServletContext();
    RequestDispatcher rd = context.getRequestDispatcher(nextJSP);
    rd.forward(request, response);
  }
  catch (SQLException e) {
    throw new ServletException("SQL call failed");
  }
  catch (Exception e) {
    throw new ServletException(e.getMessage());
  }
  finally {
    if (conn != null) {
      try {
        conn.close();
      }
      catch (SQLException e) {
        throw new ServletException("connection close failed");
      }
    }
  }
}
}
```

The request from the client is handled by the doGet method, which does the following:

► Loads the class containing the JDBC driver
► Uses the getParameter method to obtain the postal code
► Establishes a database connection
► Uses the value of the postal code to construct a SQL query
► Issues the query

▶ If the query is successful, invokes `getString` against the `ResultSet` returned by the query to obtain the weather, the city, and the state or province and uses these to set the city, stateprovince, and weather attributes in the request header

▶ Forwards the request to ReportWeather.jsp or NoWeatherAvailable.jsp

Running the Example

\OMH\cr_localweather.sql

Normally, the database table that contains the weather would be populated by a daemon process. For this example, you can use the file *cr_localweather.sql* to create the table and populate it with data for two postal codes.

When you launch the MIDlet and enter a postal code, you see this display:

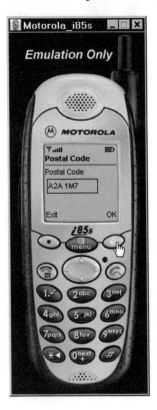

When you press OK, the request is sent to the server, and the response is displayed, as shown here:

Using HttpConnection to Query a Skills Database

In Chapter 13, you queried a skills database using a socket connection. Here's an example that queries the same database using an HttpConnection. Unlike the earlier example, which accepted a single skill as input, this example allows the user to specify multiple skills.

The Client

\OMH\com\paulsjavabooks\instantj2me\Chapter15\SkillsClient2.java

Here is the client code:

```java
/*
 * SkillsClient2.java
 *
 * Created on October 15, 2001, 6:53 PM
 */

package com.paulsjavabooks.instantj2me.Chapter15;

import javax.microedition.midlet.*;
import javax.microedition.lcdui.*;

import javax.microedition.io.Connector;
import javax.microedition.io.StreamConnection;
import javax.microedition.io.HttpConnection;

import java.io.DataInputStream;
import java.io.DataOutputStream;
import java.io.InputStream;
import java.io.IOException;
import java.io.OutputStream;

/**
 *
 * @author  paul tremblett
 * @version 1.0
 */
public class SkillsClient2 extends javax.microedition.midlet.MIDlet
    implements CommandListener {

  Display display;

  private boolean commandAvailable;
  CommandThread commandThread;

  Form inputForm;
  Form outputForm;
  ChoiceGroup skills;
  StringItem candidates;

  Command cmdBack;
  Command cmdExit;
  Command cmdOK;
```

```java
private static final String URL_BASE =
  "http://localhost/J2MEBOOK/servlet/SkillsServlet?";

private static final String[] skillList =
  {"Java","C++","Unix"};

public void startApp() {
  display = Display.getDisplay(this);

  inputForm = new Form("Skills Search");
  skills = new ChoiceGroup("Skill", Choice.MULTIPLE);
  for (int i = 0; i < skillList.length; ++i) {
    skills.append(skillList[i],null);
  }
  inputForm.append(skills);
  cmdOK = new Command("OK",Command.SCREEN,1);
  cmdExit = new Command("Exit",Command.EXIT,1);
  inputForm.addCommand(cmdOK);
  inputForm.addCommand(cmdExit);
  inputForm.setCommandListener(this);

  outputForm = new Form("Candidates");
  candidates = new StringItem(null,null);
  outputForm.append(candidates);
  cmdBack = new Command("Back",Command.BACK,1);
  outputForm.addCommand(cmdBack);
  outputForm.addCommand(cmdExit);
  outputForm.setCommandListener(this);

  commandAvailable = false;
  commandThread = new CommandThread(this);
  commandThread.start();

  display.setCurrent(inputForm);
}


public void pauseApp() {
}

public void destroyApp(boolean unconditional) {
}
```

```
public void commandAction(Command cmd, Displayable d) {
  if (cmd == cmdExit) {
    destroyApp(false);
    notifyDestroyed();
  }
  else if (cmd == cmdBack) {
    for (int i = 0; i < skills.size(); ++i) {
      skills.setSelectedIndex(i, false);
    }
    display.setCurrent(inputForm);
  }
  else if (cmd == cmdOK)
    synchronized (this) {
      commandAvailable = true;
      notify();
    }
}

class CommandThread extends Thread {
  MIDlet parent;

  boolean exit = false;

  public CommandThread(MIDlet parent) {
    this.parent = parent;
  }

  public void run() {
    while (true) {
      synchronized(parent) {
        while(!commandAvailable) {
          try {
            parent.wait();
          }
          catch (InterruptedException e) {
          }
        }
        commandAvailable = false;
      }

      getCandidates();
    }
  }
```

```
public void getCandidates() {
  HttpConnection conn = null;
  InputStream is = null;
  OutputStream os = null;
  byte[] receivedData = null;
  try {
    StringBuffer sb = new StringBuffer();
    int sz = skills.size();
    boolean[] selectedArray = new boolean[sz];
    int nsel = skills.getSelectedFlags(selectedArray);
    boolean first = true;
    for (int i = 0; i < sz; ++i) {
      if (selectedArray[i]) {
        if (first) {
          first = false;
        }
        else {
          sb.append('&');
        }
        sb.append("skills=");
        sb.append(skills.getString(i));
      }
    }
    String url = URL_BASE + urlEncode(sb.toString());
    conn = (HttpConnection)Connector.open(url);
    conn.setRequestMethod(HttpConnection.GET);
    conn.setRequestProperty("User-Agent",
      "Profile/MIDP-1.0 Configuration/CLDC-1.0");
    conn.setRequestProperty("Content-type",
      "application/x-www-form-urlencoded");
    is = conn.openInputStream();
    String contentType = conn.getType();
    int len = (int)conn.getLength();
    if (len > 0) {
      receivedData = new byte[len];
      int nb = is.read(receivedData);
    }
    else {
      receivedData = new byte[1024];
      int ch;
      len = 0;
      while ((ch = is.read()) != -1) {
        receivedData[len++] = (byte)ch;
```

```
        }
      }
      candidates.setText(new String(receivedData,0,len));
      display.setCurrent(outputForm);
    }
    catch (IOException e) {
      System.out.println(e.getMessage());
      e.printStackTrace();
    }
    finally {
      try {
        if (is != null) {
          is.close();
        }
        if (os != null) {
          os.close();
        }
        if (conn != null) {
          conn.close();
        }
      }
      catch (IOException e) {
      }
    }
  }

  private String urlEncode(String s) {
    StringBuffer sb = new StringBuffer();

    for (int i = 0; i < s.length(); ++i) {
      switch (s.charAt(i)) {
        case ' ':
          sb.append("%20");
          break;
        case '+':
          sb.append("%2b");
          break;
        case '\'':
          sb.append("%27");
          break;
        case '<':
          sb.append("%3c");
          break;
```

```
                    case '>':
                      sb.append("%3e");
                      break;
                    case '#':
                      sb.append("%23");
                      break;
                    case '%':
                      sb.append("%25");
                      break;
                    case '{':
                      sb.append("%7b");
                      break;
                    case '}':
                      sb.append("%7d");
                      break;
                    case '\\':
                      sb.append("%5c");
                      break;
                    case '^':
                      sb.append("%5e");
                      break;
                    case '~':
                      sb.append("%73");
                      break;
                    case '[':
                      sb.append("%5b");
                      break;
                    case ']':
                      sb.append("%5d");
                      break;
                    default:
                      sb.append(s.charAt(i));
                      break;
                }
              }
          return sb.toString();
        }
      }
    }
```

This MIDlet is similar to the previous one. The user interface allows selection of multiple skills by passing `Choice.MULTIPLE` as the type to the `ChoiceGroup`'s constructor. The `getSelectedFlags` method is used to determine which of the elements of the `ChoiceGroup` the user selected. This method returns an array of `boolean`s and for each element in the array that has a value of `true`, the `getString` method is called to obtain the skill. A URL suitable for use with GET is constructed repeating the skills=skillvalue pairs as many times as necessary to include all the skills the user selected. Each pair is separated by the & character. As in the previous example, the URL is encoded before it is sent to the server.

The Server
\OMH\SkillsServlet.java

The servlet that processes the request looks like this:

```java
import java.io.*;
import java.text.*;
import java.util.*;
import javax.servlet.*;
import javax.servlet.http.*;

import java.sql.*;

public class SkillsServlet extends HttpServlet {

    static final String dbURL =
        "jdbc:mysql://localhost/j2mebook?" +
        "user=j2meapps&password=bigsecret";

    public void doGet(HttpServletRequest request,
                      HttpServletResponse response)
        throws IOException, ServletException {

        Connection conn = null;

        String nextJSP = null;

        try {
            Class.forName("org.gjt.mm.mysql.Driver");
```

```
      }
      catch (ClassNotFoundException e) {
        throw new ServletException("Unable to load JDBC driver");
      }

      try {
        String[] skills = request.getParameterValues("skills");

        conn = DriverManager.getConnection(dbURL);

        Statement stmt = conn.createStatement();

        String baseQuery = "SELECT lastname, firstname " +
                      "FROM skills " + "WHERE skill IN (";

        StringBuffer sb = new StringBuffer(baseQuery);
        for (int i = 0; i < skills.length; ++i) {
          sb.append('\'');
          sb.append(skills[i]);
          sb.append('\'');
          if ((i +1) < skills.length) {
            sb.append(",");
          }
        }
        sb.append(") ORDER BY lastname");
        String query = sb.toString();

        ResultSet rs = stmt.executeQuery(query);
        nextJSP = "/ReportCandidates.jsp";
        sb = new StringBuffer();
        while (rs.next()) {
          sb.append(rs.getString(1));
          sb.append(',');
          sb.append(rs.getString(2));
          sb.append('\n');
        }
        if (sb.length() > 0) {
```

```
        request.setAttribute("candidateList",sb.toString());
      }
      else {
        nextJSP = "/NoCandidates.jsp";
      }
      conn.close();
      ServletConfig config = getServletConfig();
      ServletContext context = config.getServletContext();
      RequestDispatcher rd = context.getRequestDispatcher(nextJSP);
      rd.forward(request, response);
    }
    catch (SQLException e) {
      throw new ServletException("SQL call failed");
    }
    catch (Exception e) {
      throw new ServletException(e.getMessage());
    }
    finally {
      if (conn != null) {
        try {
          conn.close();
        }
        catch (SQLException e) {
          throw new ServletException("connection close failed");
        }
      }
    }
  }
}
```

This servlet is almost identical to the weather servlet.

Running the Example

Unless you skipped Chapter 13, you have already created the database table. If you haven't, you should do so now.

When you launch the MIDlet and select the desired skills, it displays a screen like the one shown here:

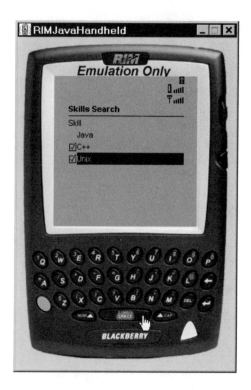

When you press OK, the candidates who match the requested skills are displayed as follows:

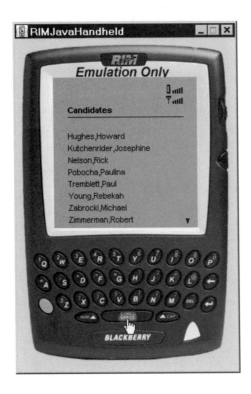

Order Status

The following example is yet another web-based version of an example from
Chapter 13. It retrieves the status of an order.

The Client

\OMH\com\paulsjavabooks\instantj2me\Chapter15\OrderStatusClient2.java

Here is the client MIDlet:

```
/*
 * OrderStatusClient2.java
 *
 * Created on October 15, 2001, 6:20 PM
 */
```

```java
package com.paulsjavabooks.instantj2me.Chapter15;

import javax.microedition.midlet.*;
import javax.microedition.lcdui.*;

import javax.microedition.io.Connector;
import javax.microedition.io.StreamConnection;
import javax.microedition.io.HttpConnection;

import java.io.DataInputStream;
import java.io.DataOutputStream;
import java.io.InputStream;
import java.io.IOException;
import java.io.OutputStream;

/**
 *
 * @author  paul tremblett
 * @version 1.0
 */
public class OrderStatusClient2 extends
javax.microedition.midlet.MIDlet implements CommandListener {

  Display display;

  private boolean commandAvailable;
  CommandThread commandThread;

  Form inputForm;
  Form outputForm;
  TextField orderNumber;
  StringItem orderStatus;

  Command cmdBack;
  Command cmdExit;
  Command cmdOK;

  private static final String URL =
    "http://localhost/J2MEBOOK/servlet/OrderStatusServlet" +
    "?orderNumber=";

  public void startApp() {
```

```
      display = Display.getDisplay(this);

      inputForm = new Form("Order Number");
      orderNumber = new TextField("Order Number",null,
        7, TextField.NUMERIC);
      inputForm.append(orderNumber);
      cmdOK = new Command("OK",Command.SCREEN,1);
      cmdExit = new Command("Exit",Command.EXIT,1);
      inputForm.addCommand(cmdOK);
      inputForm.addCommand(cmdExit);
      inputForm.setCommandListener(this);

      outputForm = new Form("Order Status");
      orderStatus = new StringItem(null,null);
      outputForm.append(orderStatus);
      cmdBack = new Command("Back",Command.BACK,1);
      outputForm.addCommand(cmdBack);
      outputForm.addCommand(cmdExit);
      outputForm.setCommandListener(this);

      commandAvailable = false;
      commandThread = new CommandThread(this);
      commandThread.start();

      display.setCurrent(inputForm);
    }


public void pauseApp() {
}

public void destroyApp(boolean unconditional) {
}

public void commandAction(Command cmd, Displayable d) {
  if (cmd == cmdExit) {
    destroyApp(false);
    notifyDestroyed();
  }
  else if (cmd == cmdBack) {
    orderNumber.setString(null);
```

```java
      display.setCurrent(inputForm);
      orderStatus.setText(null);
    }
    else if (cmd == cmdOK)
      synchronized (this) {
        commandAvailable = true;
        notify();
      }
  }

class CommandThread extends Thread {
  MIDlet parent;

  boolean exit = false;

  public CommandThread(MIDlet parent) {
    this.parent = parent;
  }

  public void run() {
    while (true) {
      synchronized(parent) {
        while(!commandAvailable) {
          try {
            parent.wait();
          }
          catch (InterruptedException e) {
          }
        }
        commandAvailable = false;
      }

      getOrderStatus();
    }
  }

  public void getOrderStatus() {
    HttpConnection conn = null;
    InputStream is = null;
    OutputStream os = null;
    byte[] receivedData = null;
    try {
      StringBuffer sb = new StringBuffer(URL);
```

```
    sb.append(orderNumber.getString());
    conn =
      (HttpConnection)Connector.open(sb.toString());
    conn.setRequestMethod(HttpConnection.GET);
    conn.setRequestProperty("User-Agent",
      "Profile/MIDP-1.0 Configuration/CLDC-1.0");
    conn.setRequestProperty("Content-type",
      "application/x-www-form-urlencoded");
    is = conn.openInputStream();
    String contentType = conn.getType();
    int len = (int)conn.getLength();
    if (len > 0) {
      receivedData = new byte[len];
      int nb = is.read(receivedData);
    }
    else {
      receivedData = new byte[1024];
      int ch;
      len = 0;
      while ((ch = is.read()) != -1) {
        receivedData[len++] = (byte)ch;
      }
    }
    orderStatus.setText(new String(receivedData,0,len));
    display.setCurrent(outputForm);
}
catch (IOException e) {
  System.out.println(e.getMessage());
  e.printStackTrace();
}
finally {
  try {
    if (is != null) {
      is.close();
    }
    if (os != null) {
      os.close();
    }
    if (conn != null) {
      conn.close();
    }
  }
  catch (IOException e) {
```

```
            }
          }
        }
      }
    }
```

The Server

\OMH\OrderStatusServer.java

Here is the servlet that process the request:

```java
import java.io.*;
import java.text.*;
import java.util.*;
import javax.servlet.*;
import javax.servlet.http.*;

import java.sql.*;

public class OrderStatusServlet extends HttpServlet {

  static final String dbURL =
    "jdbc:mysql://localhost/j2mebook?" +
    "user=j2meapps&password=bigsecret";

  public void doGet(HttpServletRequest request,
                    HttpServletResponse response)
      throws IOException, ServletException {

    Connection conn = null;

    String nextJSP = null;

    try {
      Class.forName("org.gjt.mm.mysql.Driver");
    }
    catch (ClassNotFoundException e) {
      throw new ServletException("Unable to load JDBC driver");
    }
```

```
try {
  String orderNumber = request.getParameter("orderNumber");

  conn = DriverManager.getConnection(dbURL);

  Statement stmt = conn.createStatement();

  String query = "SELECT status, dateplaced, shipdate " +
                 "FROM orders " + "WHERE ordernumber = '" +
                 orderNumber + "'";

  ResultSet rs = stmt.executeQuery(query);
  if (rs.next()) {
    request.setAttribute("orderNumber", orderNumber);
    request.setAttribute ("status", rs.getString(1));
    request.setAttribute ("datePlaced", rs.getString(2));
    String shipDate = rs.getString(3);
    if (shipDate == null) {
      shipDate = "***";
    }
    request.setAttribute ("shipDate", shipDate);
    nextJSP = "/ReportOrderStatus.jsp";
  }
  else {
    nextJSP = "/OrderNotFound.jsp";
  }
  conn.close();
  ServletConfig config = getServletConfig();
  ServletContext context = config.getServletContext();
  RequestDispatcher rd = context.getRequestDispatcher(nextJSP);
  rd.forward(request, response);
}
catch (SQLException e) {
  throw new ServletException("SQL call failed");
}
catch (Exception e) {
  throw new ServletException(e.getMessage());
}
finally {
```

```
     if (conn != null) {
       try {
         conn.close();
       }
       catch (SQLException e) {
         throw new ServletException("connection close failed");
       }
     }
   }
 }
}
```

Running the Example

The required database table should already be created. If it is not, create it now as shown in Chapter 13.

When you launch the MIDlet and enter an order number, the display looks like this:

When you press OK, the status of the order is displayed, as shown here:

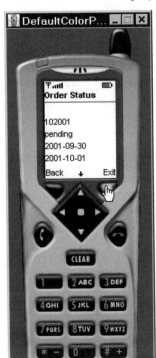

Signature Verifier

Imagine that each weekend you operate a booth at a year-round flea market. You use a phone line to validate credit cards, but you have learned from experience that checks can present a problem. Then you learn of a subscription service that will accept as input the bank number and name from a check and transmit back the signature that the bank has on file for the individual. This can be compared to the one on a check You decide that even though this can't guarantee that sufficient funds are available to cover the check, at least it can provide you with some assurance that the person who signed the check is the person whose name is imprinted on it. You at least will have a way to contact the person if the check bounces.

The service is web-based, so you could access it using a browser, but you don't want to set up a computer in a booth that you use only on weekends and you don't want to carry a laptop. Let's see how a handheld device running a MIDlet could help.

The Client

\OMH\com\paulsjavabooks\instantj2me\Chapter15\SignatureVerifier.java

Here is the code for a signature verification MIDlet:

```java
/*
 * SignatureVerifier.java
 *
 * Created on October 15, 2001, 9:47 PM
 */


package com.paulsjavabooks.instantj2me.Chapter15;

import javax.microedition.midlet.*;
import javax.microedition.lcdui.*;

import javax.microedition.io.Connector;
import javax.microedition.io.ContentConnection;

import java.io.InputStream;

/**
 *
 * @author  paul tremblett
 * @version 1.0
 */
public class SignatureVerifier extends javax.microedition.midlet.MIDlet
    implements CommandListener {

  Display display;

  private boolean commandAvailable;
  CommandThread commandThread;

  Form inputForm;
  Form outputForm;
  TextField bankNumber;
  TextField firstName;
  TextField lastName;

  ImageItem signature;
```

```java
Command cmdBack;
Command cmdExit;
Command cmdOK;

private static final String URL_BASE =
  "http://localhost/J2MEBOOK/signatures/";

public void startApp() {
  display = Display.getDisplay(this);

  inputForm = new Form(null);
  bankNumber = new TextField("Bank #", null,
    6,TextField.NUMERIC);
  inputForm.append(bankNumber);
  lastName = new TextField("Last Name",null,
    25, TextField.ANY);
  inputForm.append(lastName);
  firstName = new TextField("First Name",null,
    15, TextField.ANY);
  inputForm.append(firstName);
  cmdOK = new Command("OK",Command.SCREEN,1);
  cmdExit = new Command("Exit",Command.EXIT,1);
  inputForm.addCommand(cmdOK);
  inputForm.addCommand(cmdExit);
  inputForm.setCommandListener(this);

  outputForm = new Form(null);
  signature = new ImageItem(null,null,ImageItem.LAYOUT_CENTER,"x");
  outputForm.append(signature);
  cmdBack = new Command("Back",Command.BACK,1);
  outputForm.addCommand(cmdBack);
  outputForm.addCommand(cmdExit);
  outputForm.setCommandListener(this);

  commandAvailable = false;
  commandThread = new CommandThread(this);
  commandThread.start();

  display.setCurrent(inputForm);
}


public void pauseApp() {
```

```
    }

    public void destroyApp(boolean unconditional) {
    }

    public void commandAction(Command cmd, Displayable d) {
      if (cmd == cmdExit) {
        destroyApp(false);
        notifyDestroyed();
      }
      else if (cmd == cmdBack) {
        bankNumber.setString(null);
        lastName.setString(null);
        firstName.setString(null);
        signature.setImage(null);
        display.setCurrent(inputForm);
      }
      else if (cmd == cmdOK)
        synchronized (this) {
          commandAvailable = true;
          notify();
        }
    }


    class CommandThread extends Thread {
      MIDlet parent;

      boolean exit = false;

      public CommandThread(MIDlet parent) {
        this.parent = parent;
      }

      public void run() {
        while (true) {
          synchronized(parent) {
            while(!commandAvailable) {
              try {
                parent.wait();
              }
              catch (InterruptedException e) {
              }
```

```
      }
      commandAvailable = false;
    }

    getSignature();
  }
}

public void getSignature() {
  byte[] signatureData = null;
  int signatureLength = 0;
  try {
    ContentConnection c = null;
    InputStream is = null;
    try {
      StringBuffer sb = new StringBuffer();
      sb.append(bankNumber.getString());
      sb.append("_");
      sb.append(firstName.getString().toLowerCase());
      sb.append("_");
      sb.append(lastName.getString().toLowerCase());
      sb.append(".png");
      String url = URL_BASE + sb.toString();
      c = (ContentConnection)Connector.open(url);
      is = c.openInputStream();
      int len = (int)c.getLength();
      if (len > 0) {
        signatureData = new byte[len];
        signatureLength = is.read(signatureData);
      }
      else {
        int bufferLength = 2048;
        signatureData = new byte[bufferLength];
        int ch;
        while ((ch = is.read()) != -1) {
          signatureData[signatureLength] = (byte)ch;
          ++signatureLength;
          if (signatureLength  == bufferLength) {
            bufferLength += 2048;
            byte[] temp = new byte[bufferLength];
            for (int i = 0; i < signatureLength; ++i) {
              temp[i] = signatureData[i];
            }
```

```
            signatureData = temp;
          }
        }
      }
    }
    finally {
      if (is != null) {
        is.close();
      }
      if (c != null) {
        c.close();
      }
    }
    Image im = Image.createImage(signatureData,0,signatureLength);
    signature.setImage(im);
    display.setCurrent(outputForm);
    //yield();
  }
  catch (NumberFormatException e) {
   System.out.println("nfe " + e.getMessage());
  }
  catch (Exception e) {
    System.out.println("exception " + e.getMessage());
  }
  }
 }
}
```

This MIDlet obtains a `ContentConnection`. The `HttpConnection` you used earlier is actually a subinterface of `ContentConnection` that adds the methods and constants required to handle request headers. In this example, since only a simple request for an image is sent, the header information is unnecessary and so a `ContentConnection` can be used. The code that obtains the `ContentConnection` is as follows:

```
    c = (ContentConnection)Connector.open(url);
```

The URL is formed by concatenating its base portion, http://localhost/ J2MEBOOK/signatures, and the filename, which is formed from the bank number, last name, and first name. As was the case with the connections you have already seen, you obtain the connection by passing the URL to the static method open of class Connector. The Connection that is returned is cast to a ContentConnection object.

As its name implies, the *ContentConnection* interface is used to handle content. Invoking the getContentLength method gets the length, which is used to read the entire contents of the data stream. In this case, the contents are the bytes comprising a PNG file that contains the requested signature as an image. The byte array containing the image data is used to create an ImageItem object, which is then displayed.

Running the Example

The only server software that is involved is the Web server, so you must make sure it is started. When you launch the MIDlet and enter data into the appropriate TextFields, the display looks like this:

When you press OK, the request is sent to the Web server and the content that is returned is used to create an image, which is displayed, as shown here:

Only a portion of the signature is visible and you must scroll to view other portions, but you can indeed compare the displayed signature to the one on a check you are about to accept.

IN THIS CHAPTER:

A simple login
Using MD5 to add security
Maintaining a session

A ccess to the web-based examples you developed up to this point is unrestricted. In many cases, this is not acceptable. You would surely use a browser to view and/or alter sensitive data such as that contained in your bank account only if you were absolutely certain that you were the only person who could access such data. Controlled access usually involves a login procedure that requires the user to enter a user ID and a password known only to the user. In this chapter, we will examine two MIDlets that transmit login information to a servlet. The servlet uses JDBC to compare these to values stored in a database table and permits subsequent access only when a match occurs.

A Simple Login

The first example is a no-frills login. We will discuss its shortcomings after we use it.

The Client

\OMH\com\paulsjavabooks\instantj2me\Chapter16\Login.java

The MIDlet that implements the no-frills login is shown here:

```
/*
 * Login.java
 *
 * Created on October 9, 2001, 10:04 PM
 */

package com.paulsjavabooks.instantj2me.Chapter16;

import javax.microedition.midlet.*;
import javax.microedition.lcdui.*;

import javax.microedition.io.Connector;
import javax.microedition.io.HttpConnection;
import javax.microedition.io.StreamConnection;

import java.io.DataInputStream;
import java.io.DataOutputStream;
import java.io.InputStream;
import java.io.IOException;
import java.io.OutputStream;
```

```
/**
 *
 * @author  paul tremblett
 * @version 1.0
 */
public class Login extends javax.microedition.midlet.MIDlet
    implements CommandListener {

  Display display;

  boolean commandAvailable;
  String idPassword;
  CommandThread commandThread;

  Form inputForm;
  Form outputForm;

  TextField userid;
  TextField password;

  StringItem response;

  Command cmdExit;
  Command cmdOK;

  public void startApp() {
    display = Display.getDisplay(this);

    inputForm = new Form(null);
    userid = new TextField("User",null,
      25, TextField.ANY);
    inputForm.append(userid);
    password = new TextField("Password",null,
      15, TextField.PASSWORD);
    inputForm.append(password);
    cmdOK = new Command("OK",Command.SCREEN,1);
    cmdExit = new Command("Exit",Command.EXIT,1);
    inputForm.addCommand(cmdOK);
    inputForm.addCommand(cmdExit);
    inputForm.setCommandListener(this);

    outputForm = new Form(null);
```

```java
      response = new StringItem(null,null);
      outputForm.append(response);
      outputForm.addCommand(cmdExit);
      outputForm.setCommandListener(this);

      commandAvailable = false;
      commandThread = new CommandThread(this);
      commandThread.start();

      display.setCurrent(inputForm);
  }

public void pauseApp() {
}

public void destroyApp(boolean unconditional) {
}

public void commandAction(Command cmd, Displayable d) {
   if (cmd == cmdExit) {
     destroyApp(false);
     notifyDestroyed();
   }
   else if (cmd == cmdOK)
     synchronized (this) {
     commandAvailable = true;
     notify();
   }
}


class CommandThread extends Thread {
   MIDlet parent;

   boolean exit = false;

   public CommandThread(MIDlet parent) {
     this.parent = parent;
   }

   public void run() {
     while (true) {
       synchronized(parent) {
```

```java
      while(!commandAvailable) {
        try {
          parent.wait();
        }
        catch (InterruptedException e) {
        }
      }
      commandAvailable = false;
    }

    performLogin();
  }
}

public void performLogin() {
  HttpConnection conn = null;
  InputStream is = null;
  OutputStream os = null;
  byte[] receivedData = null;
  try {
    String url =
      "http://localhost/J2MEBOOK/servlet/LoginServlet";
    conn = (HttpConnection)Connector.open(url);
    conn.setRequestMethod(HttpConnection.POST);
    conn.setRequestProperty("User-Agent",
      "Profile/MIDP-1.0 Configuration/CLDC-1.0");
    conn.setRequestProperty("Content-type",
      "application/x-www-form-urlencoded");
    byte[] postData = createPostData();
    // In the current version of J2ME, when Content-length
    // is set using setRequestProperty(), the length is
    // sometimes transmitted as two numbers separated by
    // commas. This causes the servletcontainer to throw a
    // NumberFormatException
    //conn.setRequestProperty("Content-length",
    //   Integer.toString(postData.length));
    os = conn.openOutputStream();
    os.write(postData);
    // In the current version of J2MEWTK, flush() sometimes
    // throws an exception. Since the openInputStream() that
    // follows flushes the buffer, flush() is commented out
    //os.flush();
    is = conn.openInputStream();
```

```java
        String contentType = conn.getType();
        int len = (int)conn.getLength();
        if (len > 0) {
          receivedData = new byte[len];
          int nb = is.read(receivedData);
        }
        else {
          receivedData = new byte[1024];
          int ch;
          len = 0;
          while ((ch = is.read()) != -1) {
            receivedData[len++] = (byte)ch;
          }
        }
        response.setText(new String(receivedData,0,len));
        display.setCurrent(outputForm);
      }
      catch (IOException e) {
        System.out.println(e.getMessage());
        e.printStackTrace();
      }
      finally {
        try {
          if (is != null) {
            is.close();
          }
          if (os != null) {
            os.close();
          }
          if (conn != null) {
            conn.close();
          }
        }
        catch (IOException e) {
        }
      }
    }

    public byte[] createPostData() {
      StringBuffer sb = new StringBuffer();
      sb.append("userid=");
      sb.append(userid.getString());
      sb.append("&password=");
```

```
      sb.append(password.getString());
System.out.println("sb = <" + sb.toString() + ">");
      return sb.toString().getBytes();
    }

  }
}
```

The initial screen that is presented contains two fields into which the user enters a user ID and a password. To prevent a malicious onlooker from observing the password, the `TextField` is created as type `TextField.PASSWORD`.

After the user enters the appropriate data, the `performLogin` method is invoked. This method creates an `HttpConnection` using the URL for the servlet that will process the login request. Unlike earlier examples, which used the GET method, this example uses the POST method. A POST request is transmitted as two blocks of data. The first block contains the header information and is transmitted when the `open` method is invoked against the connection's output stream. The second block contains data pairs that take the form NAME=VALUE with each pair being separated by an & character. In the present case, the data to be transmitted is a `byte` array constructed by the `createPostData` method and transmitted to the servlet by invoking the `write` method against the connection's output stream. It takes the form userid=xxxxxxxx&password=pppppppp.

After the `performLogin` method transmits the data, it accepts the response and displays it.

NOTE

The J2MEWTK used to develop the examples is an early release that occasionally does not behave as expected. The code contains comments pointing out where this has been shown to be the case.

The Server

\OHM\LoginServlet.java

The servlet that handles the login request looks like this:

```
import java.io.*;
import java.text.*;
import java.util.*;
import javax.servlet.*;
import javax.servlet.http.*;
```

```java
import java.sql.*;

public class LoginServlet extends HttpServlet {

  static final String dbURL =
    "jdbc:mysql://localhost/j2mebook?" +
    "user=j2meapps&password=bigsecret";

  public void doPost(HttpServletRequest request,
                     HttpServletResponse response)
      throws IOException, ServletException {

    Connection conn = null;

    String nextJSP = null;

    try {
      Class.forName("org.gjt.mm.mysql.Driver");
    }
    catch (ClassNotFoundException e) {
      throw new ServletException("Unable to load JDBC driver");
    }

    try {
      String userid = (String)request.getParameter("userid");
      String password = (String)request.getParameter("password");

      conn = DriverManager.getConnection(dbURL);

      Statement stmt = conn.createStatement();
      String query = "SELECT firstname, lastname " +
                     "FROM users " + "WHERE userid = '" +
                     userid + "' AND password ='" +
                     password + "'";
      ResultSet rs = stmt.executeQuery(query);
      if (rs.next()) {
        StringBuffer fullName = new StringBuffer();
        fullName.append(rs.getString(1));
```

```
        fullName.append(" ");
        fullName.append(rs.getString(2));
        request.setAttribute ("fullName", fullName.toString());
        nextJSP = "/LoginOK.jsp";
      }
      else {
        nextJSP = "/LoginFailed";
      }
      conn.close();
      ServletConfig config = getServletConfig();
      ServletContext context = config.getServletContext();
      RequestDispatcher rd = context.getRequestDispatcher(nextJSP);
      rd.forward(request, response);
    }
    catch (SQLException e) {
      throw new ServletException("SQL call failed");
    }
    catch (Exception e) {
      throw new ServletException(e.getMessage());
    }
    finally {
      if (conn != null) {
        try {
          conn.close();
        }
        catch (SQLException e) {
          throw new ServletException("connection close failed");
        }
      }
    }
  }

  public void doGet(HttpServletRequest request,
                    HttpServletResponse response)
      throws IOException, ServletException {
    doPost(request, response);
  }
}
```

A request received by the servlet is processed by the doPost method. It first loads the class file *org.gjt.mm.mysql.Driver* that contains the JDBC driver. Two invocations of the getParameter method against the HttpRequest object passing "userid" and "password" as parameters retrieve the user ID and password. After a connection to the database is established by the getConnection method, a SQL query is constructed using the values obtained for using the values obtained for user ID and password.

If a non-empty ResultSet is returned by this query, the values entered for user ID and password are correct and the user's full name is extracted from the appropriate columns of the ResultSet and assigned as the value of the "fullName" attribute of the request using the setAttribute method. The variable nextJSP is assigned a value of "/LoginOK.jsp."

If the ResultSet returned by the query is empty, no user ID and password pair matching the one entered exists in the database. In this case, the variable nextJSP is assigned a value of "/LoginFailed."

The RequestDispatcher object is used to forward the request to the appropriate JSP, which sends the result back to the user.

\OMH\LoginOK.jsp

The code for *LoginOK.jsp* looks like this:

```
<%response.setContentType("text/plain");%>
Welcome <%= (request.getAttribute("fullName"))%>
```

\OMH\LoginFailed.jsp

The code for *LoginFailed.jsp* is as follows:

```
<%response.setContentType("text/plain");%>
Login failed!
```

Running the Example

\OMH\cr_users.sql

Before you run the example, you must create the database table that contains the users and their passwords. A file that creates and populates this table with one user is provided on the CD.

You execute this SQL by typing the command **.\cr_users.sql**. The table looks like this:

```
Command Prompt - mysql                                                    _ □ X
ERROR 1051: Unknown table 'users'
Query OK, 0 rows affected (0.00 sec)

Query OK, 1 row affected (0.00 sec)

mysql> describe users;
+-----------+-------------+------+-----+---------+-------+
| Field     | Type        | Null | Key | Default | Extra |
+-----------+-------------+------+-----+---------+-------+
| userid    | varchar(8)  | YES  |     | NULL    |       |
| password  | varchar(25) | YES  |     | NULL    |       |
| firstname | varchar(15) | YES  |     | NULL    |       |
| lastname  | varchar(25) | YES  |     | NULL    |       |
+-----------+-------------+------+-----+---------+-------+
4 rows in set (0.00 sec)

mysql> select * from users;
+--------+-------------+-----------+----------+
| userid | password    | firstname | lastname |
+--------+-------------+-----------+----------+
| jenny  | divine_ms_m | Jennifer  | Malnick  |
+--------+-------------+-----------+----------+
1 row in set (0.00 sec)

mysql> _
```

After you make sure that Apache and Tomcat have been started, launch the MIDlet. After you have entered **jenny** as a user ID and **divine_ms_m** as a password, the display looks like this:

NOTE

The version of J2MEWTK that was used to develop the examples in the book does not execute this MIDlet properly if the Default Color Phone or Default Gray Phone emulator is selected. Use the i85s emulator instead.

Since the `TextField` into which you typed the password was created as type `TextField.PASSWORD`, the value is displayed as asterisks. When you press OK, the `performLogin` method creates a POST request containing the login parameters and sends it to the servlet. When the servlet determines that the ID/password pair is valid, it sets the attribute `fullName` in the request to the name it retrieved from the database and forwards the request to *LoginOK.jsp*. The text that is output by this Java Server Page is received by the MIDlet and looks like this when displayed:

Since the sole purpose of this example is to demonstrate the login process, the only action available is Exit.

Protecting the Password Using MD5

The first login example was relatively easy to code, but it has a serious flaw. The password was hidden from prying eyes as it was typed, but is visible during transmission. But aren't all packets transmitted by devices such as pagers, cellular phones, and PDAs encrypted? As a rule, they are, but such encryption only applies when communication is with a device that can perform the appropriate decryption. The fact that you ran the previous example and observed that the servlet used the data exactly as it was received shows that the data was cleartext.

One solution to this security flaw involves the following steps:

1. The initial transmission from the MID to the servlet does not include the user ID and password, but rather, a simple notification that the MIDlet wishes to perform a login.

2. The servlet generates a token that it saves for future use and sends back to the requesting program.

3. The MIDlet accepts the password from the user, concatenates it to the token, and computes a message digest. Message digests are secure one-way hash functions that take arbitrary-size data and output a fixed-length hash value. The MIDlet transmits the user ID and the hash value, which can be safely transmitted because it is one-way and so the original text cannot be derived from it if it is intercepted.

4. When the servlet receives the user ID and hash, it retrieves the password corresponding to the user ID from the database, concatenates it to the token that it saved earlier, computes a message digest, and compares it to the message digest received from the MIDlet. If the two match, the password was correct.

The fact that the servlet applies the token from the initial request to data received in a subsequent request implies a session. You are already familiar with servlets and know that the `HttpSession` object is used to identify a user across more than one page request or visit to a web site and to store information about the user. Two mechanisms a server uses to maintain session are cookies and rewriting URLs. In this example, we will show how a MIDlet can use cookies it receives from a servlet.

The Client

\OMH\com\paulsjavabooks\instantj2me\Chapter16\MD5Login.java

Here is the code for a MIDlet that performs a login and, if the login is successful, conducts a session with the servlet:

```
/*
 * MD5Login.java
 *
 * Created on October 9, 2001, 10:04 PM
 */

package com.paulsjavabooks.instantj2me.Chapter16;

import javax.microedition.midlet.*;
import javax.microedition.lcdui.*;

import javax.microedition.io.Connector;
import javax.microedition.io.ContentConnection;
```

```java
import javax.microedition.io.StreamConnection;
import javax.microedition.io.HttpConnection;

import java.io.DataInputStream;
import java.io.DataOutputStream;
import java.io.InputStream;
import java.io.IOException;
import java.io.OutputStream;

import java.util.Vector;

import com.paulsjavabooks.instantj2me.crypto.*;

/**
 *
 * @author  paul tremblett
 * @version 1.0
 */
public class MD5Login extends javax.microedition.midlet.MIDlet
    implements CommandListener {

  Display display;

  boolean commandAvailable;
  CommandThread commandThread;
  Command cmd;

  Form loginForm;
  TextField userid;
  TextField password;

  Form counterForm;
  StringItem response;

  Command cmdExit;
  Command cmdOK;
  Command cmdNext;

  Vector cookies;
  String token;

  public void startApp() {
    display = Display.getDisplay(this);
```

```java
      loginForm = new Form(null);
      userid = new TextField("User",null,
        25, TextField.ANY);
      loginForm.append(userid);
      password = new TextField("Password",null,
        15, TextField.PASSWORD);
      loginForm.append(password);
      cmdOK = new Command("OK",Command.OK,1);
      cmdExit = new Command("Exit",Command.EXIT,1);
      loginForm.addCommand(cmdOK);
      loginForm.addCommand(cmdExit);
      loginForm.setCommandListener(this);

      counterForm = new Form(null);
      cmdNext = new Command("Next",Command.SCREEN,1);
      response = new StringItem(null,null);
      counterForm.append(response);
      counterForm.addCommand(cmdNext);
      counterForm.addCommand(cmdExit);
      counterForm.setCommandListener(this);

      commandAvailable = false;
      commandThread = new CommandThread(this);
      commandThread.start();

      token = getLoginToken();
      display.setCurrent(loginForm);
    }

    public void pauseApp() {
    }

    public void destroyApp(boolean unconditional) {
    }

    public void commandAction(Command cmd, Displayable d) {
      if (cmd == cmdExit) {
        destroyApp(false);
        notifyDestroyed();
      }
      else {
        synchronized (this) {
```

```
        this.cmd = cmd;
        commandAvailable = true;
        notify();
      }
    }
  }
  public String getLoginToken() {

    String tokenString = null;

    HttpConnection conn = null;
      InputStream is = null;
      OutputStream os = null;
      byte[] receivedData = null;
      try {
        String url =
          "http://localhost/J2MEBOOK/Login.jsp";
        conn = (HttpConnection)Connector.open(url);
        conn.setRequestProperty("User-Agent",
          "Profile/MIDP-1.0 Configuration/CLDC-1.0");
        conn.setRequestProperty("Content-type",
          "application/x-www-form-urlencoded");
        os = conn.openOutputStream();
        // In the current release of J2MEWTK, the behavior of
        // flush() is not predictable. It sometimes throws an
        // exception. Since the openInputStream(O) method that
        // follows it flushes the output stream, the flush()
        // method has been commented out
        //os.flush();
        is = conn.openInputStream();
        int headerFieldIndex = 0;
        cookies = new Vector();
        while (true) {
          String headerName = conn.getHeaderField(headerFieldIndex);
          if (headerName == null) {
            break;
          }
          String headerFieldKey = conn.getHeaderFieldKey(headerFieldIndex);
          ++headerFieldIndex;
          String hklc = headerFieldKey.toLowerCase();
          if (hklc.indexOf("cookie") < 0) {
            continue;
```

```
        }
        int scx = headerName.indexOf(';');
        String cookieValue;
        if (scx >= 0) {
          cookieValue = headerName.substring(0,scx);
        }
        else {
          cookieValue = headerName;
        }
        cookies.addElement(cookieValue);
      }

      String contentType = conn.getType();
      int len = (int)conn.getLength();
      if (len > 0) {
        receivedData = new byte[len];
        int nb = is.read(receivedData);
      }
      else {
        receivedData = new byte[1024];
        int ch;
        len = 0;
        while ((ch = is.read()) != -1) {
          receivedData[len++] = (byte)ch;
        }
      }
    tokenString = new String(receivedData,0,len).trim();
    }
    catch (IOException e) {
      e.printStackTrace();
    }
    catch (Exception e) {
      e.printStackTrace();
    }
    finally {
      try {
        if (is != null) {
          is.close();
        }
        if (os != null) {
          os.close();
        }
        if (conn != null) {
```

```
        conn.close();
      }
    }
    catch (IOException e) {
      e.printStackTrace();
    }
  }
  return tokenString.substring(tokenString.indexOf(':')+1);
}

class CommandThread extends Thread {
  MIDlet parent;

  boolean exit = false;

  public CommandThread(MIDlet parent) {
    this.parent = parent;
  }

  public void run() {
    while (true) {
      synchronized(parent) {
        while(!commandAvailable) {
          try {
            parent.wait();
          }
          catch (InterruptedException e) {
          }
        }
        commandAvailable = false;
      }
      if (cmd == cmdOK) {
        sendLogin();
      }
      else if (cmd == cmdNext) {
        visitCounter();
      }
    }
  }
}

public void sendLogin() {
  HttpConnection conn = null;
```

```
InputStream is = null;
OutputStream os = null;
byte[] receivedData = null;
try {
  String url =
    "http://localhost/J2MEBOOK/servlet/MD5LoginServlet";
  conn = (HttpConnection)Connector.open(url);
  conn.setRequestMethod(HttpConnection.POST);
  conn.setRequestProperty("User-Agent",
    "Profile/MIDP-1.0 Configuration/CLDC-1.0");
  conn.setRequestProperty("Content-type",
    "application/x-www-form-urlencoded");
  if (cookies.size() > 0) {
    StringBuffer sb = new StringBuffer();
    for (int i = 0; i < cookies.size(); ++i) {
      sb.append((String)cookies.elementAt(i));
      if ((i + 1) < cookies.size()) {
        sb.append("; ");
      }
    }
    conn.setRequestProperty("Cookie", sb.toString());
  }
  byte[] postData = assemblePostData();
  // In the current version of J2MEWTK, using setRequestProperty()
  // to set Content-length sometimes results in the transmission
  // of two instances of the length value separated by commas and
  // the servlet container throws a NumberFormatException.
  //conn.setRequestProperty("Content-length",
  //  Integer.toString(postData.length));
  os = conn.openOutputStream();
  os.write(postData);
  // See comment above about flush()
  //os.flush();
  is = conn.openInputStream();
  String contentType = conn.getType();
  int len = (int)conn.getLength();
  if (len > 0) {
    receivedData = new byte[len];
    int nb = is.read(receivedData);
  }
  else {
    receivedData = new byte[1024];
```

```
      int ch;
      len = 0;
      while ((ch = is.read()) != -1) {
        receivedData[len++] = (byte)ch;
      }
    }
    response.setText(new String(receivedData).trim());
    if (response.getText().indexOf("failed") >= 0) {
      counterForm.removeCommand(cmdNext);
    }
    display.setCurrent(counterForm);
  }
  catch (IOException e) {
    e.printStackTrace();
  }
  catch (Exception e) {
    e.printStackTrace();
  }
  finally {
    try {
      if (is != null) {
        is.close();
      }
      if (os != null) {
        os.close();
      }
      if (conn != null) {
        conn.close();
      }
    }
    catch (IOException e) {
    }
  }
}

public void visitCounter() {
  HttpConnection conn = null;
  InputStream is = null;
  OutputStream os = null;
  byte[] receivedData = null;
  try {
    String url =
      "http://localhost/J2MEBOOK/servlet/MD5LoginServlet";
```

```
conn = (HttpConnection)Connector.open(url);
conn.setRequestMethod(HttpConnection.POST);
conn.setRequestProperty("User-Agent",
  "Profile/MIDP-1.0 Configuration/CLDC-1.0");
conn.setRequestProperty("Content-type",
  "application/x-www-form-urlencoded");
if (cookies.size() > 0) {
  StringBuffer sb = new StringBuffer();
  for (int i = 0; i < cookies.size(); ++i) {
    sb.append((String)cookies.elementAt(i));
    if ((i + 1) < cookies.size()) {
      sb.append("; ");
    }
  }
  conn.setRequestProperty("Cookie", sb.toString());
}
byte[] postData = "ID=1".getBytes();
// See comment above about setting COntent-length
//conn.setRequestProperty("Content-length",
//  Integer.toString(postData.length));
os = conn.openOutputStream();
os.write(postData);
// See comment above about flush()
//os.flush();
is = conn.openInputStream();
String contentType = conn.getType();
int len = (int)conn.getLength();
if (len > 0) {
  receivedData = new byte[len];
  int nb = is.read(receivedData);
}
else {
  receivedData = new byte[1024];
  int ch;
  len = 0;
  while ((ch = is.read()) != -1) {
    receivedData[len++] = (byte)ch;
  }
}
response.setText(new String(receivedData,0,len).trim());
display.setCurrent(counterForm);
```

```
      }
      catch (IOException e) {
        e.printStackTrace();
      }
      catch (Exception e) {
        e.printStackTrace();
      }
      finally {
        try {
          if (is != null) {
            is.close();
          }
          if (os != null) {
            os.close();
          }
          if (conn != null) {
            conn.close();
          }
        }
        catch (IOException e) {
        }
      }
    }

    public byte[] assemblePostData() {
      StringBuffer sb = new StringBuffer();
      sb.append("ID=0");
      sb.append("&userid=");
      sb.append(userid.getString());
      sb.append("&MD5hash=");
      sb.append(computeMD5Hash(password.getString()));
      return sb.toString().getBytes();
    }

    public String computeMD5Hash(String password) {
      StringBuffer sb = new StringBuffer(password);
      sb.append(token);
      MD5 md5 = new MD5();
      md5.computeDigest(sb.toString().getBytes());
      return Base64.encode(md5.digest).replace('+','$');
    }
  }
}
```

\OMH\Login.jsp

After the `startApp` method creates the forms it will use and starts an instance of `CommandThread`, it invokes `getLoginToken`. This method uses an `HttpConnection` object to send a request to *Login.jsp*, which looks like this:

```
<jsp:forward page="/servlet/MD5LoginServlet" />
```

The JSP simply forwards the request to MD5LoginServlet. As you will see shortly, when the servlet receives the request, it creates a session object in which it stores a token and sends the token back to the MIDlet. The response containing the token also contains a cookie that identifies the session. The MIDlet uses `getHeaderFieldKey` to extract header fields and saves all fields containing the string "cookie" in a `Vector`.

When the MIDlet receives the token, it displays a form containing two `TextFields` into which the user enters the user ID and password. In response to the user pressing OK, the MIDlet invokes `sendLogin`. This method uses the values stored in the cookie `Vector` to construct a String whose value takes the form NAME1=VALUE1; NAME2=VALUE2;...NAMEn=VALUEn. It passes a String with a value of "Cookie" and the constructed String as arguments to `setRequestProperty`. This ensures that the server will be able to associate this request with the appropriate session. The `sendLogin` method calls `assemblePostData`, which computes the MD5 hash and constructs the second block of the POST request. The hash is converted to base 64 to facilitate transmission. All + characters in the hash are converted to $, since the HTTP protocol converts + to space. In addition to the user ID and hash, this block contains the data pair ID=1 indicating that this is to be processed as a login request.

NOTE

The version of MD5 suitable for use with MIDP is listed at the end of the chapter along with the supporting classes Base64 and Base64Exception.

If the response from the servlet indicates that the login was successful, the MIDlet displays a form containing a message indicating success and also a "Next." Each time the user presses Next, the MIDlet sends a request containing the cookies and the data pair ID=2 indicating that this is not a login request, but a page visit. It displays the "page visit" counter returned by the servlet.

The Server

\OMH\MD5LoginServlet.java

Here is the code for the servlet that processes the login request:

```java
import java.io.*;
import java.text.*;
import java.util.*;
import javax.servlet.*;
import javax.servlet.http.*;

import java.sql.*;

import java.security.MessageDigest;
import java.security.NoSuchAlgorithmException;

import com.paulsjavabooks.instantj2me.crypto.*;

public class MD5LoginServlet extends HttpServlet {

  static final String dbURL =
    "jdbc:mysql://localhost/j2mebook?" +
    "user=j2meapps&password=bigsecret";

  private static final int ID_ERROR = -1;
  private static final int ID_LOGIN = 0;
  private static final int ID_COUNT_VISITS = 1;

  String nextJSP = null;

  String fullName = null;

  public void doPost(HttpServletRequest request,
                     HttpServletResponse response)
      throws IOException, ServletException {

    String token;
    String userid;
    String receivedHash;

    HttpSession session = request.getSession();
    if (session.isNew()) {
      token = Long.toString(System.currentTimeMillis());
      session.setAttribute("TOKEN",token);
      request.setAttribute("TOKEN",token);
      request.setAttribute("ID",Integer.toString(ID_LOGIN));
      nextJSP = "/PresentLoginToken.jsp";
    }
```

```
    else {
      String screenID = request.getParameter("ID");
      if (screenID == null) {
        nextJSP = "/Error.jsp";
      }
      else {
        int id = ID_ERROR;
        try {
          id = Integer.parseInt(screenID);
        }
        catch (NumberFormatException e) {
          throw new ServletException(e.getMessage());
        }
        switch (id) {
          case ID_LOGIN:
            login(request);
            break;
          case ID_COUNT_VISITS:
            countVisits(request);
            break;
          default:
            nextJSP = "/Error.jsp";
        }
      }
    }

    try {
      ServletConfig config = getServletConfig();
      ServletContext context = config.getServletContext();
      RequestDispatcher rd = context.getRequestDispatcher(nextJSP);
      rd.forward(request, response);
    }
    catch (Exception ex) {
      ex.printStackTrace ();
    }
  }

  public void doGet(HttpServletRequest request,
                    HttpServletResponse response)
      throws IOException, ServletException {
    doPost(request, response);
  }
```

```
private void login(HttpServletRequest request)
    throws ServletException {
  HttpSession session = request.getSession();
  String token = (String)session.getAttribute("TOKEN");
  String userid = request.getParameter("userid");
  String receivedHash =
    request.getParameter("MD5hash").replace('$','+');
  if (isValid(userid, token, receivedHash)) {
    request.setAttribute("fullName", fullName);
    session.setAttribute("VisitCount",new Integer(1));
    nextJSP = "/LoginOK.jsp";
  }
  else {
    nextJSP = "/LoginFailed.jsp";
  }
}

private void countVisits(HttpServletRequest request)
    throws ServletException {
  HttpSession session = request.getSession();
  int visits = ((Integer)session.getAttribute("VisitCount")).intValue();
  ++visits;
  session.setAttribute("VisitCount",new Integer(visits));
  request.setAttribute("VisitCount",Integer.toString(visits));
  nextJSP = "/DisplayVisitCount.jsp";
}

private boolean isValid(String userid, String token,
  String receivedHash)
    throws ServletException {
  boolean userIsValid = false;
  try {
    Class.forName("org.gjt.mm.mysql.Driver");
  }
  catch (ClassNotFoundException e) {
    throw new ServletException("Unable to load JDBC driver");
  }

  Connection conn = null;

  try {
    conn = DriverManager.getConnection(dbURL);
```

```
      Statement stmt = conn.createStatement();
      String query = "SELECT firstname, lastname, password " +
                     "FROM users " + "WHERE userid = '" +
                     userid + "'";
      ResultSet rs = stmt.executeQuery(query);
      if (rs.next()) {
        StringBuffer sb = new StringBuffer();
        sb.append(rs.getString(1));
        sb.append(" ");
        sb.append(rs.getString(2));
        String password = rs.getString(3);
        String computedHash = computeHash(password, token);
        if ((userIsValid = computedHash.equals(receivedHash))) {
          nextJSP = "/LogonOK.jsp";
          fullName = sb.toString();
        }
      }
      else {
        nextJSP = "/LogonFailed";
      }
    }
    catch (SQLException e) {
      throw new ServletException("SQL call failed");
    }
    catch (Exception e) {
      throw new ServletException(e.getMessage());
    }
    finally {
      if (conn != null) {
        try {
          conn.close();
        }
        catch (SQLException e) {
          throw new ServletException("connection close failed");
        }
      }
    }
    return userIsValid;
  }

private String computeHash(String password, String token)
```

```
    throws ServletException {
  StringBuffer sb = new StringBuffer(password);
  sb.append(token);
  byte[] digest = null;
  try {
    MessageDigest md = MessageDigest.getInstance("MD5");
    digest = md.digest(sb.toString().getBytes());
  }
  catch (NoSuchAlgorithmException e) {
    throw new ServletException("no MD5 algorithm available");
  }
  return Base64.encode(digest);
  }
}
```

\OMH\PresentLoginToken.jsp

Requests sent to the servlet are processed by the doPost method. This method gets the session object, creating one if none exists. If the session has not yet been joined by the client, the servlet obtains the current time in milliseconds, converts it to a String, saves it in the session object, and stores it as an attribute in the request before forwarding the request to *PresentLoginToken.jsp*, which looks like this:

```
<%response.setContentType("text/plain");%>
Token:<%= request.getAttribute("TOKEN")%>
```

As just described, the MIDlet uses the token to compute an MD5 hash, which it sends back to the servlet along with the user ID and the data pair ID=0.

The servlet uses the value of ID as the control variable of a switch statement that determines how the request should be processed.

If the value of ID is 0, the servlet retrieves the password from the database, concatenates it to the token that is saved in the session object, computes an MD5 hash, and compares it to what was received from the MIDlet after substituting a + for each occurrence of $. It then forwards the request to either *LoginOK.jsp* or *LoginFailed.jsp* just as the first example did.

> **NOTE**
>
> *The servlet uses the MD5 algorithm provided by the* MessageDigest *class contained in the* java.security *package.*

\OMH\DisplayVisitCount.jsp

If the value of ID is 1, the servlet retrieves the attribute "VisitCount" from the session object, increments it, stores it back in the session object, stores it as an attribute in the request, and forwards the request to *DisplayVisitCount.jsp*, which looks like this:

```
<%response.setContentType("text/plain");%>
# visits = <%= request.getAttribute("VisitCount")%>
```

Running the Example

The initial screen displayed by this MIDlet is identical to the screen displayed by the first version of login. After you have entered the user ID and password as you did in the first example and press OK, the display looks like this:

Note the presence of the Next button. Each time you press this button, a screen containing the visit counter as reported by the servlet is displayed. A typical screen looks like this:

You now have all the tools required to build applications that require login and/or require a session. One such application you might want to tackle is a shopping cart.

The J2ME Version of the MD5 Algorithm

This section contains listings of the Java classes used to compute an MD5 hash and convert it to base 64 for transmission.

MD5.java

\OMH\com\paulsjavabooks\instantj2me\crypto\MD5.java

```
/*
 * MD5.java
 *
 * Created on September 23, 2001, 9:50 PM
 */
```

```java
package com.paulsjavabooks.instantj2me.crypto;

/**
 *
 * @author  paul tremblett
 * @version 1.0
 */
public class MD5 {

  public byte[] digest;

  public boolean digestValid;

  private int state[];
  private long count;
  private byte buffer[];
  private static int transformBuffer[];

  private static final int S11 = 7;
  private static final int S12 = 12;
  private static final int S13 = 17;
  private static final int S14 = 22;
  private static final int S21 = 5;
  private static final int S22 = 9;
  private static final int S23 = 14;
  private static final int S24 = 20;
  private static final int S31 = 4;
  private static final int S32 = 11;
  private static final int S33 = 16;
  private static final int S34 = 23;
  private static final int S41 = 6;
  private static final int S42 = 10;
  private static final int S43 = 15;
  private static final int S44 = 21;

  private static final int INIT_0 = 0x67452301;
  private static final int INIT_1 = 0xefcdab89;
  private static final int INIT_2 = 0x98badcfe;
  private static final int INIT_3 = 0x10325476;

  public MD5() {
    state = new int[4];
    count = 0;
```

```
    if (transformBuffer == null) {
      transformBuffer = new int[16];
    }
  buffer = new byte[64];
  digest = new byte[16];
  digestValid = false;
}

public MD5(byte mydigest[]) {
  state = new int[4];
  count = 0;
  if (transformBuffer == null) {
    transformBuffer = new int[16];
  }
  buffer = new byte[64];
  digest = mydigest;
  digestValid = false;
}

private int F(int x, int y, int z) {
  return ((x & y) | ((~x) & z));
}

private int G(int x, int y, int z) {
  return ((x & z) | (y & (~z)));
}

private int H(int x, int y, int z) {
  return ((x ^ y) ^ z);
}

private int I(int x, int y, int z) {
  return (y ^ (x | (~z)));
}

private int rotateLeft(int a, int n) {
  return ((a << n) | (a >>> (32 - n)));
}

private int FF(int a, int b, int c, int d, int x, int s, int ac) {
  a += F(b, c, d) + x + ac;
  a = rotateLeft(a, s);
  a += b;
```

```
      return a;
  }

  private int GG(int a, int b, int c, int d, int x, int s, int ac) {
    a += G(b, c, d) + x + ac;
    a = rotateLeft(a, s);
    a += b;
    return a;
  }

  private int HH(int a, int b, int c, int d, int x, int s, int ac) {
    a += H(b, c, d) + x + ac;
    a = rotateLeft(a, s);
    a += b;
    return a;
  }

  private int II(int a, int b, int c, int d, int x, int s, int ac) {
    a += I(b, c, d) + x + ac;
    a = rotateLeft(a, s);
    a += b;
    return a;
  }

  void transform(byte buf[], int offset) {
    int a, b, c, d;
    int x[] = transformBuffer;

    a = state[0];
    b = state[1];
    c = state[2];
    d = state[3];

    for (int i = 0; i < 16; i++) {
      x[i] = (int)buf[i*4+offset] & 0xff;
      for (int j = 1; j < 4; j++) {
        x[i] += ((int)buf[i*4+j+offset] & 0xff) << (j * 8);
      }
    }

    a = FF ( a, b, c, d, x[ 0], S11, 0xd76aa478);
    d = FF ( d, a, b, c, x[ 1], S12, 0xe8c7b756);
    c = FF ( c, d, a, b, x[ 2], S13, 0x242070db);
```

```
b = FF ( b, c, d, a, x[ 3], S14, 0xc1bdceee);
a = FF ( a, b, c, d, x[ 4], S11, 0xf57c0faf);
d = FF ( d, a, b, c, x[ 5], S12, 0x4787c62a);
c = FF ( c, d, a, b, x[ 6], S13, 0xa8304613);
b = FF ( b, c, d, a, x[ 7], S14, 0xfd469501);
a = FF ( a, b, c, d, x[ 8], S11, 0x698098d8);
d = FF ( d, a, b, c, x[ 9], S12, 0x8b44f7af);
c = FF ( c, d, a, b, x[10], S13, 0xffff5bb1);
b = FF ( b, c, d, a, x[11], S14, 0x895cd7be);
a = FF ( a, b, c, d, x[12], S11, 0x6b901122);
d = FF ( d, a, b, c, x[13], S12, 0xfd987193);
c = FF ( c, d, a, b, x[14], S13, 0xa679438e);
b = FF ( b, c, d, a, x[15], S14, 0x49b40821);

a = GG ( a, b, c, d, x[ 1], S21, 0xf61e2562);
d = GG ( d, a, b, c, x[ 6], S22, 0xc040b340);
c = GG ( c, d, a, b, x[11], S23, 0x265e5a51);
b = GG ( b, c, d, a, x[ 0], S24, 0xe9b6c7aa);
a = GG ( a, b, c, d, x[ 5], S21, 0xd62f105d);
d = GG ( d, a, b, c, x[10], S22,  0x2441453);
c = GG ( c, d, a, b, x[15], S23, 0xd8a1e681);
b = GG ( b, c, d, a, x[ 4], S24, 0xe7d3fbc8);
a = GG ( a, b, c, d, x[ 9], S21, 0x21e1cde6);
d = GG ( d, a, b, c, x[14], S22, 0xc33707d6);
c = GG ( c, d, a, b, x[ 3], S23, 0xf4d50d87);
b = GG ( b, c, d, a, x[ 8], S24, 0x455a14ed);
a = GG ( a, b, c, d, x[13], S21, 0xa9e3e905);
d = GG ( d, a, b, c, x[ 2], S22, 0xfcefa3f8);
c = GG ( c, d, a, b, x[ 7], S23, 0x676f02d9);
b = GG ( b, c, d, a, x[12], S24, 0x8d2a4c8a);

a = HH ( a, b, c, d, x[ 5], S31, 0xfffa3942);
d = HH ( d, a, b, c, x[ 8], S32, 0x8771f681);
c = HH ( c, d, a, b, x[11], S33, 0x6d9d6122);
b = HH ( b, c, d, a, x[14], S34, 0xfde5380c);
a = HH ( a, b, c, d, x[ 1], S31, 0xa4beea44);
d = HH ( d, a, b, c, x[ 4], S32, 0x4bdecfa9);
c = HH ( c, d, a, b, x[ 7], S33, 0xf6bb4b60);
b = HH ( b, c, d, a, x[10], S34, 0xbebfbc70);
a = HH ( a, b, c, d, x[13], S31, 0x289b7ec6);
d = HH ( d, a, b, c, x[ 0], S32, 0xeaa127fa);
c = HH ( c, d, a, b, x[ 3], S33, 0xd4ef3085);
b = HH ( b, c, d, a, x[ 6], S34,  0x4881d05);
```

```
    a = HH ( a, b, c, d, x[ 9], S31, 0xd9d4d039);
    d = HH ( d, a, b, c, x[12], S32, 0xe6db99e5);
    c = HH ( c, d, a, b, x[15], S33, 0x1fa27cf8);
    b = HH ( b, c, d, a, x[ 2], S34, 0xc4ac5665);

    a = II ( a, b, c, d, x[ 0], S41, 0xf4292244);
    d = II ( d, a, b, c, x[ 7], S42, 0x432aff97);
    c = II ( c, d, a, b, x[14], S43, 0xab9423a7);
    b = II ( b, c, d, a, x[ 5], S44, 0xfc93a039);
    a = II ( a, b, c, d, x[12], S41, 0x655b59c3);
    d = II ( d, a, b, c, x[ 3], S42, 0x8f0ccc92);
    c = II ( c, d, a, b, x[10], S43, 0xffeff47d);
    b = II ( b, c, d, a, x[ 1], S44, 0x85845dd1);
    a = II ( a, b, c, d, x[ 8], S41, 0x6fa87e4f);
    d = II ( d, a, b, c, x[15], S42, 0xfe2ce6e0);
    c = II ( c, d, a, b, x[ 6], S43, 0xa3014314);
    b = II ( b, c, d, a, x[13], S44, 0x4e0811a1);
    a = II ( a, b, c, d, x[ 4], S41, 0xf7537e82);
    d = II ( d, a, b, c, x[11], S42, 0xbd3af235);
    c = II ( c, d, a, b, x[ 2], S43, 0x2ad7d2bb);
    b = II ( b, c, d, a, x[ 9], S44, 0xeb86d391);

    state[0] += a;
    state[1] += b;
    state[2] += c;
    state[3] += d;
  }

public void init() {

  count = 0;

  state[0] = INIT_0;
  state[1] = INIT_1;
  state[2] = INIT_2;
  state[3] = INIT_3;

  digestValid = false;

  for (int i = 0; i < digest.length; i++) {
    digest[i] = 0;
  }
}
```

```
public void update(byte b) {
  int index;

  index = (int) ((count >>> 3) & 0x3f);
  count += 8;
  buffer[index] = b;
  if (index  >= 63) {
    transform(buffer, 0);
  }
}

public void update(byte input[]) {
  for (int i = 0; i < input.length; i++) {
    update(input[i]);
  }
}

public void computeDigest(byte source[]) {
  init();
  update(source);
  finish();
}

public void finish() {
  byte bits[] = new byte[8];
  byte padding[];
  int i, index, padLen;

  for (i = 0; i < 8; i++) {
    bits[i] = (byte)((count >>> (i * 8)) & 0xff);
  }

  index = (int)(count >> 3) & 0x3f;
  padLen = (index < 56) ? (56 - index) : (120 - index);
  padding = new byte[padLen];
  padding[0] = (byte) 0x80;
  update(padding);
  update(bits);

  for (i = 0; i < 4; i++) {
    for (int j = 0; j < 4; j++) {
      digest[i*4+j] = (byte)((state[i] >>> (j * 8)) & 0xff);
```

```
      }
    }
    digestValid = true;
  }

  public static void main(String[] args) {
    MD5 md5 = new MD5();
    md5.computeDigest(args[0].getBytes());
    System.out.println(Base64.encode(md5.digest));
  }
}
```

Base64.java

\OMH\com\paulsjavabooks\instantj2me\crypto\Base64.java

```
/*
 * Base64.java
 *
 * Created on September 23, 2001, 9:52 PM
 */

package com.paulsjavabooks.instantj2me.crypto;

/**
 *
 * @author  paul tremblett
 * @version 1.0
 */

public class Base64 {
  private final static char[] map = {
    'A', 'B', 'C', 'D', 'E', 'F', 'G', 'H',
    'I', 'J', 'K', 'L', 'M', 'N', 'O', 'P',
    'Q', 'R', 'S', 'T', 'U', 'V', 'W', 'X',
    'Y', 'Z', 'a', 'b', 'c', 'd', 'e', 'f',
    'g', 'h', 'i', 'j', 'k', 'l', 'm', 'n',
    'o', 'p', 'q', 'r', 's', 't', 'u', 'v',
    'w', 'x', 'y', 'z', '0', '1', '2', '3',
    '4', '5', '6', '7', '8', '9', '+', '/'
  };
```

Base64Exception.java

\OMH\com\paulsjavabooks\instantj2me\crypto\Base64Exception.java

```java
/*
 * Base64Exception.java
 *
 * Created on September 23, 2001, 9:52 PM
 */

package com.paulsjavabooks.instantj2me.crypto;

/**
 *
 * @author  paul tremblett
 * @version 1.0
 */
public class Base64Exception extends Exception {

  public Base64Exception() {
    super();
  }

  public Base64Exception(String s) {
    super(s);
  }
}
```

A Message-Forwarding Application

I n Chapter 16, you wrote a login that protected the user's password by using the MD5 algorithm. You also learned how cookies are used to maintain a session with a servlet running on a remote host. In this chapter, you will see how data can be protected during transmission.

A Minimally Secure Messaging Application

The degree to which data is protected from viewing as it is being transmitted is determined by a security policy. Let's imagine that you work for a company that is interested in exploring uses for Java-enabled handheld devices, but its security policy dictates that no data is to be transmitted as cleartext. You would like to develop a simple e-mail system. The client and server code that follow form a framework that could help you get started.

The Client

\OMH\com\paulsjavabooks\instantj2me\Chapter17\MessageRelay.java

The client code that runs on a MID is shown here:

```
/*
 * MessageRelay.java
 *
 * Created on October 18, 2001, 7:47 PM
 */

package com.paulsjavabooks.instantj2me.Chapter17;

import javax.microedition.midlet.*;
import javax.microedition.lcdui.*;
import javax.microedition.midlet.*;
import javax.microedition.lcdui.*;

import javax.microedition.io.Connector;
import javax.microedition.io.HttpConnection;
import javax.microedition.io.StreamConnection;

import java.io.DataInputStream;
import java.io.DataOutputStream;
import java.io.InputStream;
```

```java
import java.io.IOException;
import java.io.OutputStream;

import java.util.Vector;

import com.paulsjavabooks.instantj2me.crypto.*;

/**
 *
 * @author  paul tremblett
 * @version 1.0
 */
public class MessageRelay extends javax.microedition.midlet.MIDlet
     implements CommandListener {

  Display display;

  boolean commandAvailable;
  CommandThread commandThread;
  Command cmd;
  Displayable displayable;

  Form loginForm;
  TextField userid;
  TextField password;

  Form receivedMessage;
  StringItem messageID;
  StringItem messageDate;
  StringItem messageFrom;
  StringItem messageSubject;
  StringItem messageText;

  Command cmdReply;
  Command cmdDelete;

  TextBox messageBody;
  Command cmdSend;

  Form enterRecipient;
  TextField recipient;
  TextField subject;
```

```java
    List menu;
    List messageList;

    Alert alert;

    Command cmdExit;
    Command cmdOK;
    Command cmdNext;
    Command cmdPrev;
    Command cmdDone;
    Command cmdVerifyRecipient;

    String user;
    String fullName;

    Vector cookies;
    String token;

    EnigmaMachine enigmaMachine = null;

    Vector msgids = null;

    int msgCount = 0;

    String url =
        "http://localhost/J2MEBOOK/servlet/MessageRelayServlet";

    private static final int ID_ERROR =                   -1;
    private static final int ID_LOGIN =                    0;
    private static final int ID_SEND_MESSAGE =             1;
    private static final int ID_VERIFY_RECIPIENT =         2;
    private static final int ID_GET_MESSAGE_HEADERS =      3;
    private static final int ID_GET_MESSAGE_TEXT =         4;
    private static final int ID_DELETE_MESSAGE =           5;
    private static final int ID_REPLY =                    6;
    private static final int ID_LOGOUT =                   7;

    private static final int MAX_MESSAGE_SIZE = 2048;

    private static final String DELIMITER = "<<<>>>";

    public void startApp() {
        display = Display.getDisplay(this);
```

```
loginForm = new Form(null);
userid = new TextField("User",null,
  25, TextField.ANY);
loginForm.append(userid);
password = new TextField("Password",null,
  15, TextField.PASSWORD);
loginForm.append(password);
cmdOK = new Command("OK",Command.OK,1);
cmdExit = new Command("Exit",Command.EXIT,1);
loginForm.addCommand(cmdOK);
loginForm.addCommand(cmdExit);
loginForm.setCommandListener(this);

menu = new List("Menu", List.IMPLICIT);
menu.append("Get Messages",null);
menu.append("Send Message",null);
menu.append("Exit",null);
menu.setCommandListener(this);

alert = new Alert(null,null,null,null);
alert.setTimeout(Alert.FOREVER);

StringItem[] messageComponents = new StringItem[5];
messageID = new StringItem("ID:",null);
messageDate = new StringItem("Dt:",null);
messageFrom = new StringItem("From:",null);
messageSubject = new StringItem("Subj:",null);
messageText = new StringItem("Msg:",null);

receivedMessage = new Form("Message",null);
receivedMessage.append(messageID);
receivedMessage.append(messageDate);
receivedMessage.append(messageFrom);
receivedMessage.append(messageSubject);
receivedMessage.append(messageText);
cmdNext = new Command("Next",Command.SCREEN,1);
receivedMessage.addCommand(cmdNext);
cmdPrev = new Command("Prev",Command.SCREEN,1);
receivedMessage.addCommand(cmdPrev);
cmdReply = new Command("Reply",Command.SCREEN,1);
receivedMessage.addCommand(cmdReply);
cmdDone = new Command("Done",Command.SCREEN,1);
receivedMessage.addCommand(cmdDone);
```

```
        cmdDelete = new Command("Delete",Command.SCREEN,1);
        receivedMessage.addCommand(cmdDelete);
        receivedMessage.addCommand(cmdExit);
        receivedMessage.setCommandListener(this);

        messageBody = new TextBox("Message",null,
          MAX_MESSAGE_SIZE,TextField.ANY);
        cmdSend = new Command("Send",Command.SCREEN,1);
        messageBody.addCommand(cmdSend);
        messageBody.addCommand(cmdExit);
        messageBody.setCommandListener(this);

        messageList = new List("Messages",List.IMPLICIT);
        messageList.addCommand(cmdExit);
        messageList.setCommandListener(this);

        enterRecipient = new Form("Compose");
        recipient = new TextField("To:",null,
          8, TextField.ANY);
        enterRecipient.append(recipient);
        subject = new TextField("Subject:",null,
          40, TextField.ANY);
        enterRecipient.append(subject);
        cmdVerifyRecipient = new Command("Next",Command.SCREEN,1);
        enterRecipient.addCommand(cmdVerifyRecipient);
        enterRecipient.addCommand(cmdExit);
        enterRecipient.setCommandListener(this);


        commandAvailable = false;
        commandThread = new CommandThread(this);
        commandThread.start();

        token = getLoginToken();

        display.setCurrent(loginForm);
    }

    public void pauseApp() {
    }

    public void destroyApp(boolean unconditional) {
    }
```

```
public void commandAction(Command cmd, Displayable d) {
  this.displayable = d;
  if (cmd == cmdExit) {
    destroyApp(false);
    notifyDestroyed();
  }
  else {
    synchronized (this) {
      this.cmd = cmd;
      commandAvailable = true;
      notify();
    }
  }
}

public String getLoginToken() {

  String tokenString = null;

  HttpConnection conn = null;
  InputStream is = null;
  OutputStream os = null;
  byte[] receivedData = null;
  try {
    String url =
      "http://localhost/J2MEBOOK/MessageRelay.jsp";
    conn = (HttpConnection)Connector.open(url);
    conn.setRequestProperty("User-Agent",
      "Profile/MIDP-1.0 Configuration/CLDC-1.0");
    conn.setRequestProperty("Content-type",
      "application/x-www-form-urlencoded");
    os = conn.openOutputStream();
    // In the current release of J2MEWTK, the behavior of
    // flush() is not predictable. It sometimes throws an
    // exception. Since the openInputStream(O) method that
    // follows it flushes the output stream, the flush()
    // method has been commented out
    //os.flush();
    is = conn.openInputStream();
    int headerFieldIndex = 0;
    cookies = new Vector();
    while (true) {
      String headerName = conn.getHeaderField(headerFieldIndex);
      if (headerName == null) {
```

```
        break;
      }
      String headerFieldKey =
        conn.getHeaderFieldKey(headerFieldIndex);
      ++headerFieldIndex;
      String hklc = headerFieldKey.toLowerCase();
      if (hklc.indexOf("cookie") < 0) {
        continue;
      }
      int scx = headerName.indexOf(';');
      String cookieValue;
      if (scx >= 0) {
        cookieValue = headerName.substring(0,scx);
      }
      else {
        cookieValue = headerName;
      }
      cookies.addElement(cookieValue);
    }

    String contentType = conn.getType();

    int len = (int)conn.getLength();
    if (len > 0) {
      receivedData = new byte[len];
      int nb = is.read(receivedData);
    }
    else {
      receivedData = new byte[1024];
      int ch;
      len = 0;
      while ((ch = is.read()) != -1) {
        receivedData[len++] = (byte)ch;
      }
    }
  tokenString = new String(receivedData,0,len).trim();
  }
  catch (IOException e) {
    e.printStackTrace();
  }
  catch (Exception e) {
    e.printStackTrace();
  }
```

```
      finally {
        try {
          if (is != null) {
            is.close();
          }
          if (os != null) {
            os.close();
          }
          if (conn != null) {
            conn.close();
          }
        }
        catch (IOException e) {
          e.printStackTrace();
        }
      }
      return tokenString.substring(tokenString.indexOf(':')+1);
    }

class CommandThread extends Thread {
  MIDlet parent;

  HttpConnection conn = null;
  InputStream is = null;
  OutputStream os = null;
  byte[] receivedData = null;

  boolean exit = false;

  public CommandThread(MIDlet parent) {
    this.parent = parent;
  }

  public void run() {
    while (true) {
      synchronized(parent) {
        while(!commandAvailable) {
          try {
            parent.wait();
          }
          catch (InterruptedException e) {
          }
        }
```

```
      commandAvailable = false;
    }

    if (cmd == cmdOK) {
      sendLogin();
    }
    else if (cmd == cmdVerifyRecipient) {
      verifyRecipient();
    }
    else if (cmd == cmdSend) {
      sendMessage();
    }
    else if (cmd == cmdReply) {
      replyToMessage();
    }
    else if (cmd == cmdDelete) {
      deleteMessage();
    }
    else if (cmd == cmdNext) {
      displayNextMessage();
    }
    else if (cmd == cmdPrev) {
      displayPreviousMessage();
    }
    else if (cmd == cmdDone) {
      displayMessageList();
    }
    else if (cmd == List.SELECT_COMMAND) {
      if (displayable == menu) {
        processMenuItem();
      }
      else if (displayable == messageList) {
        getSelectedMessage();
      }
      else {
        alert.setTitle("ERROR");
        alert.setString("An internal error has occurred");
        alert.setType(AlertType.ERROR);
        display.setCurrent(alert,menu);
      }
    }
  }
}
```

```
private void processMenuItem() {
  switch (menu.getSelectedIndex()) {
    case 0:
      retrieveMessages();
      break;
    case 1:
      getRecipient();
      break;
    case 2:
      destroyApp(false);
      notifyDestroyed();
      break;
    default:
      alert.setTitle("ERROR");
      alert.setString("An internal error has occurred");
      alert.setType(AlertType.ERROR);
      display.setCurrent(alert,menu);
  }
}

private void getSelectedMessage() {
  int vectorIndex = messageList.getSelectedIndex();
  if (vectorIndex > msgids.size()) {
    alert.setTitle("ERROR");
    alert.setString("An internal error has occurred");
    alert.setType(AlertType.ERROR);
    display.setCurrent(alert,menu);
  }
  else {
    displaySelectedMessage(vectorIndex);
  }
}

private void displaySelectedMessage(int msgIndex) {
  String msgid = (String)msgids.elementAt(msgIndex);
  try {
    conn = (HttpConnection)Connector.open(url);
    byte[] getMessageTextRequest = assembleGetMessageText(msgid);
    sendPostRequest(conn, getMessageTextRequest);
    receivedData = getResponse(conn);
    String messageToDisplay = new String(receivedData).trim();
    String[] vals = parseMessage(messageToDisplay);
    if (vals[0].equals("--")) {
      alert.setTitle("Message Status");
```

```
          alert.setString("Can't reconstruct message!");
          alert.setType(AlertType.ERROR);
          display.setCurrent(alert,messageList);
        }
      messageID.setText(vals[1]);
      messageDate.setText(vals[2]);
      messageFrom.setText(vals[3]);
      messageSubject.setText(decode(vals[4]));
      messageText.setText(decode(vals[5]));
      display.setCurrent(receivedMessage);
    }
    catch (IOException e) {
      e.printStackTrace();
    }
    catch (Exception e) {
      e.printStackTrace();
    }
    finally {
      try {
        if (is != null) {
          is.close();
        }
        if (os != null) {
          os.close();
        }
        if (conn != null) {
          conn.close();
        }
      }
      catch (IOException e) {
      }
    }
  }

  private void replyToMessage() {
    displayNotYetImplemented();
  }

  private void deleteMessage() {
    displayNotYetImplemented();
  }

  private void displayNextMessage() {
```

```
    displayNotYetImplemented();
}

private void displayPreviousMessage() {
  displayNotYetImplemented();
}

private void displayMessageList() {
  display.setCurrent(messageList);
}

private void displayNotYetImplemented() {
  alert.setTitle("Message");
  alert.setString("This feature is not yet implemented.");
  alert.setType(AlertType.INFO);
  display.setCurrent(alert,messageList);
}

private String[] parseMessage(String s) {
  String[] vals = new String[6];
  String tempString = s;
  int delimx;
  int dlen = DELIMITER.length();
  for (int i = 0; i < vals.length; ++i) {
    delimx = s.indexOf(DELIMITER);
    String vs = s.substring(0,delimx);
    if (i == 0) {
      if (vs.startsWith("--")) {
        break;
      }
    }
    vals[i] = vs;
    s = s.substring(delimx+dlen).trim();
  }
  return vals;
}

private void retrieveMessages() {
  msgids = new Vector();
  try {
    conn = (HttpConnection)Connector.open(url);
    byte[] getMessagesRequest = assembleGetMessageHeaders();
    sendPostRequest(conn, getMessagesRequest);
```

```
    receivedData = getResponse(conn);
    String messageHeaders = new String(receivedData).trim();
    if (messageHeaders.startsWith("--")) {
      alert.setTitle("Message Status");
      alert.setString("You have no messages!");
      alert.setType(AlertType.INFO);
      display.setCurrent(alert,menu);
    }
    for (int i = 0; i < messageList.size(); ++i) {
      messageList.delete(i);
    }
    int hdx = 0;
    while (true) {
      String nextChunk = messageHeaders.substring(hdx);
      if (nextChunk.length() == 0) {
        break;
      }
      int nlix = nextChunk.indexOf('\n');
      if (nlix < 0) {
        nlix = nextChunk.length();
      }
      String header = nextChunk.substring(0,nlix);
      int tabix = header.indexOf('\t');
      String msgID = header.substring(0,tabix);
      String subject = decode(header.substring(tabix+1));
      msgids.addElement(msgID);
      messageList.append(subject,null);
      hdx += nlix + 1;
      if (hdx >= messageHeaders.length()) {
        break;
      }
    }
    display.setCurrent(messageList);
}
catch (IOException e) {
}
catch (Base64Exception e) {
}
finally {
  try {
    if (is != null) {
      is.close();
    }
```

```
      if (os != null) {
        os.close();
      }
      if (conn != null) {
        conn.close();
      }
    }
    catch (IOException e) {
      e.printStackTrace();
    }
  }
}

private String encode(String s) {
  byte[] in = s.getBytes();
  byte[] out = new byte[in.length];
  enigmaMachine.processMessage(in,out);
  return Base64.encode(out).replace('+','$');
}

private String decode(String s) throws Base64Exception {
  String s64 = s.trim().replace('$','+');
  byte[] in = Base64.decode(s64);
  byte[] out = new byte[in.length];
  enigmaMachine.processMessage(in,out);
  return new String(out);
}

private byte[] assembleGetMessageHeaders() {
  StringBuffer sb = new StringBuffer("id=");
  sb.append(Integer.toString(ID_GET_MESSAGE_HEADERS));
  sb.append("&userid=");
  sb.append(user);
  return sb.toString().getBytes();
}

private byte[] assembleGetMessageText(String msgid) {
  StringBuffer sb = new StringBuffer("id=");
  sb.append(Integer.toString(ID_GET_MESSAGE_TEXT));
  sb.append("&msgid=");
  sb.append(msgid);
  return sb.toString().getBytes();
}
```

```java
private void getRecipient() {
  recipient.setString(null);
  subject.setString(null);
  display.setCurrent(enterRecipient);
}

public void sendLogin() {
  try {
    conn = (HttpConnection)Connector.open(url);
    byte[] loginRequest = assembleLoginData();
    sendPostRequest(conn, loginRequest);
    receivedData = getResponse(conn);
    String loginResult = new String(receivedData).trim();
    if (loginResult.indexOf("OK") == 0) {
      long cipherKey = (long)(password.getString().hashCode());
      enigmaMachine = new EnigmaMachine(cipherKey);
      user = userid.getString();
      display.setCurrent(menu);
    }
    else {
      alert.setTitle("Login Failed");
      alert.setString("user or password invalid");
      alert.setType(AlertType.ERROR);
      userid.setString(null);
      password.setString(null);
      display.setCurrent(alert,loginForm);
    }
  }
  catch (IOException e) {
    e.printStackTrace();
  }
  catch (Exception e) {
    e.printStackTrace();
  }
  finally {
    try {
      if (is != null) {
        is.close();
      }
      if (os != null) {
        os.close();
      }
      if (conn != null) {
        conn.close();
```

```
          }
      }
    catch (IOException e) {
      }
    }
}

private void sendMessage() {
try {
      conn = (HttpConnection)Connector.open(url);
      byte[] messageData = assembleMessageData();
      sendPostRequest(conn, messageData);
      receivedData = getResponse(conn);
      String msgAck = new String(receivedData).trim();
      if (msgAck.startsWith("--")) {
        alert.setTitle("Error");
        alert.setString("Message not sent");
        alert.setType(AlertType.ERROR);
        messageBody.setString(null);
      }
      else {
        alert.setTitle("OK");
        alert.setString("Message sent to " + msgAck);
        alert.setType(AlertType.INFO);
      }
      display.setCurrent(alert,menu);
    }
    catch (IOException e) {
      e.printStackTrace();
    }
    catch (Exception e) {
      e.printStackTrace();
    }
    finally {
      try {
        if (is != null) {
          is.close();
        }
        if (os != null) {
          os.close();
        }
        if (conn != null) {
          conn.close();
        }
```

```java
        }
        catch (IOException e) {
        }
      }
    }

    private void sendPostRequest(HttpConnection conn, byte[] data)
        throws IOException {
      conn.setRequestMethod(HttpConnection.POST);
      conn.setRequestProperty("User-Agent",
        "Profile/MIDP-1.0 Configuration/CLDC-1.0");
      conn.setRequestProperty("Content-type",
        "application/x-www-form-urlencoded");
      if (cookies.size() > 0) {
        StringBuffer sb = new StringBuffer();
        for (int i = 0; i < cookies.size(); ++i) {
          sb.append((String)cookies.elementAt(i));
          if ((i + 1) < cookies.size()) {
            sb.append("; ");
          }
        }
        conn.setRequestProperty("Cookie", sb.toString());
      }
      OutputStream os = conn.openOutputStream();
      os.write(data);
      os.close();
    }

    private void verifyRecipient() {
      if (!recipientExists(recipient.getString())) {
        alert.setTitle("Invalid Recipient");
        alert.setString("Recipient not found in database");
        alert.setType(AlertType.ERROR);
        recipient.setString(null);
        display.setCurrent(alert,enterRecipient);
      }
      else {
        messageBody.setString(null);
        display.setCurrent(messageBody);
      }
    }

    private boolean recipientExists(String recipient) {
```

```
  boolean found = false;
  try {
      conn = (HttpConnection)Connector.open(url);
      byte[] recipientData = assembleRecipientData();
      sendPostRequest(conn, recipientData);
      receivedData = getResponse(conn);
      if (new String(receivedData).indexOf("OK") >= 0) {
        found = true;
      }
  }
  catch (IOException e) {
    e.printStackTrace();
  }
  catch (Exception e) {
    e.printStackTrace();
  }
  finally {
    try {
      if (is != null) {
        is.close();
      }
      if (os != null) {
        os.close();
      }
      if (conn != null) {
        conn.close();
      }
    }
    catch (IOException e) {
    }
  }
  return found;
}

public byte[] getResponse(HttpConnection conn)
    throws IOException {
  byte[] receivedData;
  InputStream is = conn.openInputStream();
  String contentType = conn.getType();
  int len = (int)conn.getLength();
  if (len > 0) {
    receivedData = new byte[len];
    int nb = is.read(receivedData);
```

```
        }
        else {
          byte[] temp = new byte[1024];
          int ch;
          len = 0;
          while ((ch = is.read()) != -1) {
            temp[len++] = (byte)ch;
          }
          receivedData = new byte[len];
          for (int i = 0; i < len; ++i) {
            receivedData[i] = temp[i];
          }
        }
      is.close();
      return receivedData;
    }



  public byte[] assembleLoginData() {
      StringBuffer sb = new StringBuffer("id=");
      sb.append(Integer.toString(ID_LOGIN));
      sb.append("&userid=");
      sb.append(userid.getString());
      sb.append("&MD5hash=");
      sb.append(computeMD5Hash(password.getString()));
      return sb.toString().getBytes();
    }

  public byte[] assembleMessageData() {
      StringBuffer sb = new StringBuffer("id=");
      sb.append(Integer.toString(ID_SEND_MESSAGE));
      sb.append("&messagetext=");
      sb.append(encode(messageBody.getString()));
      return sb.toString().getBytes();
    }

  public byte[] assembleRecipientData() {
      StringBuffer sb = new StringBuffer("id=");
      sb.append(Integer.toString(ID_VERIFY_RECIPIENT));
      sb.append("&recipient=");
      sb.append(recipient.getString());
```

```
      sb.append("&subject=");
      sb.append(encode(subject.getString()));
      return sb.toString().getBytes();
    }

  public String computeMD5Hash(String password) {
      StringBuffer sb = new StringBuffer(password);
      sb.append(token);
      MD5 md5 = new MD5();
      md5.computeDigest(sb.toString().getBytes());
      return Base64.encode(md5.digest).replace('+','$');
    }
  }
}
```

You have already seen most of the code in this example. It borrows the login technique from Chapter 16, as well as the code that assembles and transmits POST requests. The code that is different is that which encrypts the subject and body of each outgoing email message before transmitting it and decrypts each incoming message as it is received. In the J2SE environment, if you needed encryption, you downloaded and installed the Java Cryptography Extension (JCE). Some commercial cryptography packages for the J2ME environment are starting to appear, but we will write our own. The software emulates the Enigma machine made famous by the Germans during World War II. The machine consisted of a series of rotors that were wired together and advanced in much the same manner as a car's odometer. As each letter on a keyboard was typed, an electrical pulse was transmitted through the rotors. The rotors terminated in a special type of rotor called a reflector that was wired not to another rotor but to itself. The reflector send the signal back through the rotors to one of a series of lamps. There were as many lamps as there were keys, and as each lamp was illuminated, its assigned letter was used as the next letter in the ciphertext. The advancing of the rotors guaranteed that the encoding for each letter was different from the encoding of the preceding letter. Unlike the original machine, which only used letters and numbers, the software simulator uses bytes with values of 0 through 255 so it can accommodate a complete character set. The original machine could use a different encoding for each message by setting each rotor in the machine at starting positions known only to the sender and recipient of the messages. In the simulator, the number of rotors and their starting positions are determined from the hash code of the sender's password. This password is known only to the user and to the server software that receives the message.

The Enigma software is presented at the end of the chapter.

NOTE

The cryptographic software included with this chapter is only included to demonstrate that encoding and decoding of messages on a MID is possible. You should not assume that the algorithm is sufficiently strong for commercial or corporate purposes. The pattern generated by the Enigma can be detected by a knowledgeable cryptanalyst. Once it is determined that Enigma was used, a simple brute-force attack can be mounted by simply supplying all four billion possible values of a Java long as arguments to the constructor. You can strengthen the encryption by chaining multiple machines so that the output of one becomes the input of another. This raises the number of iterations required for a brute-force attack exponentially as machines are added. You should not, however, assume that the resultant code is unbreakable.

The Server

\OMH\MessageRelayServlet.java

Here is the server that receives e-mails, stores them in a database, and transmits them to the intended recipient when requested.

```java
import java.io.*;
import java.text.*;
import java.util.*;
import javax.servlet.*;
import javax.servlet.http.*;

import java.sql.*;

import java.security.MessageDigest;
import java.security.NoSuchAlgorithmException;

import java.util.Random;

import com.paulsjavabooks.instantj2me.crypto.*;

public class MessageRelayServlet extends HttpServlet {

  static final String dbURL =
    "jdbc:mysql://localhost/j2mebook?" +
    "user=j2meapps&password=bigsecret";

  private static final int ID_ERROR =          -1;
  private static final int ID_LOGIN =           0;
```

```
private static final int ID_SEND_MESSAGE =          1;
private static final int ID_VERIFY_RECIPIENT =      2;
private static final int ID_GET_MESSAGE_HEADERS =   3;
private static final int ID_GET_MESSAGE_TEXT =      4;
private static final int ID_DELETE_MESSAGE =        5;
private static final int ID_REPLY =                 6;
private static final int ID_LOGOUT =                7;

String nextJSP = null;

String fullName = null;
String recipientFullName = null;

HttpSession session;

long cipherKey;

EnigmaMachine enigmaMachine;

public void doPost(HttpServletRequest request,
                   HttpServletResponse response)
    throws IOException, ServletException {

  String userid;
  String receivedHash;

  session = request.getSession();
  if (session.isNew()) {
    String token = Long.toString(System.currentTimeMillis());
    session.setAttribute("token",token);
    request.setAttribute("token",token);
    request.setAttribute("id",Integer.toString(ID_LOGIN));
    nextJSP = "/PresentLoginToken.jsp";
  }
  else {
    String screenID = request.getParameter("id");
    if (screenID == null) {
      nextJSP = "/Error.jsp";
    }
    else {
      int id = ID_ERROR;
      try {
```

```
            id = Integer.parseInt(screenID);
          }
          catch (NumberFormatException e) {
            throw new ServletException(e.getMessage());
          }
          switch (id) {
            case ID_LOGIN:
              login(request);
              break;
            case ID_VERIFY_RECIPIENT:
              verifyRecipient(request);
              break;
            case ID_SEND_MESSAGE:
              sendMessage(request);
              break;
            case ID_GET_MESSAGE_HEADERS:
              getMessageHeaders(request);
              break;
            case ID_GET_MESSAGE_TEXT:
              getMessageText(request);
              break;
            default:
              nextJSP = "/Error.jsp";
          }
        }
      }

      try {
        ServletConfig config = getServletConfig();
        ServletContext context = config.getServletContext();
        RequestDispatcher rd = context.getRequestDispatcher(nextJSP);
        rd.forward(request, response);
      }
      catch (Exception ex) {
        ex.printStackTrace ();
      }
    }

    public void doGet(HttpServletRequest request,
                      HttpServletResponse response)
        throws IOException, ServletException {
      doPost(request, response);
    }
```

```java
private void login(HttpServletRequest request)
    throws ServletException {
  HttpSession session = request.getSession();
  String token = (String)session.getAttribute("token");
  String userid = request.getParameter("userid");
  String receivedHash =
    request.getParameter("MD5hash").replace('$','+');
  if (isValid(userid, token, receivedHash)) {
    request.setAttribute("status", "OK");
    session.setAttribute("userid",userid);
    session.setAttribute("fromFull",fullName);
  }
  else {
    request.setAttribute("status","--");
  }
  nextJSP = "/LoginResult.jsp";
}

private void sendMessage(HttpServletRequest request)
    throws ServletException {
  String msgText = null;
  try {
    msgText =
      decode(request.getParameter("messagetext")).replace('\'','^');
  }
  catch (Base64Exception e) {
    throw new ServletException();
  }
  String recipient = (String)session.getAttribute("recipient");
  String subject = (String)session.getAttribute("subject");
  String from = (String)session.getAttribute("userid");
  String msgTime =
    new java.util.Date(System.currentTimeMillis()).toString();
  Connection conn = null;

  try {
    conn = DriverManager.getConnection(dbURL);

    String msgid =
      Long.toString(System.currentTimeMillis()) +
      Long.toString(Math.abs((long)recipient.hashCode()));
    Statement stmt = conn.createStatement();
    String update = "INSERT INTO messages VALUES ('" +
```

```java
                        msgid + "','" + recipient + "'," +
                        "'" + from + "'," +
                        "'" + msgTime + "'," +
                        "'" + subject + "'," +
                        "'" + msgText + "')";
      int nr = stmt.executeUpdate(update);
      if (nr > 0) {
        request.setAttribute("recipientFullName",
          session.getAttribute("recipientFullName"));
      }
      else {
        request.setAttribute("recipientFullName","--");
      }
      nextJSP = "/AcknowledgeMessageSend.jsp";
    }
    catch (SQLException e) {
      throw new ServletException("SQL call failed");
    }
    catch (Exception e) {
      throw new ServletException(e.getMessage());
    }
    finally {
      if (conn != null) {
        try {
          conn.close();
        }
        catch (SQLException e) {
          throw new ServletException("connection close failed");
        }
      }
    }
  }
}

  private void getMessageHeaders(HttpServletRequest request)
      throws ServletException {
    Connection conn = null;

    String userid = (String)session.getAttribute("userid");
    try {
      conn = DriverManager.getConnection(dbURL);

      Statement stmt = conn.createStatement();
      String query = "SELECT msgid, subject " +
```

```
                    "FROM messages WHERE msgto = '" +
                    userid + "'";
    ResultSet rs = stmt.executeQuery(query);
    int numMessages = 0;
    StringBuffer sb = new StringBuffer();
    while (rs.next()) {
      sb.append(rs.getString("msgid"));
      sb.append('\t');
      sb.append(encode(rs.getString("subject").replace('^','\'')));
      sb.append('\n');
      ++numMessages;
    }
    if (sb.length() > 0) {
      request.setAttribute("msgheaders",sb.toString());
    }
    else {
      request.setAttribute("msgheaders","--");
    }
    nextJSP = "/DisplayMessageHeaders.jsp";
  }
  catch (SQLException e) {
    throw new ServletException("SQL call failed");
  }
  catch (Exception e) {
    throw new ServletException(e.getMessage());
  }
  finally {
    if (conn != null) {
      try {
        conn.close();
      }
      catch (SQLException e) {
        throw new ServletException("connection close failed");
      }
    }
  }
}

private void getMessageText(HttpServletRequest request)
    throws ServletException {

  Connection conn = null;
```

```java
String msgid = request.getParameter("msgid");
try {
  conn = DriverManager.getConnection(dbURL);

  Statement stmt = conn.createStatement();
  String query = "SELECT msgfrom, msgdate, subject, " +
                     "message FROM messages WHERE msgid = '" +
                 msgid + "'";
  ResultSet rs = stmt.executeQuery(query);
  if (rs.next()) {
    request.setAttribute("status","OK");
    String msgfrom = rs.getString("msgfrom");
    String msgdate = rs.getString("msgdate");
    String msgSubject =
      encode(rs.getString("subject").replace('^','\''));
    String message =
      encode(rs.getString("message").replace('^','\''));
    request.setAttribute("msgid", msgid);
    request.setAttribute("msgdate", msgdate);
    request.setAttribute("msgfrom", msgfrom);
    request.setAttribute("msgsubject", msgSubject);
    request.setAttribute("message", message);
  }
  else {
    request.setAttribute("status","--");
  }
  nextJSP = "/DisplayMessageText.jsp";
}
catch (SQLException e) {
  throw new ServletException("SQL call failed");
}
catch (Exception e) {
  throw new ServletException(e.getMessage());
}
finally {
  if (conn != null) {
    try {
      conn.close();
    }
    catch (SQLException e) {
      throw new ServletException("connection close failed");
    }
  }
```

```
    }
  }
  private void verifyRecipient(HttpServletRequest request)
      throws ServletException {

    Connection conn = null;

    String recipient = request.getParameter("recipient");

    try {
      conn = DriverManager.getConnection(dbURL);

      Statement stmt = conn.createStatement();
      String query = "SELECT userid, firstname, " +
                     "lastname FROM users WHERE userid = '" +
                     recipient + "'";
      ResultSet rs = stmt.executeQuery(query);
      if (rs.next()) {
        byte[] in = null;
        try {
          String msg64 =
            request.getParameter("subject").replace('$','+');
          in = Base64.decode(msg64);
        }
        catch (Base64Exception e) {
          throw new ServletException(e);
        }
        int len = in.length;
        byte[] out = new byte[len];
        enigmaMachine.processMessage(in, out);
        String subject = new String(out);
        session.setAttribute("subject",subject.replace('\'','^'));
        session.setAttribute("recipient",recipient);
        String recipientFullName =
          rs.getString("firstname") + " " +
          rs.getString("lastname");
        session.setAttribute("recipientFullName", recipientFullName);
        request.setAttribute("status","OK");
      }
      else {
        request.setAttribute("status","--");
      }
      nextJSP = "/RecipientValidation.jsp";
```

```
    }
    catch (SQLException e) {
      throw new ServletException("SQL call failed");
    }
    catch (Exception e) {
      throw new ServletException(e.getMessage());
    }
    finally {
      if (conn != null) {
        try {
          conn.close();
        }
        catch (SQLException e) {
          throw new ServletException("connection close failed");
        }
      }
    }
  }

  private boolean isValid(String userid, String token,
    String receivedHash)
      throws ServletException {
    boolean userIsValid = false;
    try {
      Class.forName("org.gjt.mm.mysql.Driver");
    }
    catch (ClassNotFoundException e) {
      throw new ServletException("Unable to load JDBC driver");
    }

    Connection conn = null;

    try {
      conn = DriverManager.getConnection(dbURL);

      Statement stmt = conn.createStatement();
      String query = "SELECT firstname, lastname, password " +
                     "FROM users " + "WHERE userid = '" +
                     userid + "'";
      ResultSet rs = stmt.executeQuery(query);
      if (rs.next()) {
        StringBuffer sb = new StringBuffer();
        sb.append(rs.getString(1));
```

```
        sb.append(" ");
        sb.append(rs.getString(2));
        String password = rs.getString(3);
        String computedHash = computeHash(password, token);
        if ((userIsValid = computedHash.equals(receivedHash))) {
          long cipherKey = (long)password.hashCode();
          enigmaMachine = new EnigmaMachine(cipherKey);
          nextJSP = "/LogonOK.jsp";
          fullName = sb.toString();
        }
      }
      else {
        nextJSP = "/LogonFailed.jsp";
      }
    }
    catch (SQLException e) {
      throw new ServletException("SQL call failed");
    }
    catch (Exception e) {
      throw new ServletException(e.getMessage());
    }
    finally {
      if (conn != null) {
        try {
          conn.close();
        }
        catch (SQLException e) {
          throw new ServletException("connection close failed");
        }
      }
    }
    return userIsValid;
}

private String encode(String s) throws Base64Exception {
  byte[] in = s.getBytes();
  byte[] out = new byte[in.length];
  enigmaMachine.processMessage(in,out);
  return Base64.encode(out).replace('+','$');
}

private String decode(String s) throws Base64Exception {
  String s64 = s.replace('$','+');
```

```
      byte[] in = Base64.decode(s64);
      byte[] out = new byte[in.length];
      enigmaMachine.processMessage(in,out);
      return new String(out);
   }

  private String computeHash(String password, String token)
      throws ServletException {
    StringBuffer sb = new StringBuffer(password);
    sb.append(token);
    byte[] digest = null;
    try {
      MessageDigest md = MessageDigest.getInstance("MD5");
      digest = md.digest(sb.toString().getBytes());
    }
    catch (NoSuchAlgorithmException e) {
      throw new ServletException("no MD5 algorithm available");
    }
    return Base64.encode(digest);
  }
}
```

Like the client, the server is similar to the one you saw in Chapter 16. It is a servlet that works in conjunction with JavaServer Pages. Its `doPost` method handles requests from the MID. Each request includes a hidden field that identifies the request. The value of this hidden field is used in a `switch` statement that determines the processing that should be performed.

When the user wishes to send a message, he or she enters the name of the intended recipient. A check is performed to ensure that the recipient exists in the *user* database table. A message intended for the recipient is encoded using a key derived from the hash code of the sender's password. When the server receives the encoded message, it decodes it since it can obtain the sender's password from the *user* database table. The message is stored as cleartext in the database, since the database can be protected. You could, if you wish, store an encrypted version of the message in the database.

When a user picks up his or her mail, the servlet encodes the message using the password of the recipient, who can decode it on the device, since the application running on the device knows the password.

The subject field of each message is also transmitted as ciphertext. All data is converted to base 64 before transmission. The normal character set used in base 64 encoding includes the + character. Before transmission, all occurrences of + are replaced by $. This is because the HTTP protocol replaces all + characters with spaces. The appropriate reverse substitution is performed on the receiving end.

Before inserting data into the *messages* database table, the server replaces all single quotes with ^. This prevents such quotes from being misinterpreted by the SQL parser as part of the query or update command. The appropriate reverse substitution is performed when the data is read from the database table.

Running
\OMH\cr_messages.sql

Before running the application, you should add new users to the *users* database table. You must also create the *messages* database table using the SQL supplied on the CD.

After you have added the new users *paul* and *kutch* and after you have created the *messages* table, you should issue the following SQL commands:

```
select * from users;
desc messages;
```

The output from these commands is shown here:

```
Command Prompt - mysql
mysql> select * from users;
+--------+-------------+-----------+--------------+
| userid | password    | firstname | lastname     |
+--------+-------------+-----------+--------------+
| jenny  | divine_ms_m | Jennifer  | Malnick      |
| paul   | g4zinta     | Paul      | Tremblett    |
| kutch  | isit42      | Josephine | Kutchenrider |
+--------+-------------+-----------+--------------+
3 rows in set (0.00 sec)

mysql> desc messages;
+---------+-------------+------+-----+---------+-------+
| Field   | Type        | Null | Key | Default | Extra |
+---------+-------------+------+-----+---------+-------+
| msgid   | varchar(25) | YES  |     | NULL    |       |
| msgto   | varchar(8)  | YES  |     | NULL    |       |
| msgfrom | varchar(25) | YES  |     | NULL    |       |
| msgdate | varchar(30) | YES  |     | NULL    |       |
| subject | varchar(15) | YES  |     | NULL    |       |
| message | blob        | YES  |     | NULL    |       |
+---------+-------------+------+-----+---------+-------+
6 rows in set (0.00 sec)

mysql>
```

One final thing you must do before you run the application is to make sure that the crypto modules are included. You do this by double-clicking on the MIDlet Suite icon, selecting the Content tab and using the Add> button to add the directory c:\OMH\com\paulsjavabooks\instantj2me\crypto.

When you launch the application, you are presented with a login screen. Log in as user *paul* using password *g4zinta*, as shown here:

After the MIDlet sends the login data to the server and receives validation, it displays the main menu as an IMPLICIT `List`, as shown here:

The next step consists of entering the name of the recipient and the subject of the message, as shown here.

When you press Next, the MIDlet sends the recipient and the subject to the servlet. If the recipient is not found in the *users* database table, an error is displayed. If it is found, a `TextBox` is displayed. You type the message into the text box like this:

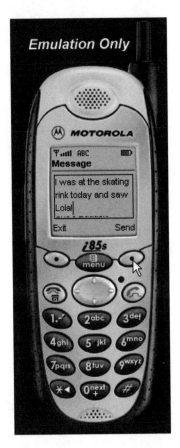

The MIDlet encodes the message and sends it to the servlet, which decodes it and store it in the *messages* table, along with the name of the sender, the subject, and the date and time when it was sent. The servlet then sends back an acknowledgement which the MIDlet displays as follows:

When the main menu is displayed again, you can send a second message. The contents of the *messages* database table now looks like this:

```
Command Prompt - mysql

Your MySQL connection id is 98 to server version: 3.23.42-nt

Type 'help;' or '\h' for help. Type '\c' to clear the buffer.

mysql> connect j2mebook
Connection id:    99
Current database: j2mebook

mysql> select * from messages;
+----------------------+-------+---------+------------------------------+------
----------------+----------------------------------------------------+
| msgid                | msgto | msgfrom | msgdate                      | subj
ect          | message                                             |
+----------------------+-------+---------+------------------------------+------
----------------+----------------------------------------------------+
| 1004476887547102416943 | kutch | paul    | Tue Oct 30 16:21:27 EST 2001 | She^
s Baaack!    | I was at the skating rink today and saw Lola!       |
| 1004476973240102416943 | kutch | paul    | Tue Oct 30 16:22:53 EST 2001 | The
Answer Is.. | The answer, which you probably already know, is 42!!!!!! |
+----------------------+-------+---------+------------------------------+------
----------------+----------------------------------------------------+
2 rows in set (0.00 sec)

mysql>
```

The next step in the process is to retrieve the message from the database. Since the messages were sent to Josephine, you must log in using her user ID and password. These are *kutch* and *isit42*, as shown here:

This time, instead of selecting Send Message from the main menu, you select Get Messages, like this:

The servlet reads from the database the message ID and subject for each message belonging to *kutch* and sends the list back to the MIDlet. The list of subjects is displayed, as shown next:

When a subject is selected from the list, its corresponding message ID is sent to the servlet. The servlet reads the message body from the database table, encrypts it using the password for *kutch*, and sends it to the MIDlet. It is displayed as a scrollable screen of `StringItems`. The top portion of the screen looks like this:

You can use the scroll button to view the bottom portion of the message, as shown here:

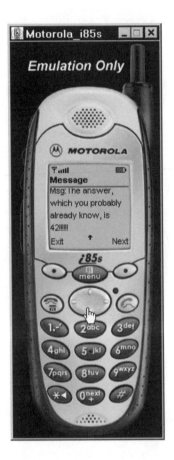

The screen that displays the message has the commands Reply, Delete, Next, and Prev associated with it. These are not implemented in the current version of the example, but empty methods are supplied if you wish to implement them as an exercise.

Enigma Code

The modules that comprise the Enigma machine are listed here.

EnigmaMachine.java

\OMH\com\paulsjavabooks\instantj2mecrypto\Enigma.java

```java
/*
 * EnigmaMachine.java
 *
 * Created on October 28, 2001, 10:33 PM
 */


package com.paulsjavabooks.instantj2me.crypto;

import java.util.Random;

/**
 *
 * @author  paul
 * @version
 */
public class EnigmaMachine extends java.lang.Object {

  EnigmaRotor[] rotors;
  int rotorCount;
  EnigmaReflector reflector;

  public EnigmaMachine(long seed) {
    Random r = new Random();
    r.setSeed(seed);
    rotorCount = Math.abs(r.nextInt() & 0x07);
    if (rotorCount < 3) {
      rotorCount = 3;
    }
    rotors = new EnigmaRotor[rotorCount];
    for (int i = 0; i < rotorCount; ++i) {
      rotors[i] = new EnigmaRotor(r.nextLong());
    }
    reflector = new EnigmaReflector(r.nextLong());
  }
```

```java
  public EnigmaMachine(long seed, int rotorCount) {
    this.rotorCount = rotorCount;
    Random r = new Random();
    r.setSeed(seed);
    rotors = new EnigmaRotor[rotorCount];
    for (int i = 0; i < rotorCount; ++i) {
      rotors[i] = new EnigmaRotor(r.nextLong());
    }
    reflector = new EnigmaReflector(r.nextLong());
  }

  public void processMessage(byte[] in, byte[] out) {
    for (int i = 0; i < in.length; ++i) {
      for (int rotorIndex = 0; rotorIndex < rotorCount; ++rotorIndex)
{
        try {
          rotors[rotorIndex].advance();
          break;
        }
        catch (EnigmaRotorTrippedException erte) {
        }
      }
      int ic = ((int)in[i]) & 0xff;
      for (int k = 0; k < rotorCount; ++k) {
        ic = rotors[k].processByte(ic, true);
      }
      ic = reflector.reflect(ic);
      for (int k = rotorCount - 1; k >= 0; --k) {
        ic = rotors[k].processByte(ic, false);
      }
      out[i] = (byte)ic;
    }
  }
}
```

EnigmaRotor.java

\OMH\com\paulsjavabooks\instantj2me\crypto\EnigmaRotor.java

```java
/*
 * EnigmaRotor.java
 *
```

```java
 * Created on October 28, 2001, 10:35 PM
 */

package com.paulsjavabooks.instantj2me.crypto;

import java.util.Random;

/**
 *
 * @author  paul
 * @version
 */
public class EnigmaRotor extends java.lang.Object {

  private int notchIndex = 0;
  private int startPosition = 0;
  private int currentIndex = 0;

  private int[] b = new int[256];
  private int[] f = new int[256];

  public EnigmaRotor(long seed) {
    int fx = 0;
    int bx;
    for (int i = 0; i < 256; ++i)
      f[i] = b[i] = -1;
    Random r = new Random();
    r.setSeed(seed);
    int rb;
    for (int i = 0; i < 256; ++i) {
      rb = r.nextInt();
      bx = rb & 0xff;
      if (b[bx] < 0) {
        b[bx] = fx;
      }
      else {
        bx = (bx + 128) % 256;
        while (true) {
          if (bx > 255)
            bx = 0;
```

```
        if (b[bx] < 0)
          break;
        bx++;
      }
      b[bx] = fx;
    }
    f[fx] = bx;
    fx++;
  }
  startPosition = currentIndex = r.nextInt() & 0xff;
}

public void setStartingPosition(int startPosition) {
  this.startPosition = currentIndex = startPosition;
}

public void advance() throws EnigmaRotorTrippedException {
  currentIndex++;
  if (currentIndex > 255) {
    currentIndex = 0;
  }
  if (currentIndex == notchIndex) {
    throw new EnigmaRotorTrippedException("notch at " +
      notchIndex + " tripped");
  }
}

public int processByte(int i, boolean forward) {
  int ri;
  int ix;
  if (forward) {
    ix = (i + currentIndex) % 256;
    ri = b[ix];
  }
  else {
    ix = i;
    ri = (f[ix] - currentIndex + 256) % 256;
  }
  return ri;
}
}
```

EnigmaReflector.java

\OMH\com\paulsjavabooks\instantj2me\crypto\EnigmaReflector.java

```java
/*
 * EnigmaReflector.java
 *
 * Created on October 28, 2001, 10:35 PM
 */


package com.paulsjavabooks.instantj2me.crypto;

import java.util.Random;

/**
 *
 * @author  paul
 * @version
 */
public class EnigmaReflector extends java.lang.Object {

  private int[] contacts = new int[256];

  public EnigmaReflector(long seed) {
    int rb;
    int[] mi = new int[256];
    for (int i = 0; i < 256; ++i)
      mi[i] = -1;
    Random r = new Random();
    r.setSeed(seed);
    int[] f = new int[2];
    for (int i = 0; i < 128; ++i) {
      for (int j = 0; j < 2; ++j) {
        rb = r.nextInt();
        int ix  = rb &0x3f;
        while (true) {
          if (mi[ix] < 0) {
            mi[ix] = 1;
            f[j] = ix;
            break;
          }
          ++ix;
```

```
        if (ix > 255) {
          ix = 0;
        }
      }
    }
    contacts[f[0]] = f[1];
    contacts[f[1]] = f[0];
  }
}

public int reflect(int i) {
  return contacts[i];
}
}
```

EnigmaRotorTrippedException.java

\OMH\com\paulsjavabooks\instantj2me\crypto\EnigmaRotorTrippedException.java

```java
/*
 * EnigmaRotorTrippedException.java
 *
 * Created on October 28, 2001, 10:36 PM
 */

package com.paulsjavabooks.instantj2me.crypto;

/**
 *
 * @author  paul
 * @version
 */
public class EnigmaRotorTrippedException extends java.lang.Exception {

  public EnigmaRotorTrippedException() {
    super();
  }

  public EnigmaRotorTrippedException(String msg) {
    super(msg);
  }
}
```

In Conclusion

If you have explored all the MIDlets presented in the book, you should now feel comfortable writing MIDlets. As is the case with any new technology, you will become really proficient at using it by writing your own applications. I would like to suggest that the best practice you can get is to search the Web for the hundreds of applications that have already been developed for Palm devices. Don't look at the code, but simply note what each application does. Pick a few applications that appeal to you and write their MIDlet equivalents. Since the success of any programming language is proportional to the number of applications in which it is used, each MIDlet you develop will contribute to the acceptance and success of J2ME. I wish you success.

Installing Prerequisite Software

Τhis Appendix briefly describes how to obtain the software that was used to develop the sample programs used in the book. Instructions for installing the software are available from each download site.

NOTE

The URLs mentioned here were correct at the time this book was written. It is not uncommon for Web sites to be rearranged. If you encounter problems accessing any of the URLs, you should try to access the home page of the site in question and then follow the links to the software you are trying to download.

Forte For Java Community Edition

This component is optional but highly recommended. While it is possible to develop J2ME applications using your favorite editor and the command line, using an IDE is much easier. If you choose to use Forte, and you want to integrate it with the Java 2 Microedition Wireless Toolkit (J2MEWTK), you *must* install Forte first.

Forte for Java Community Edition is available at no cost from Sun at http://www.sun.com/forte/ffj. Like most software, this product is subject to a license agreement. You will be asked to view the license and agree to its terms as part of the download process.

The software downloads as an executable. When you run the executable, it installs Forte.

Java 2 Microedition Wireless Toolkit

This component contains everything you need for start-to-finish development of J2ME applications for devices that support the MID Profile. In addition to the JAR file containing the MIDP APIs, the Toolkit contains a byte-code preverifier, several emulators, the KToolbar, and a plug-in module that lets you run the tools under Forte. As previously mentioned, if you wish to use the plug-in, you *must* install Forte first.

The Java 2 Micro Edition Wireless Toolkit is available from http://java.sun.com/products/j2newtoolkit/download.html. Like Forte, it downloads as an executable that installs the Toolkit when you run it. When the installer presents the dialog box asking whether you want standalone or integrated, you should choose the integrated option if you wish to use the Toolkit in conjunction with Forte.

Palm OS Emulator (POSE)

One of the more popular emulators that can be launched from the KToolbar or Forte is the Palm OS Emulator (POSE). It is available at no charge under license from http://www.palmos.com/dev/tech/tools/emulator. In order to run the emulator, you will need a Palm ROM of OS 3.5 or later. If you own a Palm, you can transfer the ROM from it using RomTransfer.prc. If you do not own a Palm device, you can obtain a ROM from Palm by joining their developer program.

MySQL Relational Database Management System

MySql is an Open Source SQL database from the Swedish company MySQL AB. It is available at no charge from http://www.mysql.com/downloads/mysql-3.23.html. It uses the GNU General Public License to define what you may and may not do with the code.

The software is distributed as a Zip file that you extract using WinZIP.

NOTE

You can use another database if you wish. If this is the case, you can skip this section and the following section. You must, however, modify the examples to reflect the name of your JDBC driver. You might also have to modify the SQL that creates the database tables.

JDBC Driver For mySQL

There are several JDBC drivers for mySQL. One of the more widely used type IV drivers, and the one used in this book, is MM.Mysql. It is available from http://mmmysql.sourceforge.net/#downloads under the LGPL license. Installation consists of simply placing the JAR file in a directory that appears in your CLASSPATH.

Apache Web Server

Apache is the most popular web server is use today in installations large and small. It is available under the Apache Software license from http://www.apache.org. Detailed instructions for installing the server are available from the download site.

NOTE

Any J2EE-compliant web server can be used. If you already have such a server installed, you can skip this section and the following two sections.

Tomcat Servlet Container

Some of the examples in the book use `HttpConnection` to communicate with servlets that use JavaServer Pages to deliver output. Tomcat provides the environment for running servlets and JSPs. It is available under terms of the Apache Software license from jakarta.apache.org, and several documents are available that describe the installation procedure.

mod_jk

Typically, requests that simply ask for a Web page or image and requests that require servicing by a servlet are both sent to Apache, which sends requests that are targeted at a servlet to Tomcat. The software that enables Apache to communicate with Tomcat is mod_jk. It is available under terms of the Apache Software license from http://jakarta.apache.org/builds/jakarta-tomcat/release/v3.2.3/bin/win32/i386.

Software From The CD

The software used in this book is divided into four categories:

- ▶ MIDlets
- ▶ SQL For Creating Database Tables
- ▶ Standalone Programs and Servers
- ▶ J2EE Software

Installation of software from the CD depends upon the category. Each is described as follows.

MIDlets

All of the MIDlets are contained in the file MIDlets.zip, which unzips into the directory \OMH. Use the Filesystems tab in Forte's Explorer window to mount this directory. If you only want to run the sample programs, all you have to do is right-click on a MIDlet Suite icon and select Execute. If you want to explore and possibly modify the source code, you can do so by double-clicking on the MIDlets icon.

SQL For Creating Database Tables

The file SQL.zip contains the SQL you will need to create the database tables. You can unzip this file into any directory, but \OMH is recommended. If you use a database other than MySQL, you might have to modify these files.

Standalone Program and Servers

Programs in this category are contained in the file StandAlone.zip. You can extract the contents of this file into any directory, but \OMH is recommended.

J2EE Software

Software in this category is available from two sources on the CD. The first is the file J2MEBOOK.war. If you have properly installed Apache and Tomcat or if you have a J2EE-compliant web server already installed, you can simply place a copy of J2MEBOOK.war in the webapps directory and restart the server. When the server starts, it will create the context J2MEBOOK and extract the contents of J2MEBOOK.war into the proper directories.

If you are not using a J2EE-compliant server, you can extract the servlets and JSPs from the file J2EE.zip and move the components to the appropriate directories.

NOTE

The instructions in this appendix assume that you are using Windows. All of the software mentioned is also available for Linux.

B

The MIDP API

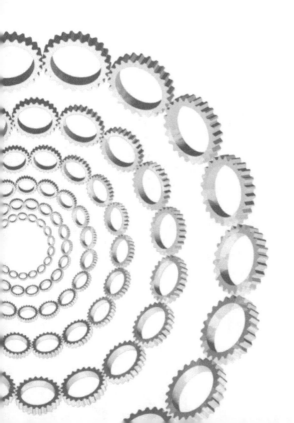

T his appendix is intended to provide a quick reference to the methods of each of the classes and interfaces found in the six packages that comprise the MIDP API. It does not contain detailed information about each of the classes and interfaces and does not describe constructors. The exceptions that can be thrown by a method and detailed explanations of each exception are not shown. Detailed information can be found in the javadoc that is delivered with MIDP.

Package java.io

This package provides for system input and output through data streams.

Interface DataInput

Method	Description
boolean readBoolean( )	Reads 1 byte. Returns true if byte is non-zero. Returns false if byte is zero.
byte readByte( )	Reads 1 input byte.
char readChar( )	Reads one input char.
void readFully(byte[ ] b)	Reads b bytes. Blocks until b bytes are available or end of file is detected.
void readFully(byte[ ]b, int off, int len)	Reads len bytes. Blocks until len bytes are available or end of file is detected.
int readInt( )	Reads 4 input bytes and returns an int.
long readLong( )	Reads 8 bytes and returns a long.
short readShort( )	Reads 2 bytes and returns a short.
int readUnsignedByte( )	Reads 1 byte, zero extends it to an int and returns an int in the range 0–255.
int readUnsignedShort( )	Reads 2 bytes and returns an int in the range 0–65535.
String readUTF( )	Reads a String that was encoded using a modified UTF-8 format. The first 2 bytes read are used to form an unsigned 16-bit integer that indicates the number of bytes to read.
int skipBytes(int n)	Attempts to skip over and discard n bytes.

Interface DataOutput

Method	Description
void write(byte[ ] b)	Writes the bytes in array *b*.
void write(byte[ ] b, int off, int len)	Writes *len* bytes from array *b* starting at off.
void write(int b)	Writes the 8 low-order bits of *b*.
void writeBoolean(boolean v)	Writes a boolean.
void writeByte(int v)	Writes the 8 low-order bits of *v*.
void writeChar(int v)	Writes a char comprised of 2 bytes.
void writeChars(String s)	Write all characters in *s*, 2 bytes per character.
void writeInt(int v)	Writes an int.
void writeLong(long v)	Writes a long.
void writeShort(int v)	Writes a short.
void writeUTF(String s)	Writes 2 bytes of length information followed by each character in *s* using the Java modified UTF representation.

Class ByteArrayInputStream

Method	Description
int available( )	Returns the number of bytes that can be read without blocking.
void close( )	Closes the input stream.
void mark(int readAheadLimit)	Sets the current marked position.
boolean markSupported( )	Returns true if ByteArrayInputStream supports mark/reset.
int read( )	Reads the next byte and returns it as an int in the range 0–255.
int read(byte[ ] b, int off, int len)	Reads up to *len* bytes of data into the byte array *b*. Returns the actual number of bytes read, which can be less than or equal to *len*. Returns –1 if end of file is detected.
void reset( )	Resets buffer to marked position.
long skip (long n)	Skips *n* bytes.

Class ByteArrayOutputStream

Method	Description
void close( )	Closes the output stream.
void reset( )	Resets the count field to zero so that all currently accumulated output is discarded.
int size( )	Returns the current size of the buffer.
byte[ ] toByteArray( )	Copies the contents of the buffer to a newly allocated byte array and returns the array.
String toString( )	Copies the buffer to a String translating bytes into characters according to the platform's default encoding and returns the String.
void write(byte b, int off, int len)	Writes *len* bytes from *b* starting at off.
void write(int b)	Writes *b*.

Class DataInputStream

Method	Description
int available( )	Returns the number of bytes that can be read without blocking.
void close( )	Closes the stream.
void mark(int readLimit)	Marks the current position in the input stream.
boolean markSupported( )	Returns true if the input stream supports the mark and reset methods.
int read( )	Reads the next byte.
int read(byte[ ] b)	See Interface DataInput.
int read(byte[ ] b, int off, int len)	See Interface DataInput.
boolean readBoolean( )	See Interface DataInput.
byte readByte( )	See Interface DataInput.
char readChar( )	See Interface DataInput.
void readFully(byte[ ] b)	See Interface DataInput.
void readFully(byte[ ] b, int off, int len)	See Interface DataInput.
int readInt( )	See Interface DataInput.
long readLong( )	See Interface DataInput.
short readShort( )	See Interface DataInput.
int readUnsignedByte( )	See Interface DataInput.

Method	Description
int readUnsignedShort( )	See Interface DataInput.
String readUTF( )	See Interface DataInput.
String readUTF(DataInput in)	Reads a unicode character string from the stream in and returns it as a Java String.
void reset( )	Repositions stream to point where mark method was last called.
long skip(long n)	Skips *n* bytes.
int skipBytes(int n)	See Interface DataInput.

Class DataOutputStream

Method	Description
void close( )	Closes the stream.
void flush( )	Flushes the stream.
void write(byte[ ] b, int off, int len)	Writes *len* bytes from *b* starting at off.
void write(int b)	Writes the 8 low-order bits of *b*.
void writeBoolean(boolean v)	Writes a boolean as 1 byte.
void writeByte(int v)	Writes a byte.
void writeChar(char v)	Writes a char as a 2-byte value, high byte first.
void writeChars(String s)	Writes the String *s*.
void writeInt(int v)	Writes an int as 4 bytes, high byte first.
void writeLong(long v)	Writes a long as 8 bytes, high bytes first.
void writeShort(short v)	Writes a short as 2 bytes, high byte first.
void writeUTF(String s)	Writes the String *s* using UTF-8 encoding.

Class InputStream

Method	Description
int available( )	Returns the number of bytes that can be read without blocking.
void close( )	Closes the stream.
void mark( )	Marks the current position in the stream.
boolean markSupported( )	Returns true if the stream supports mark and reset.
abstract int read( )	Reads the next byte.

Method	Description
int read(byte[ ] b)	Reads bytes into the byte array *b*. Returns the actual number of bytes read.
int read(byte b, int off, int len)	Reads up to *len* bytes into *b* starting at off. Returns the actual number of bytes read.
void reset( )	Resets the stream to the position when mark was last called.
long skip(long n)	Skips over *n* bytes.

Class InputStreamReader

Method	Description
void close( )	Closes the stream.
void mark( )	Marks the current position in the stream.
boolean markSupported( )	Returns true if the stream supports mark and reset.
int read( )	Reads a single character.
int read(char[ ] cb, int off, int len)	Reads *len* characters into *ca* starting at off. Returns the actual number of characters read.
boolean ready( )	Returns true if the stream is ready to be read.
void reset( )	Resets the stream to the position when mark was last called.
long skip(long n)	Skips *n* characters.

OutputStream

Method	Description
void close( )	Closes the stream.
void flush( )	Flushes the stream.
void write(byte[ ] b)	Writes all the bytes in *b*.
void write(byte[ ] b, int off, int len)	Writes *len* bytes from *b* starting at off.
abstract void write(int b)	Writes the byte *b*.

Class OutputStreamWriter

Method	Description
void close( )	Closes the stream.
void flush( )	Flushes the stream.
void write(char[ ] cb, int off, int len)	Writes *len* chars from *ca* starting at off.
void write(char c)	Writes the single character *c*.
void write(String s, int off, int len)	Writes *len* characters from *s* staring at off.

Class PrintStream

Method	Description
boolean checkError( )	Flushes stream and checks error state.
void close( )	Closes the stream.
void flush( )	Flushes the stream.
void print(boolean b)	Prints a boolean.
void print(char c)	Prints a char.
void print(char[ ] s)	Prints a character array.
void print(int i)	Prints an int.
void print(long l)	Prints a long.
void print(Object o)	Prints a String representation of an object.
void print(String s)	Prints a String.
void println( )	Terminates the current line by writing a line separator string as defined in System.properties.
void println(boolean b)	Prints a boolean and terminates the line.
void println(char)	Prints a char and terminates the line.
void println(char[ ] s)	Prints a character array and terminates the line.
void println(int i)	Prints an int and terminates the line.
void println(long l)	Prints a long and terminates the line.

Method	Description
void println(Object o)	Prints an object and terminates the line.
void println(String s)	Prints a String and terminates the line.
protected void setError( )	Sets the error state of the stream to true.
void write(byte[ ] b, int off, int len)	Writes *len* bytes from *b* starting at off to the stream.
void write(int b)	Writes *b* to the stream.

Class Reader

Method	Description
abstract void close( )	Closes the stream.
void mark( )	Marks the current position in the stream.
boolean markSupported( )	Returns true if the stream supports mark.
int read( )	Reads a single character.
int read(char[ ] cb)	Reads characters into *cb*. Returns the actual number of characters read.
abstract int read(char[ ] cb, int off, int len)	Reads up to *len* characters into *cb* starting at off.
boolean ready( )	Returns true if the stream is ready to be read.
void reset( )	Resets the stream.
long skip(long n)	Skips *n* characters.

Class Writer

Method	Description
abstract void close( )	Closes the stream.
abstract void flush( )	Flushes the stream.
void write(char[ ] cb)	Writes the characters in *cb*.
void write(char[ ] cb, int off, int len)	Writes *len* chars from *cd* starting at off.
void write(int c)	Writes a single character.
void write(String s)	Writes all of the characters in *s*.
void write(String s, int off, int len)	Writes *len* characters from *s* starting at off.

Package java.lang

This package contains MID Profile Language classes included from Java 2 Standard Edition.

Interface Runnable

Method	Description
void run( )	Called when a thread is started if that thread was created using an Object that implements Runnable.

Class Boolean

Method	Description
boolean booleanValue( )	Returns the value as a boolean primitive.
boolean equals(Object o)	Runs true if and only if *o* is not null and is a Boolean object that represents the same Boolean value as this object.
int hashCode( )	Returns the object's hash code.
String toString( )	Returns a String object representing this object's Boolean value.

Class Byte

Method	Description
byte byteValue( )	Returns the value of this object as a byte.
boolean equals(Object o)	Compares this object to *o*.
int hashCode( )	Returns the object's hash code.
static byte parseByte(String s)	Returns a byte containing the value represented by *s*.
static byte parseByte(String s, radix r)	Returns a byte containing the value represented by *s* using radix *r*.
String toString( )	Returns a String representing this object's byte value.

Class Character

Method	Description
char charValue( )	Returns the char value of the object.
static int digit(char c, int r)	Returns the numeric value of c in radix r.
boolean equals(Object o)	Compares this object to o.
int hashCode( )	Returns the object's hash code.
static boolean isDigit(char c)	Returns true if c is a digit.
static boolean isLowerCase(char c)	Returns true if c is a lowercase character.
static boolean isUpperCase(char c)	Returns true if c is an uppercase character.
static char toLowerCase(char c)	Returns c mapped to its lowercase equivalent.
String toString( )	Returns a String representing this object's character value.
static char toUpperCase(char c)	Returns c mapped to its uppercase equivalent.

Class Class

Method	Description
static Class forName(String cn)	Returns the Class object associated with the class named cn.
String getName( )	Returns a String containing the fully qualified name of the class, interface, array class, primitive type, or void represented by this Class object.
InputStream getResourceAsStream(String s)	Finds a resource with the name s.
boolean isArray( )	Returns true if this Class object represents an array class.
boolean isAssignableFrom(Class cl)	Returns true if the class or interface represented by this Class object is either the same as or a superclass or superinterface of the class or interface represented by cl.
boolean isInstance(Object o)	Returns true if o is assignment-compatible with the object represented by this class.
boolean isInterface( )	Returns true if the specified Class object represents an interface.
String newInstance( )	Creates a new instance of a class.
String toString( )	Returns a String representing the object.

Class Integer

Method	Description
byte byteValue( )	Returns the value of this Integer as a byte.
boolean equals(Object o)	Compares this object to *o*.
int hashCode( )	Returns the object's hash code.
int intValue( )	Returns the value of this Integer as an int.
long longValue( )	Returns the value of this Integer as a long.
static int parseInt(String s)	Parses *s* as a signed decimal integer.
static int parseInt(String s, int radix)	Parses *s* as a signed decimal integer in radix *r*.
short shortValue( )	Returns the value of this Integer as a short.
static String toBinaryString(int i)	Returns a String representing the argument as an unsigned integer in base 2.
static String toHexString(int i)	Returns a String representing the argument as an unsigned integer in base 16.
static String toOctalString(int i)	Returns a String representing the argument as an unsigned integer in base 8.
String toString( )	Returns a String representing this Integer's value.
String toString(int i)	Returns a String representing the argument.
String toString(int , int r)	Returns a String representing the first argument in radix *r*.
static Integer valueOf(String s)	Returns an Integer object initialized to *s*.
static Integer valueOf(String s, int r)	Returns an Integer object initialized to *s* in radix *r*.

Class Long

Method	Description
boolean equals(Object o)	Compares this object to *o*.
int hashCode( )	Returns the object's hash code.
long longValue( )	Returns the value of this object as a long.
static long parseLong(String s)	Returns a String representing *s* as a signed decimal long.
static long parseLong(String s, int r)	Returns a String representing *s* as a signed decimal long in radix *r*.
String toString( )	Returns a String representing this object's value.
static String toString(long l)	Returns a String representing the argument.
static String toString(long l, int r)	Returns a String representing the argument in radix *r*.

Class Math

Method	Description
static int abs(int a)	Returns the absolute value of a.
static long abs(int b)	Returns the absolute value of b.
static int max(int a, int b)	Returns the greater of a and b.
static long max(long a, long b)	Returns the greater of a and b.
static int min(int a, int b)	Returns the lesser of a and b.
static long min(long a, long b)	Returns the lesser of a and b.

Class Object

Method	Description
boolean equals(Object o)	Returns true if o is equal to this object.
Class getClass( )	Returns the object's runtime class.
int hashCode( )	Returns the object's hash code.
void notify( )	Wakes up a single thread that is waiting on this object's monitor.
void notifyAll( )	Wakes up all threads that are waiting on this object's monitor.
String toString( )	Returns a String representing this object.
void wait( )	Causes the current thread to wait until another thread notifies this object.
void wait(long t)	Causes the current thread to wait at most t milliseconds for another thread to notify this object.
void wait(long t, int n)	Causes the current thread to wait at most $(1000000 * t) + n$ nanoseconds for another thread to notify this object.

Class Runtime

Method	Description
void exit( )	Terminates the current application.
long freeMemory( )	Returns the amount of free memory in the system.

Method	Description
void gc( )	Requests that the virtual machine run the garbage collector.
static Runtime getRuntime( )	Returns the Runtime object associated with the current application.
long totalMemory( )	Returns the total amount of memory in the virtual machine.

Class Short

Method	Description
boolean equals(Object o)	Compares this object to *o*.
int hashCode	Returns the object's hash code.
static short parseShort(String s)	Returns the short represented by *s*.
static short parseShort(String s, int r)	Returns the short represented by *s* in radix *r*.
short shortValue( )	Returns the value of this object as a short.
String toString( )	Returns a String representing this object.

Class String

Method	Description
char charAt(int index)	Returns the character at index.
int compareTo(String s)	Returns −1, 0, 1 depending on whether *s* is lexicographically less than this object, equal to this object, or greater than this object.
String concat(String s)	Returns a String that is the concatenation of this String and *s*.
boolean endsWith(String s)	Returns true if this String ends with *s*.
boolean equals(String s)	Returns true if this String equals *s*.
byte[ ] getBytes( )	Returns an array of bytes resulting from converting this String according to the platform's default encoding.
byte[ ] getBytes(String e)	Returns an array of bytes resulting from converting this String according to the encoding specified by *e*.
void getChars(int sb, int se, char[ ] d, int db)	Copies characters from this String starting at *sb* up to *se* into *d* beginning at *db*.

Method	Description
int hashCode( )	Returns the object's hash code.
int indexOf(int ch)	Returns the index of *ch* in this String.
int indexOf(int ch, int st)	Returns the index of *ch* is this String starting the search at *st*.
int indexOf(String s)	Returns the position in this String at which the substring *s* begins.
int indexOf(String s, int st)	Returns the position in this String at which the substring *s* begins, starting the search at *st*.
int lastIndexOf(int ch)	Returns the index of the last occurrence of *ch* in this String.
int lastIndexOf(int ch, int st)	Returns the index of the last occurrence of *ch* in this String starting the search at *st*.
int length( )	Returns the length of this String.
boolean regionMatches(boolean ignrCase, int off, String s, int so, int len)	Returns true if *len* bytes of this String starting at off match *len* bytes of *s* starting at *so* with case sensitivity determined by ignrCase.
String replace(ch old, ch new)	Returns a String that is a copy of this String with all occurrences of *old* replaced by *new*.
boolean startsWith(String s)	Returns true if this String starts with *s*.
boolean startsWith(String s, int off)	Returns true if this String beginning at off starts with *s*.
String substring(int b)	Returns the substring of this String from *b* to the end.
String substring(int b, int e)	Returns the substring of this String beginning at *b* and ending at *e*.
char[ ] toCharArray( )	Returns this String converted to a character array.
String toLowerCase( )	Returns a copy of this String converted to lowercase.
String toString( )	Returns itself.
String toUpperCase( )	Returns a copy of this String converted to uppercase.
String trim( )	Returns a copy of this String with white space removed from each end.
static String valueOf(boolean b)	Returns a String representing *b*.
static String valueOf(char c)	Returns a String representing *c*.

Method	Description
static String valueOf(char[ ] ca)	Returns a String representing the character array *ca*.
static String valueOf(char[ ] ca, int off, int len)	Returns a String representing *len* characters in *ca* starting at off.
static String valueOf(int i)	Returns a String representing the argument.
static String valueOf(long l)	Returns a String representing *l*.
static String valueOf(Object o)	Returns a String representing *o*.

Class StringBuffer

Method	Description
StringBuffer append(boolean b)	Appends the string representation of *b* to the StringBuffer.
StringBuffer append(char c)	Appends the string representation of *c* to the StringBuffer.
StringBuffer append(char[ ] ca)	Appends the string representation of *ca* to the StringBuffer.
StringBuffer append(char[ ] ca, int off, int len)	Appends *len* characters from *ca* starting at off to the StringBuffer.
StringBuffer append(int v)	Appends the string representation of *v* to the StringBuffer.
StringBuffer append(long l)	Appends the string representation of *l* to the StringBuffer.
StringBuffer append(Object o)	Appends the string representation of *o* to the StringBuffer.
StringBuffer append(String s)	Appends *s* to the StringBuffer.
int capacity( )	Returns the capacity of the StringBuffer.
char charAt(int index)	Returns the character at index.
StringBuffer delete(int b, int e)	Collapses the StringBuffer by removing the substring starting at *b* and ending at *e*.
StringBuffer deleteCharAt(int index)	Collapses the StringBuffer by removing the character at index.
void ensureCapacity(int mc)	Ensures that the capacity is at least *mc*.
void getChars(int sb, int se, char[ ] dest, int dl)	Copies *dl* characters from position *sb* to position *se* from the StringBuffer to *dest*.

Method	Description
StringBuffer insert(int off, boolean b)	Inserts a String representing *b* into the StringBuffer starting at off.
StringBuffer insert(int off, char c)	Inserts a String representing *c* into the StringBuffer starting at off.
StringBuffer insert(int off, char[ ] ca)	Inserts a String representing *ca* into the StringBuffer starting at off.
StringBuffer insert(int off, int i)	Inserts a String representing the second argument into the StringBuffer starting at off.
StringBuffer insert(int off, long l)	Inserts a String representing *l* into the StringBuffer starting at off.
StringBuffer insert(int off, Object o)	Insert the String representation of *o* into the StringBuffer starting at off.
StringBuffer insert(int off, String s)	Inserts *s* into the StringBuffer starting at off.
int length( )	Returns the length of the StringBuffer.
StringBufffer reverse( )	Reverses the StringBuffer.
void setCharAt(int index, char ch)	Sets the character at index to *ch*.
void setLength(int len)	Sets the length of the StringBuffer.
String toString( )	Returns a String containing the contents of the StringBuffer.

Class System

Method	Description
static void arrayCopy(Object os, int osp, Object od, int dsp, int len)	Copies *len* bytes of array *os* starting at *osp* to the array *od*.
static long currentTimeMillis( )	Returns the current time in milliseconds.
static void exit(int status)	Terminates the application returning status.
static void gc( )	Suggests that the virtual machine call the garbage collector.
static String getProperty(String key)	Gets the system property identified by key.
static int identityHashCode(Object o)	Returns the hash code for *o* even if *o* has overridden getHashCode.

Class Thread

Method	Description
static int activeCount( )	Returns the current number of active threads in the virtual machine.
static Thread currentThread( )	Returns a reference to the currently executing thread.
int getPriority( )	Returns this thread's priority.
boolean isAlive( )	Returns true if this thread is alive.
void join( )	Waits for this thread to die.
void run( )	Calls the run method of the Runnable used to create this thread or return if this thread was not created from a Runnable.
void setPriority(int p)	Sets the thread's priority to p.
static void sleep(long t)	Ceases this thread's execution for t milliseconds.
void start( )	Instructs the virtual machine to begin execution of this thread by invoking its start method.
String toString( )	Returns a String containing an identifier for this thread and its priority.
static void yield( )	Causes the current thread to temporarily pause and allow other threads to execute.

Class Throwable

Method	Description
String getMessage( )	Returns a String containing this Throwable's error message.
void printStackTrace( )	Prints this Throwable and a trace to the standard output stream.
String toString( )	Returns a String containing a description of this Throwable.

Package java.util

This package contains MID Profile utility class included from Java 2 Standard Edition.

Interface Enumeration

Method	Description
boolean hasMoreElements( )	Returns true if this enumeration has more elements.
Object nextElement( )	Returns the next element in the enumeration.

Class Calendar

Method	Description
boolean after(Object when)	Returns true if the time field of this Calendar is after the argument's time field.
boolean before(Object when)	Returns true if the time field of this Calendar is before the argument's time field.
boolean equals(Object when)	Returns true if the time fields of this Calendar is the same as the time field of the argument.
int get(int field)	Returns the specified time field.
static Calendar getInstance( )	Returns an instance of Calendar created using the default time zone and locale.
static Calendar getInstance(TimeZone tz)	Returns an instance of Calendar created using time zone *tz* and the default locale.
Date getTime( )	Returns the Calendar's current time.
protected long getTimeMillis( )	Returns the Calendar's current time as the number of milliseconds since 1 Jan 1970 0:00:00 GMT.
TimeZone getTimeZone( )	Returns the Calendar's time zone.
void set(int field, int value)	Sets the time field specified by the first argument to the value specified by the second argument.

Method	Description
void setTime(Date date)	Sets the Calendar's time to the value of the argument.
protected void setTimeInMillis(long t)	Sets the Calendar's time using the value of *t*.
void setTimeZone(TimeZone tz)	Sets the Calendar's time zone to *tz*.

Class Date

Method	Description
boolean equals(Object o)	Returns true if this date is equal to the specified argument.
long getTime( )	Returns the time in milliseconds.
int hashCode( )	Returns the object's hash code.
void setTime(long t)	Sets the time using the value *t*.

Class Hashtable

Method	Description
void clear( )	Clears the Hashtable so that it contains no keys.
boolean contains(Object obj)	Returns true if the Hashtable contains the specified object.
boolean containsKey(Object key)	Returns true if the Hashtable contains the specified key.
Enumeration elements( )	Returns an enumeration of the values in the Hashtable.
Object get(Object key)	Returns the value to which the specified key is mapped in the Hashtable.
boolean isEmpty( )	Returns true if the Hashtable is empty.
Enumeration keys( )	Returns an enumeration of the keys in the Hashtable.
Object put(Object key, Object value)	Maps the specified value to the specified key.
protected void rehash( )	Rehashes the contents of this Hashtable into a new, larger Hashtable.

Method	Description
Object remove(Object key)	Removes the key and its corresponding value from the Hashtable.
int size( )	Returns the size of the Hashtable.
String toString( )	Returns a String representation of the Hashtable.

Class Random

Method	Description
protected int next(int bits)	Generates the next pseudorandom number.
int nextInt( )	Returns the next pseudorandom, uniformly distributed int.
long nextLong( )	Returns the next pseudorandom, uniformly distributed long.
void setSeed(long seed)	Seeds the generator using the specified argument.

Class Stack

Method	Description
boolean empty( )	Returns true if the stack is empty.
Object peek( )	Returns the object on the top of the stack without popping it.
Object pop( )	Removes an object from the stack and returns it.
Object push(Object o)	Places the specified object on the stack.
int search(Object o)	Returns the position of the specified object on the stack with 1 being the first position.

Class Timer

Method	Description
void cancel( )	Terminates the timer, discarding any currently scheduled tasks.
void schedule(TimerTask t, Date d)	Schedules task t to execute at time d.

Method	Description
void schedule(TimerTask t, Date d, long p)	Schedules task *t* to execute at time *d* and to repeat execution *p* milliseconds after the start time.
void schedule(TimerTask t, long d)	Schedules task *t* to start after a delay of *d* milliseconds.
void schedule(TimerTask t, long d, long p)	Schedules task *t* to start after a delay of *d* milliseconds and to execute repeatedly after *p* milliseconds.
void scheduleAtFixedRate(TimerTask t, Date dt, long p)	Schedules task *t* to execute at *dt* and to repeat at intervals of *p*.
void scheduleAtFixedRate(TimerTask t, long d, long p)	Schedules task *t* to execute after a delay of *d* milliseconds and to repeat after *p* milliseconds.

Class TimerTask

Method	Description
boolean cancel( )	Cancels this timer task.
abstract void run( )	This method contains the actual task to be executed.
long scheduledExecutionTime( )	Returns the scheduled execution time of the most recent actual execution of this task.

Class TimeZone

Method	Description
static String[ ] getAvailableIDs( )	Returns a list of all supported IDs.
static TimeZone getDefault( )	Returns the default ID.
String getID( )	Returns the ID of this time zone.
abstract int getOffset(int era, int year, int month, int day, int wkday, int millis)	Gets offset for current date.
abstract int getRawOffset( )	Returns GMT offset for this time zone.
static TimeZone getTimeZone(String ID)	Returns the time zone for the specified ID.
abstract boolean useDaylightTime( )	Returns true if this time zone uses daylight savings time.

Class Vector

Method	Description
void addElement(Object o)	Adds the specified object to the Vector.
int capacity( )	Returns the current capacity.
boolean contains(Object o)	Returns true if the Vector contains the specified element.
void copyInto(Object[ ] array)	Copies all elements of the Vector into array.
Object elementAt(int index)	Returns the element at index.
Enumeration elements( )	Returns an enumeration of all elements in the Vector.
void ensureCapacity(int c)	Increases the capacity to accommodate a minimum of c elements.
Object firstElement( )	Returns the first element in the Vector.
int indexOf(Object o)	Returns the index of the specified element.
int indexOf(Object o, int index)	Returns the index of the specified object starting the search at index.
void insertElementAt(Object, int index)	Inserts the specified object at index.
boolean isEmpty( )	Returns true if the Vector is empty.
Object lastElement( )	Returns the last element in the vector.
int lastIndexOf(Object o)	Returns the index of the last occurrence of o.
int lastIndexOf(Object o, int index)	Returns the index of the last occurrence of o searching backwards for it from index.
void removeAllElements( )	Removes all elements and sets size to zero.
void removeElement(Object o)	Removes the object o.
void removeElementAt(int index)	Remove the element at index.
void setElementAt(Object o, int index)	Adds the specified object at index, replacing any object already at index.
void setSize(int sz)	Sets the size to sz.
int size( )	Returns the current size.
String toString( )	Returns a String representing the Vector.
void trimToSize( )	Trims the capacity to the current size.

Package javax.microedition.io

This package provides networking support based on the GenericConnection
framework from the Connected Limited Device Configuration.

Interface Connection

Method	Description
void close( )	Closes the connection.

Interface ContentConnection

Method	Description
String getEncoding( )	Returns a String describing the encoding of the content.
long getLength( )	Returns the length of the content.
String getType( )	Returns a String describing the type of the content.

Interface Datagram

Method	Description
String getAddress( )	Returns the address of the Datagram.
byte[ ] getData( )	Returns the buffer.
int getLength( )	Returns the length.
int getOffset( )	Returns the offset.
void reset( )	Zeroes the read/write pointer as well as offset and length.
void setAddress(Datagram d)	Uses the address of *d* to set this Datagram's address.
void setAddress(String addr)	Sets the address to *addr*.
void setData(byte[ ] b, int off, int len)	Sets the buffer, offset, and length.
void setLength(int len)	Sets the length to *len*.

Interface DatagramConnection

Method	Description
int getMaximumLength( )	Returns the maximum length a Datagram can be.
int getNominalLength( )	Returns the nominal length.
Datagram newDatagram(byte[ ] da, int sz)	Creates a new Datagram.
Datagram newDatagram(byte[ ] ba, int sz, String addr)	Creates a new Datagram.
Datagram newDatagram(int sz)	Creates a new Datagram.
Datagram newDatagram(int sz, String addr)	Creates a new Datagram.
void receive(Datagram d)	Receives a Datagram.
void send(Datagram d)	Sends a Datagram.

Interface HttpConnection

Method	Description
long getDate( )	Returns the value of the date header field.
long getExpiration( )	Returns the value of the expires header field.
String getFile( )	Returns the file portion of the URL of this connection.
String getHeaderField(int index)	Returns the header field at index.
String getHeaderField(String name)	Returns the header field with the specified name.
long getHeaderFieldDate(String name, int def)	Returns the named field parsed as a date using field *def* if named field does not exist.
int getHeaderFieldInt(String name, int def)	Returns the named field parsed as a number using field *def* if the named field does not exist.
String getHeaderFieldKey(int n)	Returns the header field key at *n*.
String getHost( )	Returns the host information from the URL of this connection.
long getLastModified( )	Returns the value of the last-modified header field.

Method	Description
int getPort( )	Returns the network port number from the URL of this connection.
String getProtocol( )	Returns the protocol name from the URL of this connection.
String getQuery( )	Returns the query portion of the URL for this connection.
String getRef( )	Returns the ref portion of the URL for this connection.
String getRequestMethod( )	Returns the current request method.
String getRequestProperty(String key)	Returns the value of the named request property.
int getResponseCode( )	Returns the response code.
String getResponseMessage( )	Returns the response message.
String getURL( )	Returns a String representing this connection's URL.
void setRequestMethod(String method)	Sets the request method to one of: POST, GET, HEAD.
void setRequestProperty(String key, String value)	Sets the value of a request property.

Interface InputConnection

Method	Description
DataInputStream openDataInputStream( )	Opens and returns a data input stream for the connection.
InputStream openInputStream( )	Opens and returns an input stream for the connection.

Interface OutputConnection

Method	Description
DataOutputStream openDataOutputStream( )	Opens and returns a data output stream for the connection.
OutputStream openOutputStream( )	Opens and returns an output stream for the connection.

Interface StreamConnection

This interface combines the InputConnection and OutputConnection interfaces.

Interface StreamConnectionNotifier

Method	Description
StreamConnection acceptAndOpen( )	Returns a StreamConnection that represents a server-side socket connection.

Class Connector

Method	Description
static Connection open(String name)	Creates and opens a connection.
static Connection open(String name, int mode)	Creates and opens a connection for the specified access mode.
static Connection open(String name, int mode, boolean timeouts)	Creates and opens a connection for the specified access mode indicating whether the caller wants timeout exceptions.
static DataInputStream penDataInputStream(String name)	Creates and opens a connection input stream.
static DataOutputStream openDataOutputStream(String name)	Creates and opens a connection output stream.
static InputStream openInputStream (String name)	Creates and opens a connection input stream.
static OutputStream openOutputStream(String name)	Creates and opens a connection output stream.

Package javax.microedition.lcdui

This package contains the API that provides a set of features for implementing a user interface in MIDP applications.

Interface Choice

Method	Description
int append(String stringPart, Image imagePart)	Appends an element to the Choice.
void delete(int index)	Deletes an element from the Choice.
Image getImage(int index)	Returns the image part of the specified element.
int getSelectedFlags(boolean[ ] ba)	Sets the elements of *ba* to reflect the selected state of the corresponding elements and returns the number of selected elements.
int getSelectedIndex( )	Returns the index of the selected element.
String getString(int index)	Returns the string part of the specified element.
void insert(int index, String stringPart, Image imagePart)	Inserts an element prior to index.
boolean isSelected(int index)	Returns true if the specified element is selected.
void set(int index, String stringPart, Image imagePart)	Replaces the element at index.
void setSelectedFlags(boolean[ ] ba)	Uses the contents of *ba* to set the selected state of every element.
void setSelectedIndex(int index, boolean selected)	Sets the element at index to the specified selected state.
int size( )	Returns the number of elements in the Choice.

Interface CommandListener

Method	Description
void commandAction(Command cmd, Displayable d)	Called in response to a command event.

Interface ItemStateListener

Method	Description
void itemStateChanged(Item item)	Called when the user changes the state of the item indicated by the argument.

Class Alert

Method	Description
void addCommand(Command cmd)	This method always throws an IllegalStateException. Commands are not allowed on Alerts.
int getDefaultTimeout( )	Returns the default timeout for Alerts.
Image getImage( )	Returns the image used by this Alert.
String getString( )	Returns the Alert's string.
int getTimeout( )	Returns the Alert's timeout.
AlertType getType( )	Returns the type of Alert.
void setCommandListener (CommandListener l)	This method always throws an IllegalStateException. Listeners are not allowed on Alerts.
void setImage(Image im)	Sets the Alert's image.
void setString(String s)	Sets the Alert's string.
void setTimeout(int t)	Sets the Alert's timeout.
void setType(AlertType t)	Sets the Alert's type.

Class AlertType

Method	Description
boolean playSound(Display display)	Plays the sound for this alert type.

Class Canvas

Method	Description
int getGameAction(int keycode)	Returns the game action associated with *keycode*.
int getHeight( )	Returns the height of the displayable area in pixels.
int getKeyCode(int gameAction)	Returns the key code that corresponds to the specified game action.
String getKeyName(int keycode)	Returns a String describing the specified key code.
int getWidth( )	Returns the width of the displayable area in pixels.
boolean hasPointerEvents( )	Returns true if the platform supports pointer press and release events.
boolean hasPointerMotionEvents( )	Returns true if the platform supports pointer motion events (pointer dragged).
boolean hasRepeatEvents( )	Returns true if the platform can generate repeat events when a key is held down.
protected void hideNotify( )	Called by the implementation shortly after the Canvas has been removed from the display.
boolean isDoubleBuffered( )	Returns true if the Graphics is double buffered by the implementation.
protected void keyPressed(int keycode)	Called when a key is pressed.
protected void keyReleased(int keycode)	Called when a key is released.
protected void keyRepeated( )	Called when a key is repeated (held down).

Method	Description
protected abstract void paint(Graphics g)	Renders the Canvas.
protected void pointerDragged(int x, int y)	Called when the pointer is dragged.
protected void pointerPressed(int x, int y)	Called when the pointer is pressed.
protected void pointerReleased(int x, int y)	Called when the pointer is released.
void repaint( )	Requests a repaint for the entire screen.
void repaint(int x, int y, int w, int h)	Requests a repaint for the region of the screen below and to the right of the coordinate (x,y) that is w pixels wide and h pixels high.
void serviceRepaints( )	Forces any pending repaint requests to be serviced immediately.
protected void showNotify( )	Called by the implementation immediately before the Canvas is made visible on the display.

Class ChoiceGroup

Method	Description
int append(String stringPart, Image imagePart)	Appends an element to the Choice.
void delete(int index)	Deletes the element at index.
Image getImage(int index)	Returns the image part of the element at index.
int getSelectedFlags(boolean[ ] ba)	Sets the elements of ba to the selected state of the elements in the Choice.
int getSelectedIndex( )	Returns the index of the selected element.
String getString(int index)	Returns the string part of the element at index.
void insert(int index, String stringPart, Image imagePart)	Inserts an element just prior to index.
boolean isSelected(int index)	Returns true if the element at the specified index is selected.
void set(int index, String stringPart, Image imagePart)	Sets the element at index overwriting any existing element.
void setLabel(String label)	Sets the label of the Choice.
void setSelectedFlags(boolean[ ] ba)	Uses the boolean values in ba to set the selected state of all elements in the Choice.
void setSelectedIndex(int index, boolean selected)	Sets the selected state of the element at index.
int size( )	Returns the number of elements in the Choice.

Class Command

Method	Description
int getCommandType( )	Returns the type.
String getLabel( )	Returns the label.
int getPriority( )	Returns the priority.

Class DateField

Method	Description
Date getDate( )	Returns the date field.
int getInputMode( )	Returns the input mode.
void setDate(Date dt)	Sets the date field to the specified value.
void setInputMode(int mode)	Sets the input mode.
void setLabel(String label)	Sets the label.

Class Display

Method	Description
void callSerially(Runnable r)	Requests that *r* have its run method called later, serialized with the event stream, soon after completion of the repaint cycle.
Displayable getCurrent( )	Returns the current Displayable object.
static Display getDisplay( )	Gets the Display object unique to this MIDlet.
boolean isColor( )	Returns true if the device supports color.
int numColors( )	Returns the number of colors or number of gray levels the device supports.
void setCurrent(Alert a, Displayable next)	Requests that the specified Alert be made visible on the display and that the Displayable designated by the second argument be displayed after the Alert is dismissed.
void setCurrent(Displayable next)	Requests that the specified Displayable be made visible on the display.

Class Displayable

Method	Description
void addCommand(Command cmd)	Adds the specified command.
boolean isShown( )	Returns true if the Displayable is actually visible on the screen.
void removeCommand(Command cmd)	Removes the specified command.
void setCommandListener (CommandListener l)	Sets a listener, replacing any existing listener.

Class Font

Method	Description
int charsWidth(char[ ] ca, int off, int len)	Returns the advance width of the *len* characters in *ca* starting at off.
int charsWidth(char ch)	Returns the advance width of the specified character.
int getBaselinePosition( )	Returns the distance in pixels from the top of the text to the text's baseline.
static Font getDefaultFont( )	Returns the system's default Font.
int getFace( )	Returns the face of the Font.
static Font getFont(int face, int style, int size)	Returns an instance of Font having the specified face, style, and size.
int getHeight( )	Returns the standard height of a line of text in this Font.
int getSize( )	Returns the size of the Font.
int getStyle( )	Returns the style of the Font.
boolean isBold( )	Returns true if this Font is bold.
boolean isItalic( )	Returns true if this Font is italic.
boolean isPlain( )	Returns true if this Font is plain.
boolean isUnderlined( )	Returns true if this Font is underlined.
int stringWidth(String s)	Returns the total advance width required to show the specified String in this Font).
int substringWidth(String s, int off, int len)	Returns the total advance width required to display *len* characters of the specified String starting at off in this Font.

Class Form

Method	Description
int append(Image im)	Appends the specified Image.
int append(Item item)	Appends the specified Item.
int append(String s)	Appends the specified String.
void delete(int itemNum)	Deletes the Item at itemNum.
Item get(int itemNum)	Returns the Item at itemNum.
void insert(int itemNum, Item item)	Inserts the specified Item just prior to itemNum.
void set(int itemNum, Item item)	Sets the Item at itemNum to the specified Item, overriding any existing Item.
void setItemStateListener (ItemStateListener listener)	Sets the ItemStateListener for the Form, replacing any existing listener.
int size( )	Returns the number of items in the Form.

Class Gauge

Method	Description
int getMaxValue( )	Returns the maximum value for this Gauge.
int getValue( )	Returns the current value of the Gauge.
boolean isInteractive( )	Returns true if the Gauge is interactive.
void setLabel(String s)	Sets the label.
void setMaxValue(int val)	Sets the maximum value.
void setValue(int val)	Sets the current value.

Class Graphics

Method	Description
void clipRect(int x, int y, int w, int h)	Intersects the current clip with the specified rectangle.
void drawArc(int x, int y, int w, int h, int startAngle, int arcAngle)	Draws the outline of an arc covering the specified rectangle.
void drawChar(char ch, int x, int y, int anchor)	Draws the specified character.

Method	Description
void drawChars(char[ ] ca, int off, int len, int x, int y, int anchor)	Draws the specified characters.
void drawImage(Image im, int x, int y, int anchor)	Draws the specified Image.
void drawLine(int x1, int y1, int x2, int y2)	Draws a straight line connecting the two specified points.
void drawRect(int x, int y, int w, int h)	Draws the specified rectangle.
void drawRoundRect(int x, int y, int w, int h, int arcWidth, int arcHeight)	Draws the specified rounded corner rectangle.
void drawString(String s, int x, int y, int anchor)	Draws the specified String.
void drawSubstring(String s, int off, int len, int x, int y, int anchor)	Draws the specified substring.
void fillArc(int x, int y, int w, int h, int startAngle, int arcAngle)	Fills an arc covering the specified rectangle.
void fillRect(int x, int y, int x, int h)	Fills the specified rectangle.
void fillRoundRect(int x, int y, int w, int h, int arcWidth, int arcHeight)	Fills the specified rounded corner rectangle.
int getBlueComponent( )	Returns the blue component of the current color.
int getClipHeight( )	Returns the height of the current clipping area.
int getClipWidth( )	Returns the width of the current clipping area.
int getClipX( )	Returns the X offset of the current clipping area, relative to the coordinate system origin of the graphics context.
int getClipY( )	Returns the Y offset of the current clipping area, relative to the coordinate system origin of the graphics context.
int getColor( )	Returns the current color.
Font getFont( )	Returns the current font.
int getGrayScale( )	Returns the current grayscale value of the current color.
int getGreenComponent( )	Returns the green component of the current color.
int getRedComponent( )	Returns the red component of the current color.
int getStrokeStyle( )	Returns the current stroke style.

Method	Description
int getTranslateX( )	Returns the X coordinate of the translated origin of the graphics context.
int getTranslateY( )	Returns the Y coordinate of the translated origin of the graphics context.
void setClip(int x, int y, int w, int h)	Sets the clip to the specified rectangle.
void setColor(int RGB)	Sets the current color to the specified RGB values.
void setColor(int r, int g, int b)	Sets the current color to the specified RGB values.
void setFont(Font f)	Sets the current font.
void setGrayScale(int val)	Sets the current grayscale value.
void setStrokeStyle(int style)	Sets the current stroke style.
void translate(int x, int y)	Translates the origin of the graphics context to the point (x,y) in the current coordinate system.

Class Image

Method	Description
static Image createImage(byte[ ] data, int off, int len)	Creates an immutable image, which is decoded using *len* bytes from data starting at off.
static Image createImage(Image im)	Creates an immutable image from the specified source image.
static Image createImage(int w, int h)	Creates a mutable image for offscreen drawing.
static Image createImage(String name)	Creates an immutable image from decoded data obtained from the specified resource.
Graphics getGraphics( )	Returns a Graphics object that renders to this image.
int getHeight( )	Returns the height of the image in pixels.
int getWidth( )	Returns the width of the image in pixels.
boolean isMutable( )	Returns true if the image is mutable.

Class ImageItem

Method	Description
String getAltText( )	Returns the text string to be used if the image exceeds the device's capacity to display it.
Image getImage( )	Returns the image contained within the ImageItem.
int getLayout( )	Returns the layout directives.
void setAltText(String s)	Sets the alternate text to the specified string.
void setImage(Image im)	Sets the image.
void setLabel(String s)	Sets the label to the specified string.
void setLayout(int layout)	Sets the layout.

Class Item

Method	Description
String getLabel( )	Returns the Item's label.
void setLabel(String s)	Sets the label to the specified string.

Class List

Method	Description
int append(String stringPart, Image imagePart)	Appends an element to the Choice.
void delete(int index)	Deletes the specified element.
Image getImage(int index)	Returns the image part of the specified element.
int getSelectedFlags(boolean[ ] ba)	Sets the elements of *ba* to the corresponding selected state of all elements in the Choice.
int getSelectedIndex( )	Returns the number of the selected element.
String getString(int index)	Returns the string part of the specified element.
void insert(int index, String stringPart, Image imagePart)	Inserts an element just prior to the specified element.
boolean isSelected(int index)	Returns true if the specified element is selected.
void set(int index, Strring stringPart, Image imagePart)	Sets the specified element, replacing any existing element.

Method	Description
void setSelectedFlags(boolean[ ] ba)	Uses the contents of *ba* to set the selected state of all elements.
void setSelectedIndex(int index, boolean b)	Sets the selected state of the specified element.
int size( )	Returns the number of elements in the Choice.

Class Screen

Method	Description
Ticker getTicker( )	Returns the Ticker used by this screen
String getTitle( )	Returns the screen's title.
void setTicker(Ticker t)	Sets the screen's Ticker.
void setTitle(String s)	Sets the screen's title.

Class StringItem

Method	Description
String getText( )	Returns the text contents of the StringItem.
void setLabel(String s)	Sets the label.
void setText(String s)	Sets the text contents.

Class TextBox

Method	Description
void delete(int off, int len)	Deletes *len* characters starting at off.
int getCaretPosition( )	Returns the current input position.
int getChars(char[ ] ca)	Copies the contents of the TextBox into *ca* starting at zero.
int getConstraints( )	Returns the input constraints.
int getMaxSize( )	Returns the maximum number of characters that can be stored in the TextBox.
String getString( )	Returns the contents of the TextBox.
void insert(char[ ] ca, int off, int len, int pos)	Inserts *len* characters from *ca* starting at off into the TextBox starting at *pos*.
void insert(String s, int pos)	Inserts the specified String at the specified position.
void setChars(char[ ] ca, int off, int len)	Sets the contents of the TextBox using *len* characters from *ca* starting at off.

Method	Description
void setConstraints(int constraints)	Sets the input constraints of the TextBox.
int setMaxSize(int maxSize)	Sets the maximum number of characters that can be stored in the TextBox.
void setString(String text)	Uses string to set the contents of the TextBox.
int size( )	Returns the number of characters currently in the TextBox.

Class TextField

Method	Description
void delete(int off, len)	Deletes *len* characters starting at off.
int getCaretPosition( )	Returns the current input position.
int getChars(char[ ] ca)	Copies the contents of the TextField into *ca*.
int getConstraints( )	Returns the TextField's input constraints.
int getMaxSize( )	Returns the maximum number of characters the TextField can hold.
String getString( )	Returns the contents of the TextField as a String.
void insert(char[ ] ca, int off, int len, int pos)	Inserts *len* characters from *ca* starting at off into the TextField starting at *pos*.
void insert(String s, int pos)	Inserts *s* into the TextField starting at *pos*.
void setChars(char[ ] ca, int off, int len)	Sets the contents of the TextField using *len* characters from *ca* starting at off.
void setConstraints(int constraints)	Sets the input constraints.
void setLabel(String s)	Sets the TextField's label to *s*.
int setMaxSize(int sz)	Sets the maximum number of characters the TextField can hold.
void setString(String s)	Uses the String *s* to set the contents of the TextField.
int size( )	Returns the current size of the TextField.

Class Ticker

Method	Description
String getString( )	Returns the string currently being scrolled by the Ticker.
void setString(String s)	Sets the Ticker's String.

Package javax.microedition.midlet

This package defines Mobile Information Device Profile applications, the interactions between such applications, and the environment in which they run.

Class MIDlet

Method	Description
protected abstract void destroyApp (boolean conditional)	Signals the MIDlet to terminate and enter the *Destroyed* state.
String getAppProperty(String key)	Returns the property named by key.
void notifyDestroyed( )	Notifies the Application Management Software that the MIDlet has entered the *Destroyed* state.
void notifyPaused( )	Notifies the Application Management Software that the MIDlet no longer wishes to be active and has entered the *Paused* state.
protected abstract void pauseApp( )	Signals the MIDlet to stop and enter the *Paused* state.
void resumeRequest( )	Notifies the Application Management Software that the MIDlet wishes to enter the *Active* state.
protected abstract void startApp( )	Signals the MIDlet that it has entered the *Active* state.

Package javax.microedition.rms

This package contains the mechanism used by MIDlets to store data persistently and retrieve it.

Interface RecordComparator

Method	Description
int compare(byte[ ] rec1, byte[ ] rec2)	Returns RecordComparator.PRECEDES, RecordComparator.FOLLOWS or RecordComparator.EQUIVALENT, depending on whether rec1 precedes, follows, or is equal to rec2 in sort order.

Interface RecordEnumeration

Method	Description
void destroy( )	Frees internal resources used by the Enumeration.
boolean hasNextElement( )	Returns true if more elements exist in the *next* direction.
boolean hasPreviousElement( )	Returns true if more elements exist in the *previous* direction.
boolean isKeptUpdated( )	Returns true if the Enumeration keeps its enumeration current with changes in the store.
void keepUpdated(boolean b)	Uses the value of *b* to instruct the Enumeration as to whether it should keep its enumeration current with changes in the store.
byte[ ] nextRecord( )	Returns the next record.
int nextRecordId( )	Returns the recordID of the next record.
int numRecords( )	Returns the number of records in the Enumeration.
byte[ ] previousRecord( )	Returns the previous record.
int previousRecordId( )	Returns the recordID previous record.
void rebuild( )	Updates the Enumeration to reflect the current state of the record store.
void reset( )	Resets the Enumeration to the same state as when it was newly created.

Interface RecordFilter

Method	Description
boolean matches(byte[ ] candidate)	Returns true if the candidate record meets application-defined criteria for inclusion in an Enumeration.

Interface RecordListener

Method	Description
void recordAdded(RecordStore rs, int recid)	Called when a record has been added to the store.
void recordChanged(RecordStore rs, int recid)	Called when a record in the store has been changed.
void recordDeleted(RecordStore rs, int recid)	Called when a record has been deleted from the store.

Class RecordStore

Method	Description
int addRecord(byte[ ] data, int off, off nb)	Writes *nb* bytes of data starting at off to the next record in the store and returns the recordID.
void addRecordListener(RecordListener l)	Adds the specified listener to the RecordStore.
void closeRecordStore( )	Closes the RecordStore.
void deleteRecord(int recid)	Deletes the specified record.
static void deleteRecordStore(String name)	Deletes the named RecordStore.
RecordEnumeration enumerateRecords(RecordFilter f, RecordComparator c, boolean keepUpdated)	Returns an Enumeration.
long getLastModified( )	Returns the last time the RecordStore was modified.
String getName( )	Returns the RecordStore's name.
int getNextRecordID( )	Returns the recordID of the next record to be added to the store.

Method	Description
int getNumRecords( )	Returns the number of records currently in the RecordStore.
byte[ ] getRecord(int recid)	Returns the record identified by *recid*.
int getRecord(int recid, byte[ ] data, int off)	Writes the records identified by *recid* to the data array starting at off.
int getRecordSize(int recid)	Returns the size in bytes of the specified record.
int getSize( )	Returns the number of bytes that the RecordStore occupies.
int getSizeAvailable( )	Returns the number of bytes available for growth.
int getVersion( )	Returns the current version of the RecordStore.
static String[ ] listRecordStores( )	Returns a list of all record stores in the current MIDlet Suite.
static RecordStore openRecordStore(String name, boolean create)	Opens the named RecordStore using the value of *create* to determine whether to create it if it does not exist.
void removeRecordListener (RecordListener l)	Removes the specified listener.
void setRecord(int recid, byte[ ] data, int off, int len)	Writes *len* bytes from data starting at off.

Index

INTERNATIONAL CONTACT INFORMATION

AUSTRALIA
McGraw-Hill Book Company Australia Pty. Ltd.
TEL +61-2-9417-9899
FAX +61-2-9417-5687
http://www.mcgraw-hill.com.au
books-it_sydney@mcgraw-hill.com

CANADA
McGraw-Hill Ryerson Ltd.
TEL +905-430-5000
FAX +905-430-5020
http://www.mcgrawhill.ca

**GREECE, MIDDLE EAST,
NORTHERN AFRICA**
McGraw-Hill Hellas
TEL +30-1-656-0990-3-4
FAX +30-1-654-5525

MEXICO (Also serving Latin America)
McGraw-Hill Interamericana Editores S.A. de C.V.
TEL +525-117-1583
FAX +525-117-1589
http://www.mcgraw-hill.com.mx
fernando_castellanos@mcgraw-hill.com

SINGAPORE (Serving Asia)
McGraw-Hill Book Company
TEL +65-863-1580
FAX +65-862-3354
http://www.mcgraw-hill.com.sg
mghasia@mcgraw-hill.com

SOUTH AFRICA
McGraw-Hill South Africa
TEL +27-11-622-7512
FAX +27-11-622-9045
robyn_swanepoel@mcgraw-hill.com

**UNITED KINGDOM & EUROPE
(Excluding Southern Europe)**
McGraw-Hill Education Europe
TEL +44-1-628-502500
FAX +44-1-628-770224
http://www.mcgraw-hill.co.uk
computing_neurope@mcgraw-hill.com

ALL OTHER INQUIRIES Contact:
Osborne/McGraw-Hill
TEL +1-510-549-6600
FAX +1-510-883-7600
http://www.osborne.com
omg_international@mcgraw-hill.com

About the CD

The CD contains the code for:

- ► All of the MIDlets in the book
- ► The standalone servers accessed by the MIDlets
- ► The servlets and JavaServer Pages accessed by the MIDlets
- ► The SQL needed to create the database tables used by the standalone servers and servlets

Installation instructions can be found in Appendix A.